Organizational Entry

*Recruitment, Selection, Orientation,
and Socialization of Newcomers*

Second Edition

Organizational Entry

Recruitment, Selection, Orientation, and Socialization of Newcomers

Second Edition

John Parcher Wanous
The Ohio State University

 Addison-Wesley Publishing Company
Reading, Massachusetts • Menlo Park, California • New York
Don Mills, Ontario • Wokingham, England • Amsterdam • Bonn
Sydney • Singapore • Tokyo • Madrid • San Juan • Milan • Paris

In memory of my parents,
Leo H. Wanous and Dorothy Parcher Wanous

Library of Congress Cataloging-in-Publication Data

Wanous, John P.
   Organizational entry: recruitment, selection, orientation, and socialization of newcomers / John Parcher Wanous.
       p   . cm.
   Includes bibliographical references and indexes.
   ISBN 0-201-51480-X
   1.   Employees—Recruiting.   2.   Employee selection.
   3.   Employee orientation.   I.   Title.
   HF5549.5.R44W36   1991
   658.3'11—dc20
                                                        91-27636
                                                           CIP

ISBN 0-201-51480-X
1 2 3 4 5 6 7 8 9 10-BA-9594939291

The Addison-Wesley Series on Managing Human Resources

Series Editor: John Parcher Wanous, The Ohio State University

Merit Pay: Linking Pay Increases to Performance Ratings
Robert L. Heneman, The Ohio State University

Assessment Centers in Human Resource Management
George C. Thornton, III, Colorado State University

Fairness in Selecting Employees, Second Edition
Richard D. Arvey, University of Minnesota and
Robert H. Faley, Kent State University

Organizational Entry: Recruitment, Selection, Orientation, and Socialization of Newcomers, Second Edition
John P. Wanous, The Ohio State University

Increasing Productivity through Performance Appraisal
Gary P. Latham, University of Toronto, and
Kenneth N. Wexley, Michigan State University

Managing Conflict at Organizational Interfaces
L. David Brown, Boston University

Employee Turnover: Causes, Consequences and Control
William H. Mobley, Texas A & M University

Managing Careers
Manuel London, AT&T and Stephen A. Stumpf, New York University

Managing Employee Absenteeism
Susan R. Rhodes, Syracuse University and
Richard M. Steers, University of Oregon

Foreword

This is an exciting time for the Managing Human Resources Series. Originally conceived in 1977, the first six books were published between 1979 and 1982. These books were uniformly well received by academic and business professionals alike. They have been extensively cited by researchers in human resources as state-of-the-art monographs. Moreover, students—both under-graduate and graduate—have found the series books to be both readable and informative.

The series is now in its second phase. *Fairness in Selecting Employees* (1979) by Rich Arvey was revised by Arvey and Robert Faley and published in 1988. This was followed by *Managing Employee Absenteeism* by Susan Rhodes and Rick Steers. My own book on *Organizational Entry* (1980) has been revised and reis-sued in 1992. Two new titles also appear in 1992. The first is *Merit Pay* by Rob Heneman, and the second is *Assessment Centers in Human Resource Management* by George Thornton. The commit-ment from Addison-Wesley to continue and expand the series has been crucial.

As always, this series is dedicated to the articulation of new solutions to human resources problems. My charge to authors has been to produce books that will summarize and extend cutting-edge knowledge. These authors must be intellectual leaders. In addition, they must make their books readily accessible to college students and human resource professionals alike. Readability need not and must not be sacrificed at the alter of academic scholarship. Both are achievable, as evidenced by the first books in this series. The present ones continue this tradition.

John Parcher Wanous
Series Editor

Preface

It has been 12 years since *Organizational Entry* was first published. Since then, interest in this topic has increased dramatically. In many cases the number of research studies now available has increased two to fourfold. What were tentative conclusions in 1980 are now much firmer. In addition, new topics have emerged, including the effects of job interviewers on job candidates and the development of "structured" job interviews.

This edition differs considerably from the first one, even though many of the chapter titles and headings are identical. The contents have changed. For example, the Matching Model has been revised in accordance with recent research. The types of recruiting sources that yield fewer turnover-prone employees have been slightly revised and have been re-named "inside" sources, rather than "informal" sources. Field experiments continue to show greater job survival rates for those recruited with a realistic job preview. The chapter on organizational choice now includes recent material on judgment errors and biases in human decision making. A chapter on newcomer orientation has been added, and the title of the book now reflects this. The chapter on selection has been completely rewritten. Its focus is now on selection methods that, while designed to assess competence to perform a job, also communicate realistic job information to candidates. The chapter has an extensive section on selecting personnel for their "fit" to the climate and culture of an organization. The chapter on organizational socialization places this topic in the larger context of research on persuasion from social psychology. Newcomers are also viewed as members of groups that can be in various stages of development, so that group development issues must be jointly considered with those of newcomer socialization. Throughout the book all material has been updated through the early part of 1991, when the manuscript was completed. Approximately 200 new references have been added for this edition.

This edition has been a lot of work and I thoroughly enjoyed every minute of it.

My wife and colleague Arnon Reichers was helpful and supportive throughout this effort. My toddler son Evan Reichers Wanous did his very best to mess up my notes, articles and books, and to destroy my word processor (which he called the "T.V.") Nevertheless, his presence in our lives the last two years has been, simply, the best.

Columbus, Ohio   **J.P.W.**

Contents

1 **What is Organizational Entry?** 1
Four Phases of Organizational Entry 2
Why the Study of Organizational Entry is Important 5
A Model of Matching Individuals and Organizations 7
Conclusions 19
The Plan of This Book 20

2 **Organizational Recruitment** 21
Relationship of Recruitment to the Model of Organizational
Entry 21
Conflicts During Organizational Entry 22
What do "Outsider" Individuals Know About
Organizations? 23
Consequences of Unrealistic Expectations: Low
Satisfaction 31
Sources Used By Organizations to Find Newcomers 34
Contrasting Philosophies of Recruitment 41
Purpose and Theory of Realistic Recruitment 48
Conclusions 52

3 **Realistic Recruitment** 53
Diagnosis of the Need for Realistic Recruitment 53
A Case Study of Diagnosis 56
Guidelines for When to Use Realistic Recruitment 59
Guidelines for Designing RJPs 61
Realistic Recruitment in Practice 64
Evaluation of Realistic Recruitment 70
Evaluating the Impact of Realistic Recruitment 74

Evaluating the Theory of Realistic Recruitment 82
Other Applications of Realism 84
Conclusions 86

4 Choice of an Organization 89
Organizational Choice Versus Vocational Choice 90
Two Views of Organizational Choice 91
Evaluating the Two Views of Organizational Choice 99
Should Individuals Make Rational Career and Organizational
   Choices? 103
Is It Possible for People to Be Rational? 107
Relationship of Organizational Choice to Recruitment 111
Organizational Choice and the Job Interview 112
Conclusions 120

5 Selection of Newcomers by an Organization 123
Realistic Selection Methods 124
Selection for Organizational Climates 152
Conclusions 163

6 Newcomer Orientation 155
What is Newcomer Orientation? 166
Ways to Manage Stress 173
Three Studies of Newcomer Orientation 178
Design Guidelines for ROPES 182
Conclusions 184

7 Organizational Socialization 187
Socialization Versus Orientation 188
Organizational Control Is the Basic Objective 189
Socialization and Selection 192
Who and What Changes During Socialization? 194
Stages of Socialization 200
The Psychology of Socialization: Persuasion 214
Socialization Tactics 221
Examples of Organizational Socialization 224
Conclusions 234

Appendix 237

References 241

Index 265

1

What Is Organizational Entry?

Organizational entry includes the wide variety of events occurring when new members join organizations. By its very nature the entry process must be considered from the perspective of both the individual and the organization. Individuals choose to apply, organizations select newcomers from among applicants, and job candidates choose from among offers.

Organizational entry concerns movement into businesses, schools, the armed forces, etc. Because of the focus on crossing the boundary from outside to inside, the immediate concern of organizational entry is to identify those factors affecting this move. To put this another way, it is important to distinguish between the decision to *participate* in an organization and the decision to *perform well* in that organization (March & Simon, 1958). This is a book more concerned with participation than performance.

One purpose of Chapter 1 is to introduce readers to various issues facing newcomers and the organizations they enter during the four phases of organizational entry. Examples are then given to show how expensive and inefficient the entry process can be to an organization. Finally, a schematic model of organizational entry is presented that shows the major factors of this process and how they relate to each other. This model serves as a common reference point throughout the book. Since it will be referred to in each chapter, the reader is advised to study it well.

Four Phases of Organizational Entry

Table 1.1 shows four phases of organizational entry, beginning with two preentry phases, *recruitment* and *selection*. These two are followed by two postentry phases, *orientation* and *socialization*. The four phases of entry are described in terms of two perspectives: that of the individual newcomer and that of the organization being entered. Viewing organizational entry from both of these two perspectives is a central theme here. It is hoped that both potential employees and employers can benefit from reading this book.

Although the four phases of entry have distinct names and are placed in a sequence, the reality of this process is much less tidy than might be implied by the graphic representation in Table 1.1. For example, the two preentry phases are frequently intertwined, rather than occurring one after the other. In other words, it is sometimes difficult to separate the processes of mutual attraction and mutual choice while they are happening because they affect each other in a very dynamic way (Porter, Lawler, & Hackman, 1975). (This interdependence between recruitment and selection is discussed in Chapter 2.)

Organizational recruitment is called the process of mutual attraction between a potential job candidate and an organization. From the individual's perspective, several questions have concerned researchers. First, how do people find out about job openings? Second, after learning about openings, how do they learn something specific about a particular organization? Related to this second question is the accuracy of the information they have gotten about an organization. Third, what do individuals do after considering the information they have about an organization? Do they apply or not?

The organizational perspective of organizational recruitment can also be divided into some specific questions. First, what are good sources of new recruits? For example, are employment agencies as effective as referrals by current employees? Related to this is the meaning of "effective" sources: What constitutes effectiveness? Is it the job performance of newcomers, or is it retaining new employees, or is it both performance and retention together? Second, what type of strategy is to be used to attract job candidates to be interested in joining up. Chapter 2 focuses considerable attention on the differences between two basically different strategies,

Table 1.1
Individual and Organizational Issues at Four Stages of Entry

Phase of Organizational Entry	Whose Perspective?	
	The Newcomer Individual	The Organization Being Entered
1. **Recruitment:** The process of mutual attraction	• Finding sources of information about job openings • Determining the accuracy of information about particular oganizations	• Finding sources of effective job candidates • Attracting candidates with appropriate strategy ("selling" vs. "realism")
2. **Selection:** The process of mutual choice	• Coping with job interviews and other assessment methods • Deciding whether or not to apply • Choosing from among job offers	• Assessing candidates for future job performance and retention
3. **Orientation:** The process of initial adjustment	• Coping with the stress of entry	• Managing both emotional and information needs of newcomers
4. **Socialization:** The process of mutual adjustment	• Moving through typical stages • Detecting one's success	• Influencing newcomers with various tactics • Using the psychology of persuasion

the traditional "selling the organization" and "realistic recruitment." The latter recruitment strategy will be advocated in this book.

The selection phase of entry can likewise be separated into individual and organizational perspectives. From the job candidates' viewpoint, people are concerned with coping while the organization is assessing them. They must cope with job interviews since virtually all organizations use this as one assessment method. They must also cope with other assessment techniques such as psychological testing. Finally, they must choose an organization from among those making job offers.

The organizational perspective of selection has been the topic of much research during the twentieth century. The primary focus of these efforts has been to define the necessary knowledge, skills, and abilities for particular jobs, and then to design corresponding methods that will reveal these qualities during the preentry selection phase. Perhaps the best example of work in this direction is the considerable effort that has gone into the development of useful psychological tests. This history is only briefly covered in this book since it has been the topic of several others (e.g., Anastasi, 1982; Arvey & Faley, 1988; Guion, 1965).

The primary focus in the organizational selection of job candidates is on a subset of assessment techniques that have in common the dual perspectives of individual and organization that are emphasized in this book. This particular group of techniques is unique in that it tries to accomplish two objectives: (1) to provide information to the organization about a job candidate's suitability for a job, and (2) to provide information to a job candidate about the desirability of a particular job. This group's three techniques are realistic work sample tests and simulations (Asher & Sciarrino, 1974); assessment centers and simulations (Gaugler, Rosenthal, Thornton & Bentson, 1987; Stumpf, 1990; Thornton, 1992); and "structured" interviews (Janz, Hellervick & Gilmore, 1986; Latham, Saari, Pursell & Campion, 1980). These are discussed in Chapter 5.

The final two stages concern the postentry "adjustment" of newcomers and organizations to each other. Newcomer orientation is a topic new to this edition. As will be argued in Chapter 6, it is important that a particular type of orientation be held for newcomers. Furthermore, orientation is seen as sufficiently different from socialization that treating it as a separate topic is warranted. The theme of the orientation chapter is how organizations can help newcomers cope with the considerable stress associated with organizational entry. In the final postentry stage, newcomer socialization is described as one way (along with selection) to maintain the status quo in an organization. Socialization will be examined as a process of adjusting to both a new work group and the culture of the larger organization. From the perspective of newcomers, there will be a discussion of how to detect the "success" of your own assimilation, as you move through the typical stages of socialization. From the perspective of organizations, the psychology of persuasion is described and tactics for socialization are discussed.

Why the Study of Organizational Entry Is Important

The most important reason why considerable attention should be placed on the entry of new organization members is that the cost of "premature" turnover is quite high. It takes a while for almost all organizations to get newcomers to "pay their own way" by being sufficiently productive to repay the costs associated with their recruitment, selection, orientation, and training. The costs vary widely from job to job and organization to organization, but there are *always* costs—even for the lowest level, lowest paid jobs.

As an example of how replacement costs are calculated, consider the case of bank tellers from my own experience (Dean & Wanous, 1984). This particular bank estimated that it cost them $2800 each time there was an early quit, i.e., someone left during the first six months after beginning work. In today's dollars (figuring 5 percent inflation per year), the replacement cost would be about 40 percent higher, or about $4000 per teller. The cost breakdown is as follows: $200 for hiring costs, $100 for orientation, $2000 for three weeks of training, $500 for the cost of continuing training while on the job, and $1200 for the cost of "lost production" while the new teller becomes fully competent. This last cost element is necessary because a newcomer is simply less efficient than a more experienced teller—it usually takes 20 weeks of on-the-job experience for the average teller to become fully competent.

The fact that turnover is expensive is certainly a good reason to look more carefully at entry from the individual's viewpoint. This conclusion is further reinforced by also recognizing that the *highest turnover rates are found among the newly hired employees*. Most companies calculate turnover rates as a percentage. For example, if a small manufacturing company had a steady average work force of 500 employees throughout a full year, but it hired 75 people during that period, the annual turnover rate for the whole company would be 15 percent. Such rates can also be calculated for departments or smaller units within the organization, and they can be calculated for particular groups of employees based on sex, age, race, or how new they are to the organization. For example, some companies calculate the turnover rates for new MBAs hired. When calculated on a basis other than the total organization, rates can be quite high—often over 100 percent per year within particular types of jobs.

One of the most extreme examples of low job survival among the newly hired was reported in a study of self-service gas station attendants (Avner, Guastello & Aderman, 1982). Of the 437 new hires, about 80 percent quit within two months of being hired—an annualized turnover rate of 480 percent. The remaining 20 percent all quit within the next seven months, so that after a mere nine months, *all* of the newcomers were gone.

A study of new job placements through the New York State Employment service (Wanous, Stumpf & Bedrosian, 1979) clearly shows that the highest turnover rates are for newcomers. Table 1.2 shows the percentage of new hires who dropped out during each of seven time periods of four weeks each. Although these data come from only one study, the persons included were placed in a wide variety of jobs and organizations throughout the entire state, so they are reasonably representative.

An interesting approach to combining replacement costs and attrition is taken by the U.S. Navy (Morrison, 1990). The first calculation is how much it costs in recruitment and training to graduate one new recruit from whatever training school they attended. This varies considerably with the skill and complexity of some specialties. For example, the highest cost specialty (fire control technician for ballistic missiles, $101,000) is *17 times* more expensive than that for the lowest cost job (boatswain's mate, $5800). However, when the Navy takes into account the degree of attrition from each specialty, the cost figures increase dramatically. The type of calculation made is the total cost to the Navy to obtain *one* person in an occupational specialty through subsequent reenlistments. This calculation, thus, incorporates the initial costs, plus the varying attrition rates from each specialty. Considering the high cost specialty of fire control technician for ballistic missiles, the total cost to have just one person remain in the Navy through the third enlistment is over $700,000. The same figure for the lowest cost specialty is about $58,000 for the boatswain's mate.

Table 1.2
Turnover Rates for Newcomers to Organizations

Time Period	Percentage Who Left During Period	Cumulative Percent	Annual Turnover Rate
Weeks 1–4	33.5	33.5[†]	402% (first month)
5–8	9.7	43.2	
9–12	6.9	50.1	
13–16	1.7	51.8	
17–20	2.3	54.1	
21–24	1.0	55.1	
25–28[*]	2.3	57.4[†]	115% (after 6 months)

[*]A total of 1736 persons was tracked for 29 weeks. Of this group, 1239 left and only 497 remained at work longer than 28 weeks.
[†]The annual turnover rate is twelve times the cumulative % for the first month and two times the cumulative percent for the first 6 months.

A Model of Matching Individuals and Organizations

A major theme in the examination of the entry process is the "matching" of individual and organization. A model of this process is shown here and will be referred to repeatedly throughout the entire book as the Matching Model.

Figure 1.1 is based on the Minnesota studies of *vocational* adjustment (Dawis & Lofquist, 1984; Lofquist & Dawis, 1969) that has been changed to an *organizational* focus (Wanous, 1978, 1980). It shows two ways in which individuals and organizations get matched to each other. The upper portion of the diagram shows that the capabilities of an individual are matched to the organization's job requirements. This matching process is the traditional view of organizational selection. The major consequence of a *mis*match is on the newcomer's job performance at work. Over the years the concern of matching people and organizations has been most often expressed as the upper portion of this figure. Clearly

Figure 1.1
Matching Individual and Organization

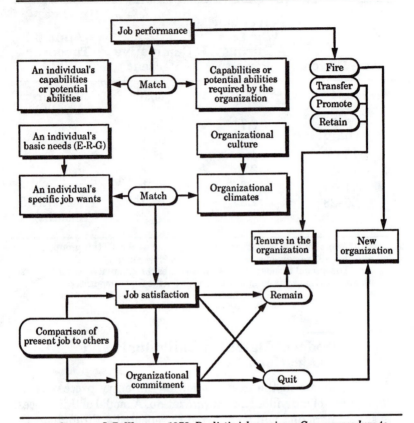

Source: J. P. Wanous, 1978, Realistic job previews: Can a procedure to reduce turnover also influence the relationship between abilities and performances? Personnel Psychology *31: 250. Reprinted by permission.*

this represents the viewpoint of the organization rather than that of the individual.

In contrast, the lower part of the figure shows a second type of matching process, that between the specifically wanted job outcomes of human beings and the capacity of organizational climates to *reinforce* those wants. The impact of a mismatch is directly on job *satisfaction* and indirectly on *commitment* to the organization, rather than on the level of job *performance*.

Table 1.3
Examples of Specific Job Wants in Each of Three Needs Categories

Existence Needs

Salary level
Fringe benefits
Fairness in pay
Physical safety at work
Physical aspects of working conditions

Relatedness Needs

Work or live with friendly people
Get respect from others (customers, friends, co-workers)
Get support from other people
Remain open in communications with others
Desire feeling of prestige from others

Growth Needs

Degree of challenge at work
Desire for activities in which you are independent
Degree that your abilities are used to their fullest
Personal involvement at work
Feeling of self-esteem

Having shown this general model, several questions still remain. First, what is the difference between an individual's basic needs and specific job wants? Second, what is the difference between an organization's culture and its various climates? Third, what is the factual basis for the Matching Model? Fourth, can a mismatch at the "top" of Figure 1.1 also affect job satisfaction and commitment? Can a mismatch at the "bottom" influence job performance?

Needs Versus Specific Job Wants

For years psychologists have searched for a comprehensive set of basic human needs that would be representative of most people. This resulted in a variety of different "lists" of what should be considered basic, but relatively little agreement among the various investigators who proposed them. It is crucial to realize, however, that the term "needs" refers to a *category* of specific job wants rather than to a single factor (Lawler, 1973). Table 1.3 shows this relationship for a three-category system of human needs: Existence, Relatedness, and Growth (Alderfer, 1972).

The three-category system, E-R-G for short, seems to be in accord with research that has been done. (Alderfer, 1972; Wahba & Bridwell, 1976; Wanous & Zwany, 1977). For the sake of comparison, Figure 1.2 shows how E-R-G compares with the well-known, five-category system proposed many years ago by Maslow (1943).

The advantage in using E-R-G is that each of the three categories refers to a different focus or orientation of the individual. For example, Existence needs refer to one's desire for material things—a very tangible type of need. Relatedness needs refer to one's relationships with other people. Finally, Growth needs refer to an inward orientation toward one's self or one's personal growth.

Culture Versus Climate

The relationship between culture and climate parallels that between individual needs and specific job wants. That is, organizational culture is a more basic idea, i.e., a concept that is at a higher

Figure 1.2
Comparison of Maslow and E-R-G Needs Categories

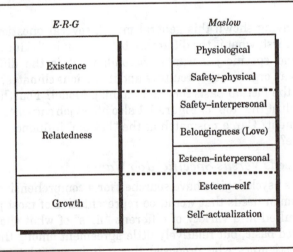

level of abstraction, than organizational climate. Culture refers to the subconscious assumptions, shared meanings, and ways of interpreting things that pervade an entire organization (Reichers & Schneider, 1990). On the other hand, organizational climate refers to the shared perceptions of "the way things are around here." For example, an organization is usually considered to have many particular climates (Schneider, 1975a) such as the climate for service, safety, cooperation, and the rewards/punishments for good/poor performance. When people are asked to describe what it is like to work in their organization, the characteristics that they mention most often are called the various climates of the organization.

As in the case of human needs and specific job wants, in the organizational environment there appears to be a link between the broader, more basic concept (culture) and the more specific one (climate). This model shows organizational culture as causing specific climates to emerge in an organization. Thus "matching" for organizational entry occurs between a newcomer's specifically wanted job outcomes and the capacity of various organizational climates to fulfill those wants.

What Is the Factual Basis for the Matching Model?

The Matching Model shown in Figure 1.1 is actually quite complex. There are many components, and the relationships among them are fairly intricate. To conduct research on the model is actually quite difficult. As a result, no single study has tried to examine the model in its entirety. However, a number of studies have focused on various components of the model. Thus the validity of the model rests on being able to "put all the pieces together," as if one were assembling a puzzle. Although this may be unsettling to some readers, it is the best that can be done at the present time. A more optimistic view is that there is considerably more research now than when I first proposed the model (Wanous, 1978).

One research study of 1736 new hires throughout New York State (Wanous, Stumpf & Bedrosian, 1979) was designed to test some of the connections shown in the Matching Model. To do so, it was first necessary to separate voluntary and involuntary turnover. Then measures of performance and satisfaction were obtained. According to the model, job satisfaction should be lower for those who quit voluntarily than it is for those who leave involuntarily, and this is what was found. Furthermore, job performance ratings by supervisors should be higher for those who stay in the organization or who leave voluntarily as compared with those who leave involuntarily. This was also found to be the case. Finally, there should be moderately strong relationships between job performance and involuntary turnover on the one hand, and job satisfaction and voluntary turnover on the other. This was also found to be true. Although this study examined the consequences of *both* match-ups, there were no direct measures of the match-ups themselves.

Other research studies have not examined both match-ups, but they have been fairly comprehensive in their concern with those relationships at the "bottom" of the model, i.e., the effect that matching has on job satisfaction, and the relationships among job satisfaction, commitment, and job quitting. Probably the most comprehensive of these studies was one of 393 information systems and data processing personnel from nine major insurance companies (Vandenberg & Scarpello, 1990). This study measured the degree of employee match-up and related it to subsequent levels of job satisfaction, organizational commitment, and voluntary turnover. Their results supported the model. In fact, their data and that of others to be discussed here led to a revision in the model. In the present version, organizational commitment is an *indirect* result of the matching process.

Two other studies also confirm that job satisfaction and organizational commitment are separate factors, and that commitment is most likely a result of one's job satisfaction, because commitment is a stable attitude that develops over time (Werbel & Gould, 1984). The first of these two studies reexamined data from two previously published reports (Bluedorn, 1982; Michaels & Spector, 1982), which were studies of 106 mental health workers and 157 insurance company employees. The second of the two studies (Farkas & Tetrick, 1989) looked at 440 male Navy recruits during their first 20–21 months in the service. Taken together, these studies pointed to job satisfaction as being the direct result of a newcomer's matching between his or her specific desires and the fulfillment of those desires by the organization's various climates. Other studies have confirmed that organizational commitment is a direct cause of a newcomer's desire to stay or to quit (Porter, Crampon & Smith, 1976; Werbel & Gould, 1984). One recent review of 35 studies of organizational commitment found that the average correlation between job survival and commitment is about −.20 (Randall, 1990). However, another recent review reported a –.28 correlation, indicating an even greater rate of turnover stemming from low commitment (Mathieu & Zajac, 1990). (See the Appendix for an explanation of the correlation coefficient.)

Of all the studies examining the matching of individual job wants to organizational climates, only one was actually an experiment in which newcomers were categorized by their specific wants and then placed in "appropriate" working environments (Morse, 1975). Clerical employees ($N = 35$) were divided into two groups according to whether they wanted to work in a highly complex and ambiguous environment or in the opposite sort of environment. A third group of newcomers was placed on jobs without taking into account those wants (this is called the "control" group). After eight months on the job, both experimental groups (each being appropriately matched, even though their respective working environments were quite different) felt much more competent and able to cope with the demands of their jobs than those in the control group.

The emphasis in the Matching Model of Figure 1.1 is on matching an individual's specific job wants to various organizational climates. Up to now nothing has been said about matching a newcomer's basic needs to the culture of the organization. This is because it seems less likely that this type of more "distant" match-up will have as great an impact. Nevertheless, several studies (Bretz, Ash & Dreher, 1989; Caldwell & O'Reilly, 1990; Chatman, 1989; McClelland & Boyatzis, 1982) have attempted to study this type of matching. The results of need-culture matching are not that clear-cut. With the exception of one study (McClelland & Boyatzis, 1982), which did find a clear effect of this type of match, the others did not actually examine the entry of newcomers, and their results are not as strong. This is as would be expected, given the way that the Matching Model is presented in its current version. (The original version did not distinguish between these two types of individual-organization match-ups as is done in the current version.)

One final issue about the Matching Model—the effect of job performance on turnover—has been debated among those who study employee turnover. One review of this issue found no clear relationship, i.e., sometimes high performance was linked to *low* turnover, but at other times it was linked to *high* turnover (Jackofsky, 1984). It was concluded that the best explanation is that performance is positively related to *voluntary* turnover (good performers leave because they *can* leave) and negatively related to *involuntary* turnover (poor performers *must* leave). If this were true, it would suggest adding an extra link to the Matching Model. However, a more recent and comprehensive review of this issue suggests otherwise (McEvoy & Cascio, 1987). That is, high performance is linked to *staying* in the organization, and poor performance is linked to having to leave, as the Matching Model shows. There was no support for the idea that the best performers leave.

Individual Capabilities and Organizational Requirements

The top portion of Figure 1.1 shows that a mismatch between one's capabilities and the job requirements results in poor performance at work. The evidence for this link comes from years of research on the validity of selection procedures for predicting the future performance of job candidates. Ghiselli (1966) summarized all the available studies from 1920–1966 and concluded that it was easier to predict success in training programs than in actual on-the-job performance (average correlations of .29 versus .19).[1] In an update (Ghiselli, 1973), the averages increased to a correlation of .39 for the prediction of training success and .22 for the prediction of job performance.

More recently, reviews and summaries of various assessment methods for predicting future job performance have come to more optimistic conclusions, particularly regarding mental ability testing (Hunter & Hunter, 1984). One major review of Ghiselli's data, plus new studies completed afterwards, concluded that the average validity of ability tests is about .50 (Hunter & Hunter, 1984, p. 90). That is, the average correlation between test scores taken from job candidates *correlates* .50 with later measures of actual job performance. Another review of the testing research focused only on those studies that had been published in scientific journals (Schmitt, Gooding, Noe & Kirch, 1984). They found average correlations of mental (and physical) abilities closer to .30. Regardless of which review is more persuasive, both conclude that

---

1. A correlation is an index number used to show how closely two things are related to each other. It can have values of −1.00 to +1.00. A correlation of zero indicates no relationship at all between two things. Increases away from zero (in either a positive or negative direction) mean that two things *are* related to each other. See the Appendix.

ability testing is an accurate way to predict future job performance. Since these tests are usually less expensive than alternative methods for selection, they can be quite useful to employers.

As an example of this renewed interest, consider the U.S. Army as an example of the largest employer of new personnel in this country. A massive project designed to develop a complete selection and placement system was conducted between 1983 and 1988 (see the entire issue of *Personnel Psychology* for the summer of 1990 for a report of this project). During a typical year, the Army screens 300,000 to 400,000 applicants and selects 120,000 to 140,000 (Campbell, 1990). Those selected must then be appropriately placed in one of 276 entry-level positions (called MOS, for Military Occupational Specialties). The magnitude of this effort needs accurate, yet inexpensive methods to handle such an overwhelming number of people and positions. Testing to measure a person's capabilities/potential is the key to being successful. When a battery of tests was used to predict a newcomer's performance, very strong results were obtained. Specifically a study of 4039 newcomers in nine very different MOS found that the Army's ability test battery predicted on-the-job performance with a multiple correlation of $R = .65$ and predicted "general soldiering proficiency" with $R = .69$ (McHenry, Hough, Toquam, Hanson & Ashworth, 1990).

The example of the U.S Army is a particularly good one because it shows how one very large organization was able to carefully define the required capabilities/potential, and then use tests to estimate these factors in newcomers so that they could be placed in appropriate MOS. The results of doing this are quite strong, and they lend considerable support to the upper portion of the Matching Model.

The conclusion I reach about the overall Matching Model is that the evidence available today is much more extensive than when this was first proposed (Wanous, 1978, 1980), and that the evidence is much more convincing. This is true with respect to both of the key match-ups in the model.

The increased enthusiasm for ability testing to facilitate the "upper" match-up is probably more the result of better methods for analyzing the research that has been conducted than of major breakthroughs in new testing methods. The particular method of assembling individual research studies and combining their results is called "meta-analysis." It refers to how we go about trying to make sense of the many individual research reports that frequently reach different conclusions. This method is explained more fully in the Appendix.

The version of meta-analysis used in the personnel testing area today (Hunter & Schmidt, 1990) was first developed in 1977 (Schmidt & Hunter, 1977). The technique was designed to assess the degree to which different results from different research studies could be explained in terms of the small samples of people usually used in personnel testing research. (It has been estimated that the average size of a study is about only 70 people.) Everyone knows that the conclusions reached from a study of only a few people are questionable. The reason for this is that small samples yield results that are not representative. Because they are not representative, small-sample research studies are likely to produce unpredictable results—results that can be much lower *or much higher* than would have been found if a larger group of people had been studied. It is this "volatility" of results from small samples that makes an entire area of research appear as if there are no general conclusions. The unique contribution of the meta-analysis technique developed by Schmidt and Hunter is its ability to remove concerns about drawing conclusions from a body of research in which there appears to be wide disagreement. This is done by attributing most of the apparent disagreement among studies to the high degree of sampling error that each study has by itself. In plain language, it is now perfectly reasonable to trust the *average* results from a large body of research without worrying too much about the level of disagreement among the studies that compose the body.

Thus the support for the individual capabilities and organizational requirements match-up comes mostly from reanalyzing the large body of research that has been done on personnel selection. In contrast, the support for the matching of individual job wants and organizational climates comes from new research conducted during the last 10–15 years. Remember that this body of research is not nearly as large as that from personnel selection testing. Even though the research support is positive and encouraging, the total amount of study on the matching of individual job wants to organizational climates is still relatively small and needs to be increased.

Some people have questioned the very nature of trying to represent human behavior at work as has been done in Figure 1.1

(Salancik & Pfeffer, 1978; Schneider, 1987). The crux of the argument is that it is impossible to separate individuals and organizations as entities that are relatively independent of one another. Instead, they argue that people and organizations cannot be separated because they influence each other so much that any separation would be purely arbitrary. Basically the critics of the Matching Model approach are saying that individual-organization relationships are so dynamic that they preclude representing either individuals or organizations as separate entities, as has been done here.

Despite this valid criticism, I believe the approach is still quite useful. The main reason for this is that the Matching Model is used to represent the *entry* process. In this particular context of newcomers joining an already established system, it still makes very good sense to consider individuals and organizations as separate entities that need to be matched for both effective job performance and for personal job satisfaction. It is only some time *after* newcomers join organizations that the "boundary" between the two becomes increasingly less clear. Since this book is about the joining and entering process, it seems perfectly valid to represent that process as has been done in Figure 1.1.

Are There Other Consequences of Mismatches?

Can a mismatch between specific job wants and organizational climates also have an impact on job performance? Can satisfaction be influenced by a mismatch between capabilities and job requirements? The answer in both cases is yes, in some instances. Since these examples are less frequent than those shown in Figure 1.1 these linkages are omitted from the model and discussed here instead.

Most studies of mismatches between individual job wants and organizational climates (i.e., low commitment and job dissatisfaction) focus on their probable influences on turnover and absenteeism. Many have also been concerned with job performance, however. In fact much of management theory has been preoccupied with the possible link between job satisfaction and performance, which has been unfortunate. (See Schwab & Cummings, 1970, for a review of this history).

Contrary to what many people believe to be true, the relationship between satisfaction and performance is not as strong as has been thought. The average correlation between the two is about .15 to .20 (Brayfield & Crockett, 1955; Iaffaldano & Muchinsky, 1985; Petty, McGee & Cavender, 1984; Vroom, 1964; Wanous, Sullivan & Malinak, 1989). Satisfaction and performance may be linked in a particular organization (e.g., Wanous, 1974) or in a specific situation (Cherrington, Reitz & Scott, 1971), however. Chris Argyris (1964) has done a good job of identifying instances in which low satisfaction resulted in the employee's poor performance as a way of retaliating against the organization that is the cause of the dissatisfaction. Sometimes this can go to extremes, e.g., sabotage.

A study of 307 U.S. Navy personnel found that job *performance* could be affected by the degree of match/mismatch between specific job wants and organizational climates (O'Reilly, 1977). The Navy personnel were divided into those who regarded work as merely something that one does to get money and security ("instrumental" orientation) and those who regarded work as an opportunity to experience personal growth and achievement ("expressive" orientation). The types of jobs these personnel did were divided into those that were more complex and challenging and those that offered little challenge. The results clearly showed that the "expressive" personnel were more satisfied and committed to the Navy when they were on "challenging" jobs, as would be predicted by the Matching Model. These personnel were also higher performers, too. Since the type of matching done here primarily concerned the nature of work performed, perhaps these results are not too surprising. If the matching had been done on climates other than the nature of work, the effects on job performance would probably not be as strong. Nevertheless, this is an example of how one type of match-up can affect a wider range of outcomes than would normally be expected.

When abilities and job requirements are mismatched, turnover can result. This is most likely to occur when the individual is *over*qualified for a job, rather than underqualified. In this case, quitting is the most likely result, depending on the number of available jobs elsewhere. As an example, a telephone company used to have the operator-hiring policy of wanting college graduates or those with at least some college experience. This policy was relaxed when it became clear that operators with too much education were difficult to retain. This example also serves to reinforce the usefulness of the Matching Model. Had this company taken the comprehensive view of entry illustrated in Figure 1.1, it would not have required its operators to have so much education. The company's focus on job performance led it to the "more is better" policy regarding education and prevented it from realizing the policy's potential impact on turnover. Had the company recognized that overqualified operators might also be mismatched in terms of specifically wanted job outcomes and organizational climate, it might have avoided costly turnover problems. It took the company about two years to get that policy changed, and then the turnover rate was lowered.

A recent study on the topic of "person-job fit" examined the consequences of matching *one's own assessment of competence* as compared to the types of competence required for success in the organization (Caldwell & O'Reilly, 1990). This study of seven diverse organizations is unusual in that the assessment of competence/skills was made by the individuals themselves, rather than by some form of testing/assessment by the organization. It is a noteworthy study in that it presents a new way of measuring the concept of "fit," or "matching." This method is too complex to be explained here, however, but will undoubtedly become quite useful in the future because it *quantifies* the degree of matching on a high-to-low scale. The study is also noteworthy in that it shows that job satisfaction can be affected by a mismatch in capabilities and job requirements, although the analysis mainly focused on the more likely consequences on job performance.

In summary, the main point in listing these exceptions to the Matching Model is simply to show that organizational reality is always more complex than any schematic model can represent. In mentioning these "exceptions" to the major predictions of the Matching Model, do not forget that the bulk of the research on newcomers shows that the links in the model are the most likely consequences. However, other effects of the matching process will always occur in certain situations.

Conclusions

1. Organizational entry is a two-sided process in which individuals choose organizations and organizations select individuals.
2. It is important to study the entry of newcomers to organizations because the exit of valued employees is very expensive. Not all turnover is costly, however, since

it is clearly desirable to have poor performers leave. Thus it is important to distinguish between voluntary and involuntary turnover.

3. The entry process can be represented schematically as a *dual matching process*. One match is between the individual's specific job wants and the capacity of the organizational climates to fulfill them. The direct consequence of this match is on job satisfaction, and, indirectly on organizational commitment and voluntary turnover. The other match is between the individual's capabilities/potential and the requirements of a particular job. The direct consequence of this match is on job performance, and, indirectly, on *in*voluntary turnover.

The Plan of This Book

The chapters that follow can be divided into the four phases of the entry process. The next two chapters focus on recruitment—the process of mutual attraction. In Chapter 2, it will be seen that outsiders to organizations really know very little about them. Two philosophies of recruitment are contrasted, traditional and realistic, and a preference for the latter expressed. In Chapter 3, the second chapter on recruitment, how to do realistic recruitment is described in detail. Results from organizations using realism are summarized. In these two chapters on recruitment, the perspectives of the individual and organization are both taken into account.

The second phase—the process of mutual choice—also contains two chapters. The first of these, Chapter 4, is written primarily from the perspective of the newcomer individual; it concerns how one makes the choice to join a new organization. Chapter 5, however, is written from an organizational viewpoint; it focuses on how newcomers are selected for job offers by organizations. The third phase is orientation—the process of initial adjustment. Chapter 6 discusses the immediate period after entry in terms of orientation programs to help ease the transition. Chapter 7 concerns the fourth phase of entry called organizational socialization—the process of mutual adjustment.

2

Organizational Recruitment

Recruitment is examined from the dual perspective of the individual and the organization. This chapter is divided into five parts, each of which will (1) show the relationship of recruitment to the entry model already developed, (2) identify conflicts between individuals and organizations during recruitment, (3) describe what "outsider" individuals really know about organizations, (4) show the most effective sources used by organizations to find newcomers, and (5) differentiate between two very different philosophies of recruitment. Chapter 3, Realistic Recruitment, goes into greater depth and detail about how realistic recruitment has been done in various types of organizations, and its effectiveness for increasing the job survival of newcomers.

Relationship of Recruitment to the Model of Organizational Entry

In Chapter 1, the Matching Model of individual and organization was presented (Fig. 1.1). Two different types of matchings were shown: (a) between capabilities (and/or potential) *and* organizational job requirements, and (b) between specifically wanted job outcomes *and* organizational climates. Keeping these two matchings separate, it can be argued that *recruitment* has its greatest impact on the latter matching, whereas *selection* (Chapter 5) has its greatest effect on the former matching. The Matching Model demonstrates further that the effectiveness of *recruitment* can be best assessed by examining employee job satisfaction, organizational commitment, and voluntary turnover. On the other hand, the effectiveness of *selection* methods is better judged by examining the job performance and involuntary turnover of new employees.

It is, however, overly simplistic to treat the twin matchings as existing separately from each other because they are closely linked. The twin processes of matching individual and organization are interrelated due to a rather high degree of tension that constantly exists between them, as will be discussed in the next section.

Conflicts During Organizational Entry

One of the clearest statements about the conflicts surrounding the dual nature of choice during organizational entry can be found in the work of Porter, Lawler, and Hackman (1975). Figure 2.1 summarizes the four types of conflict they have identified.

Two of the conflicts (numbers 1 and 2) occur between individuals and organizations. Type 1 occurs because individuals need to have complete information about an organization, and the information needs to be accurate. Without such information, the individual cannot make a very wise choice, i.e., one that matches specific job wants with organizational climates. The conflict occurs because the typical actions that organizations use to attract, or recruit, newcomers (1) do *not* give *full* information (usually they only give positive information, and (2) do *not* give *accurate* information (sometimes the recruiters give biased descriptions).[1]

The second conflict between individual and organization occurs for many of the same reasons as the first. Most individuals feel that it's important to generate as many job offers as possible, in an attempt to obtain one that will be highly desirable. Because of this desire, individuals are not prone to disclose their own shortcomings and quite often describe their desired job in terms of what they think the organization has to offer (rather than in terms of what they would really prefer).

Conflicts 3 and 4 are internal to either the organization or the individual. The third conflict indicates that recruitment efforts may hinder effective selection of new personnel. The goals of any

---

1. The motives behind this type of recruiter strategy, called here the *traditional method,* are discussed later in this chapter and are contrasted with *realistic recruitment.*

Figure 2.1
Conflicts During Organizational Entry

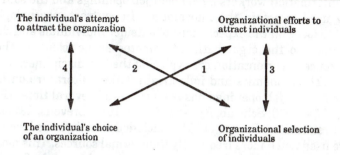

The individual's attempt to attract the organization

Organizational efforts to attract individuals

4   2   1   3

The individual's choice of an organization

Organizational selection of individuals

Source: L. W. Porter, E. E. Lawler, III, and R. J. Hackman, 1975, Behavior in Organizations, p. 134, Reprinted by permission of the McGraw-Hill Book Company.

personnel input function are to *both select and retain* competent people. Thus typical recruitment practices that emphasize information limited only to the positive aspects of the organization may result in a mismatch between individual specific job wants and organizational climates, as shown in the Matching Model. The fourth conflict can be explained in somewhat the same fashion. When individuals misrepresent themselves to appear more attractive to an organization, they run the risk of being offered jobs ill suited to their own capabilities and wants. The individual's final choice of a job depends on those that are actually offered. Therefore, an individual's efforts to appear overly attractive do influence *which* jobs are offered. Consequently the individual's own choice of an organization is limited to those that offer admittance.

What Do "Outsider" Individuals Know About Organizations?

Researchers have tried to answer this question in two ways: (a) how do outsiders find out about job openings, and (b) how accurate is the information outsiders have about those organizations with job openings.

Information About Job Openings

Labor economists and industrial relations specialists have studied the information workers have about job openings and the sources they used to obtain the information. In contrast, psychologists tend to focus on the expectations of outsider individuals and their reactions to the organizational climates as newcomers. These differences in orientation are typical of the two disciplines.

The economics and industrial relations literature on how workers find job openings has been reviewed several times (Parnes, 1954, 1970; Schwab, Rynes & Aldag, 1987; Stevens, 1977). In the first review, Parnes (1954) concluded that *informal* sources were used much more frequently than formal sources. This meant that workers found out about job openings by word of mouth through friends and relatives in about 80 percent of the cases. This conclusion was based on Parnes's interpretation of six studies which included ten groups of workers on 16 different jobs (Heneman, Fox & Yoder, 1948; Kerr, 1942; Myers & MacLaurin, 1943; Myers & Schultz, 1951; Reynolds, 1951; and de Schweinitz, 1932). A review by Stevens (1977) concluded that blue-collar workers used friends or just applied directly to jobs about two-thirds of the time. Besides using informal sources, workers were also not considered very rational (in the sense of obtaining full labor-market information) because they made job choice decisions based on certain minimum standards. If an opening came along that met a worker's personal standards, it was usually taken. Classical economic theory, in contrast, holds that workers should have continued to search for alternative job openings in the hope of finding one that would be a perfect match, not just one that was minimally satisfactory.

In a second review by Parnes (1970) a different picture emerged due to the addition of other studies. The second review concluded that the behavior of white-collar workers differs considerably from the behavior of blue-collar workers. In particular, white-collar workers fit more closely the image of economic rationality because they tend to obtain much more information about job openings than do blue-collar workers. (See Foltman, 1968; Rees, 1966; Sheppard & Belitsky, 1966.) Rather than relying on informal sources about 80 percent of the time, white-collar workers obtain job openings information from formal sources about 50 percent of the time. This same conclusion has been reached by a more recent review (Schwab et al., 1987).

Information About Organizations Themselves

Based on the earlier discussion of the organizational entry Matching Model (Fig. 1.1) and the conflicts occurring during entry (Fig. 2.1), it should be quite clear that individuals need complete and valid information to make effective organizational choices for themselves. This raises the issue of how much the typical "outsider" job candidate knows in comparison to more experienced "insider" members of organizations. Research on this issue has been conducted in business, the armed forces, and education.

Business. The most comprehensive, and longest in duration, of the studies in business organizations was conducted at the American Telephone and Telegraph (AT&T) company (Bray, Campbell & Grant, 1974; Howard & Bray, 1988). This study, known as the Management Progress Study, includes a wealth of data. A total of 274 college recruits, who were hired in the summers of 1956, 1957, 1959, and 1960, were assessed thoroughly by a team of professional industrial psychologists at the time of hiring. For the first twenty years, their job performance, promotions, and job attitudes were monitored by the personnel research unit of AT&T. After eight years, the group had shrunk to 167, and after twenty years, it was down to 137. A group of 148 non-college graduates was also hired in 1958–1960 and followed for twenty years, when 129 remained.

The first indication of unrealistic expectations held by these recruits came in the analysis of two sets of data: (1) what the recruits *wanted* in a job, and (2) what they *expected* to find at AT&T. The analysis of these two responses showed that the recruits expected to find jobs almost exactly like the ones they wanted (the correlation between expectations and wants was .87). This was interpreted as completely unrealistic because it is a good example of how one's *wants* can influence one's *expectations*.

When attitudes toward AT&T were measured, there was a steady downward trend for the first eight years. The new recruits did not find the reality of organizational life to be quite as they had expected. Figure 2.2 shows this trend. Attitudes fell from initially high, positive levels for the college graduate management group to lower levels over the first eight years and dropoff occurred for *all* employees, both high and low job performers. (The definition of successful performance was whether or not the employee

Figure 2.2
Attitudes at Work for AT&T Managers

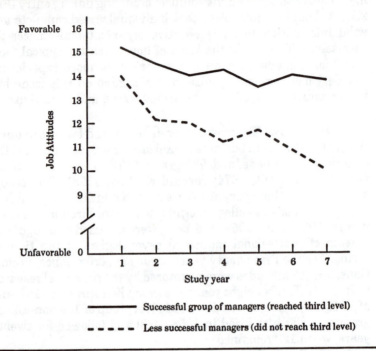

Source: D. W. Bray, R. J. Campbell & D. L. Grant, 1974, Formative Years in Business, *p. 158. Copyright © 1974 by John Wiley & Sons, Inc. Reprinted by permission of John Wiley & Sons, Inc.*

had reached the third level of management, called middle management, by the eighth year with AT&T.)

The drop off in expectations did not continue beyond the seventh or eighth year, however (Howard & Bray, 1988). This leveling off of negative attitudes was found in both the college and non-college groups. Thus the newcomers to AT&T took quite a few years to adjust to the system, but they did finally adjust. Other studies (to be discussed later) also show the decline in attitudes after newcomers enter organizations. These AT&T results are particularly important because they represent both college and non-college graduates in both management and nonmanagement jobs, and particularly because the newcomers were tracked for the first *twenty* years—a feat that no other study has come close to duplicating.

The Ford Motor Company also tried to assess why some managers stayed and others left (Dunnette, Arvey & Banas, 1973). From a total group of more than 1000, they divided the employees into Stayers (525) and Terminators (495), based on whether or not the person stayed or left within the first four years of employment.

For the Stayer group, the researchers found that four of the five *most important* job characteristics also had the largest *discrepancies* between expectations and the employees' present experiences on the job. When the discrepancies were calculated for the *first* jobs held, three of the five most important characteristics were among those with the largest discrepancies between expectations and reality. Figure 2.3 shows these results.

The fact that the largest discrepancies found were for those job facets that were rated as most important had very significant implications for Ford management. Note also that the greatest *dis*confirmation of expectations by reality occurs for one's *first* job, rather than for later jobs held within the company. This may be because people can switch to jobs that are closer to their expectations. A second reason for the smaller discrepancy for subsequent job choices is that insider experience teaches individuals what to expect. Of the important job characteristics, pay level was the closest to what was expected. This is probably because pay is easy to measure and job candidates can check on it, as found earlier by Wanous (1972b).

There are several other studies of newcomer expectations among entry-level workers in service industries, who are typically low paid, e.g., telephone operators, bank tellers, and nurses. These studies are particularly interesting and somewhat surprising because they come to the same conclusions as those of management personnel just described. These service jobs are probably more "visible" to job candidates than the typical management job because these job candidates probably have been customers of the service already. Therefore, you would expect the candidates for these service jobs to have had fairly realistic expectations.

A study of telephone operators (Wanous, 1976a) found that expectations measured prior to entry were higher than subsequent reports of actual on-the-job experiences one and three months later. These declines were found on virtually all questions that were asked. A similar study of supermarket checkout clerks

Figure 2.3

Discrepancies Between Job Expectations and Job Experiences for First Jobs and Later Jobs at the Ford Motor Company

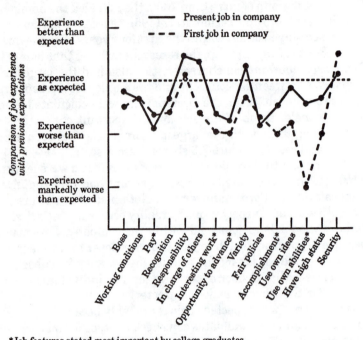

Present job in company
--- *First job in company*

Comparison of job experience with previous expectations

Experience better than expected

Experience as expected

Experience worse than expected

Experience markedly worse than expected

Boss, Working conditions, Pay*, Recognition, Responsibility, In charge of others, Interesting work*, Opportunity to advance*, Variety, Fair policies, Accomplishment*, Use own ideas, Use own abilities*, Have high status, Security

*Job features stated most important by college graduates

and baggers (Dugoni & Ilgen, 1981) found more inflated expectations than accurate ones, but in a few cases, newcomer expectations were actually worse than later realized. A study of bank tellers (Colella, 1989) followed 175 new hires through their training and into the first three months on the job. The most highly inflated expectations concerned the rewards they might expect from the job (pay and promotions). There were slightly inflated expectations about the nature of teller work and relatively accurate expectations with regard to interpersonal relationships (those with the boss, co-workers, and customers).

Because of the traditionally high turnover in nursing, there have been several studies of this particular occupation. Fisher (1985) followed 366 graduates of nursing school through their first six months on the job (where the group had dwindled to 210). When expectations were compared to later perceptions about the job, *not one person said that things were better than expected.* In fact, three out of four nurses reported either moderate or high levels of disconfirmed expectations. The greatest number of unmet expectations was found at three rather than six months. This is probably because "learning the ropes" occurs right away. Less dramatic results, but still quite similar, have been reported in two other studies of nurses' first few months on the job (Hom & Griffeth, 1985; Pierce & Dunham, 1987).

Where do job candidates get such inflated expectations? There is no definitive answer to this, although research on MBA graduates from the Harvard Business School identifies one source—recruiters from business itself (Ward & Athos, 1972). This study, conducted by two professors at that school, examined the expectations of 378 students. The students' expectations for a particular company were compared with the recruiters' descriptions of the same company. There were very few differences between these two sources of data across 14 different types of work expectations. The correlation between the students' expectations and the recruiters' job descriptions was .48, indicating the strong influence of recruiters on student expectations.

The Armed Forces. Since the advent of the all-volunteer armed services, the various services have become increasingly interested in studying the problems of recruitment, selection, and reenlistment of volunteers. The armed forces now face many of the same problems as private industry.

The single most comprehensive study of expectations in the military was done on 7989 Navy personnel in six diverse occupational specialties (Hoiberg & Berry, 1978). These recruits were surveyed four times over the first two years: (a) the first day of training, (b) midway through training, (c) at graduation from training, and (d) after one year of active duty. The authors report that expectations were inflated and that the degree to which they were met was positively related to staying in the Navy. The sheer magnitude and the diversity of this study make it particularly persuasive. There have been other studies of newcomer expectations in the military, but many of them are unpublished and thus generally unavailable. However, Wiskoff (1977) summarized the following conclusions from this body of research:

1. Regardless of the country (Australia, Canada, the United Kingdom, or the United States), youth seem to hold similar attitudes about life in the armed services.
2. The expectations of preservice individuals are usually in error and are usually inflated, but with a few important exceptions.
3. The exceptions to the general trend of inflated expectations are pay levels and the severity of basic training. Pay is better than expected and basic training is not as bad as feared.
4. Recruiters are the major source for creating expectations of those not already in the military service.
5. Intentions to remain in service decline the longer someone is in the service.

Educational Organizations. Similar results can be found in educational organizations, too. For example, a study of nursing school students (Katzell, 1968) found that first-year expectations were unrealistically high and that dropping out of the program was related to them. The most detailed study done in schools was of three different graduate schools of business administration in New York City (Wanous, 1976a). The incoming MBA candidates filled out questionnaires at three points during entry into these schools: (1) as outsiders in the summer before entry, (2) as newcomers during the fall of the first year, and (3) as insiders at the end of the spring term.

The 15 specific questions asked these individuals could be collapsed into two broad categories: (1) *intrinsic* to the process of education, e.g., excellent teaching, competition for grades, practical skills being taught, and chances for personal growth, and (2) *extrinsic* to the learning process, e.g., reasonable tuition, location of school, getting credit for previous work, and an attractive atmosphere. Of these two categories, there was a clear decline for the intrinsic, not extrinsic, factors from naive (i.e., inflated) levels to more realistic (i.e., lower) levels. In contrast, the students seemed to have fairly realistic expectations about concrete, practical matters. The best explanation for these results is that the intrinsic factors were too abstract for students to obtain solid information. On the other hand, a factor such as tuition could be accurately assessed by outsiders who have not actually been inside the organization.

Consequences of Unrealistic Expectations: Low Satisfaction

It is quite reasonable to predict that newcomers to organizations will be disappointed when they realize that many of their expectations will not be met. This has been called the "theory of met expectations" (Porter & Steers, 1973). This theory was offered as one explanation of why employees quit—particularly newcomers who have by far the highest turnover rates. Even though it may seem like common sense, the theory of met expectations is somewhat complicated. First, it really has two aspects: (a) unmet expectations cause low job satisfaction, and (b) low satisfaction causes newcomers to quit. Second, the theory really only applies to those expectations that are "important" to newcomers, e.g., salary and chances for promotions. When newcomers' expectations about relatively *un*important factors are disconfirmed, the typical reaction is more one of surprise than dissatisfaction (Greenhaus, Seidel & Marinis, 1983; Locke, 1976).

The theory of met expectations has been particularly appealing to those who study the behavior of newcomers. It is seen as a reasonable explanation of two well-established characteristics of newcomers: (a) their inflated expectations regarding most aspects of the work environment, and (b) their much lower job survival rates compared to employees who have been in the organization for a longer period of time.

Only recently has anyone tried to examine the met expectations research that has been done in order to see if this enthusiasm is warranted (Wanous, Poland, Premack & Davis, 1991). Our review covered 31 studies of 17,241 people, and we specifically examined the effects of met expectations on initial job satisfaction, organizational commitment, the intention to quit, and whether or not the newcomer actually quit. The results of this review are quite consistent with the Matching Model developed in Chapter 1 (Fig. 1.1).

That is, the strongest effects of unmet expectations are found on job satisfaction and organizational commitment, followed by one's intent to remain in the organization and then by actual job survival (stay or leave). The effect of met expectations is fairly strong, too. When met expectations were related to satisfaction/commitment; the average correlation was .39; with intent to remain, it was .29; and with job survival, it was .17. Since newcomers actually decide whether to quit or to stay long after initial job satisfaction and initial organizational commitment are typically measured, it is not surprising that the effects of unmet expectations get weaker over time (Hulin, Henry & Noon, 1990).

From a research perspective, the preceding studies are probably the best evidence for the effects of met expectations on the attitudes and behavior of newcomers. From a practical perspective, however, many managers and students do not know how to interpret a correlation coefficient. (See the Appendix.) Thus a second type of research study may be more convincing. This type of study follows newcomers from the time of entry, through the first few months, and in some cases through the first few years on the job. When such a study clearly shows that newcomer satisfaction decreases over time, the results are also consistent with the theory of met expectations, and they are a bit easier to understand.

Five studies of newcomers to organizations have examined satisfaction with various aspects of the organization. Once again the AT&T study (Bray et al., 1974) contains significant data gathered on a yearly basis for the first eight years with that company. The AT&T researchers divided their questions into those concerning *personal* versus *job* satisfaction. For *personal* satisfaction, there was a decline up to the third year, a slight rise for the next two years, and then a slight falling. The difference between the first and last measurements was not statistically significant, although personal satisfaction was lower at the end of the study. The group of managers was split into those who made it to third level (i.e., middle) management and those who did not. As might be expected, there were few initial differences. After the third year, these two groups became quite different in terms of personal satisfaction. The successful group's average continued to rise from the third year on, whereas the unsuccessful group showed only a slight rise after year three and then a decline.

The *job* satisfaction trend for the AT&T managers was different from the personal satisfaction trend. Instead of dropping in the first three years, job satisfaction rose slightly. This, however, was followed by a steady decline to the extent that the final level of job satisfaction was significantly lower than the initial level. In contrast to personal satisfaction, there were few differences in job satisfaction between successful and less successful groups.

A study done at Sears (Smith, Roberts & Hulin, 1976) gathered job satisfaction data from over 98,000 blue- and white-collar employees at 132 branches located throughout the United States. Data were collapsed into three time periods extending over a ten-year span of time (1963–1969, 1967–1970, 1971–1972). A total of seven areas were measured (supervision, financial rewards, career future, kind of work, etc.).

On an overall basis, the Sears data show a downward trend for five of the seven areas of job satisfaction. One area did not change (amount of work done), and one area dropped and then rose (financial rewards). To try to isolate trends for the newly entered employees, those with less than one year's tenure in the 1967–1970 group were compared with those with one to five years of service in the 1971–1972 group. There was a decline for five of the seven areas (supervision, amount of work done, co-workers, physical surroundings, and career future). Kind of work done and financial rewards both increased.

The AT&T and Sears studies show a general decrease in satisfaction with increasing tenure in an organization. In both cases, however, no data were gathered *prior* to entry into these two companies. Three other studies did obtain both preentry and postentry data. The most ambitious of these three traced the attitudes of college accounting majors as they took jobs after graduation (Lawler, Kuleck, Rhode & Sorenson, 1975). An initial group of 711 provided data prior to making an organizational choice; 431 continued in the study by responding to the post-choice questionnaire; 197 provided data after one year on the job. The attractiveness of the accounting firm chosen for one's first job increased immediately after making the choice, but fell in the one-year follow-up. Remember that the immediate post-choice data were gathered *prior* to entry.

A smaller study of Carnegie–Mellon graduates found the same decreasing satisfaction phenomenon (Vroom, 1966; Vroom & Deci, 1971). After one year on the job, 31 of 39 subjects (80 percent) saw their chosen company as less attractive than they saw it initially. After 3.5 years, 12 subjects had changed jobs and were more satisfied than those who remained in their original organizations. Similar results were found in a study of college graduates entering MBA programs (Wanous, 1976a) in three New York City graduate schools of business administration. The satisfaction trend decreased from preentry to postentry. The attractiveness of each school steadily dropped prior to entry, to two months after entry, to eight months after entry.

The most recent research on newcomers has also found the falling satisfaction phenomenon after newcomers enter organizations. For example, a study of 158 Cleveland-area nurses measured a drop between the third week on the job and four months later (Hom & Griffeth, 1985). This finding is particularly interesting because the sample of nurses studied was divided into two groups. One of these was given a "realistic job preview" (to be discussed in Chapter 3) designed to ease the entry into a new organization. The preview worked as planned, i.e., it made initial expectations more realistic and increased job survival for those who saw it. Nevertheless, those who saw the realistic job preview still had falling satisfaction, as did the control group.

Sources Used by Organizations to Find Newcomers

Organizations recruit newcomers from a variety of sources, e.g., newspaper ads, employment agencies, school placement services, in-house notices of job openings, rehires, referrals from employees or friends of job seekers, and sometimes job candidates just "walk-in" seeking employment. Personnel managers are interested in which sources are likely to produce effective newcomers. As it turns out, certain sources are more effective than others. Personnel researchers observing this have tried to explain *why* some sources are better than others. This section summarizes the results of research on recruitment sources by showing which sources are best and for what purpose. It also discusses why certain sources should be better than others.

Effectiveness of Sources

An "effective" newcomer can mean several things. It could mean someone who is particularly competent on the job, or who has high potential for promotion to more complex and responsible jobs.

Effectiveness can also mean that a newcomer does not leave the organization shortly after being hired. Early quits are expensive, as shown in Chapter 1. Ideally, newcomers are both good performers *and* they are motivated to remain in the organization.

When the first edition of this book was written, only four studies had been done on the effectiveness of recruitment sources. These few studies showed that newcomers from such sources as being referred by a present employee or being rehired tended to have longer "job survival" than those from such sources as newspaper ads or employment agencies. In an attempt to make sense of this pattern, I referred to the former sources as "informal" and the latter as "formal." It seemed to me that job candidates from the informal sources were more likely to have realistic expectations about an organization because of the contacts made prior to entry, and that this more complete and accurate information would result in a greater percentage of newcomers remaining with an organization for the first year or so. (See the end of this chapter for details on why realistic expectations should enhance job survival.)

It may, however, make more sense to call those sources associated with greater job survival "inside" sources because they provide "insider" information not typically available to others from "outside" sources. Following this line of thinking, inside information should be provided by the following sources: rehires, referrals, and in-house notices that are typically targeted at current employees. Outside sources are those typically providing less specific information about the organization as a place to work: newspaper ads, employment agencies, and school placement offices. The "walk-in" is difficult to categorize as either an inside or an outside source because it is simply not clear what motivated the person to walk in. If it was particular knowledge of the organization, the person could have insider information. However, some walk-ins could just be those motivated by a whim, desperation, or some other reason not related to their knowledge of the organization. Thus I have assigned the results of the research on recruitment sources to these three categories: inside, outside, and walk-in.

At the present time, 14 research studies have been conducted, and 12 of these assessed job survival rates from various sources (two others concerned job performance and did not report survival rates). These 12 are summarized in Table 2.1.

The first thing to notice in Table 2.1 is that inside sources are virtually always the ones with higher job survival rates for

Table 2.1
Sources of Newcomers and Subsequent Job Survival

Research Study				Rate of Job Survival		
Year	Authors	Number of People Studied and Job Type	Length of Time from Entry	Inside Sources	Outside Sources	Walk-ins
1966	Ullman	144 clerical 114 clerical	1 year 1 year	25% 62%	12% 32%	N.A.[3]
1971	Gannon	6390 bank	1 year	76%	65%	71%
1972	Reid	279 metal trades	1 year	39%	20%	25%
1979	Decker & Cornelius	514 bank 1793 ins. agent 199 service	1 year 1 year 1 year	67% 69% 95%	59% 60% 86%	57% 64% 90%
1983	Caldell & Spivey	1400 store clerks	1 month	22% white 13% black	19% white 21% black	N.A.
1983[1]	Taylor & Schmidt	300 seasonal packaging plant	6 months	58%	37%	45%
1984	Breaugh & Mann	99 social serivce	1 year	83%	76%	87%
1985	Swaroff, Barclay, & Bass	618 technical sales trainees	2 years	78%	75%	N.A.
1986	Conard & Ashworth	7255 insurance sales agents	1 year	48%	37%	52%
1989[2]	Kirnan, Farley & Girsinger	5037 insurance sales agents	1 year	41.6 wks.	38.2 wks.	N.A.
1989	Colella & Wanous	63 bank tellers	1 month	83%	62%	97%
1990	Williams, Labig & Stone	234 nurses	1 year	67%	63%	72%

1. This is the mean amount of tenure expressed as a percentage of the number of possible days that could have been worked since it was only seasonal employment.
2. Average number of weeks employed was reported; not job survival rates.
3. N.A. means not available.

newcomers, and that most of the studies looked at survival rates for the first year on the job. One way to calculate how effective inside sources are in obtaining longer term employees is to determine the percentage increase in job survival rates compared to those from outside sources. For example, if the survival rate for an outside source is 50 percent for the first year (i.e., of all those hired in a particular period, half stay and half leave by the end of the first year), and the survival rate for inside sources is 60 percent, this represents a 20 percent increase ($[60 - 50] \div 50 = 20\%$) .

There are two ways to calculate the percentage gain in job survival from inside sources: an average gain across all the studies and an average gain across studies when each study is "weighted" by the number of people in the study. The former method treats all studies equally even though they have substantially different numbers of people. The latter method gives more weight to a study with a large number of people. Both methods are used here. The reason for calculating both average gains in job survival is that the overall average can be dramatically affected by a single large sample study. In the present case two studies of life insurance agents are much larger than those of other job types. By comparing the weighted and unweighted average gains, it is possible to see how these two large sample studies affect the overall average. This is a procedure that has been recommended by statisticians (e.g., Hunter & Schmidt, 1990). The average gain in job survival using inside sources is 36 percent when the studies are simply averaged, and it is 24 percent when the studies are weighted by their respective sample sizes before averaging them.

An average difference between the two sources can be misleading, however. For example, an organization with a job survival rate of 90 percent from outside sources cannot be easily improved. Even if the inside sources increased this all the way up to 100 percent, the gain would be only 11 percent ($[100 - 90] \div 90 = 11\%$). Thus it should be clear that the *lower* the job survival rate, the greater the chance for a high percentage improvement using an inside source. Figure 2.4 shows the relationship between job survival rate for outside sources and the *percentage gain* when compared to inside sources. The correlation between these two factors is –.75. As can be seen in Figure 2.4, one study is an "outlier," i.e., its results are quite different from all the rest. When this one study (Caldwell & Spivey, 1983) is removed, the correlation increases in strength to –.90. Therefore, an almost perfect

Figure 2.4
How the Gain in Job Survival from Inside Recruitment Is Affected by the Job Survival Rate

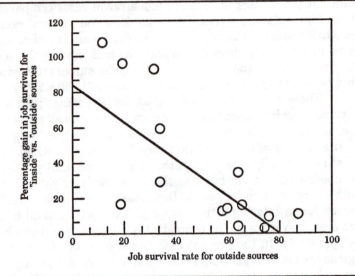

relationship exists between the percentage gain for inside recruiting sources and the basic level of job survival for outside sources. As was said at the outset, the greater the problem of low job survival, the greater the gain to be made from using inside sources. Nevertheless, there are always gains to be made, even at the highest levels of job survival.

The conclusion from Table 2.1 and Figure 2.4 is that organizations have quite a lot to gain in terms of increased job survival rates for newcomers when they have severe retention problems. These gains can be made by using the inside sources as much as possible and by decreasing reliance on outside sources. It may not always be possible to emphasize one type of source at the expense of another in certain types of labor markets, but this research does indicate the direction toward which an organization should move in order to increase retention among newcomers.

Research on differences among recruitment sources has also examined both job performance and attendance (see a review of these by Wanous & Colella, 1989). Far fewer studies have been done on these two indicators of new employee effectiveness. Only two studies of absenteeism have been conducted, so there simply is not sufficient data to detect any trends at this time. There have been five studies of job performance, but no conclusive trends have emerged here either. (As will be seen later in this chapter, there is no strong reason to expect recruiting sources to be related to job performance. Thus the absence of any trend is about what one would expect to find.)

Explanations for Increased Survival

Personnel researchers have been curious as to why inside sources so consistently produce newcomers who are less likely to quit. Two primary reasons have been given for this. The first reason is the realistic information explanation that was briefly mentioned earlier. Hill (1970) first mentioned it, but it was given more credence and exposed to a wider audience in the first edition of this book. At that time, the theory of realistic recruitment not only explained the effects of inside recruiting sources, but also the effects of realistic job previews (see Chapter 3). To a researcher, having a reasonable explanation of this relationship makes the relationship more believable and less likely to be considered a fluke.

According to the realistic information explanation, newcomers from an inside source are a better "match" to the organization because they had the opportunity to drop out from further consideration (self-selection). Thus those from inside sources (who continue to pursue an offer) are more likely to be those who believe they will "fit into" the new organization. Furthermore, those from inside sources are better equipped to cope with a strange new environment upon entry because of the more complete and accurate expectations they have developed. Recruits from outside sources presumably do not have these two advantages. In fact, it is likely that they will have substantial amounts of *mis*information, based on the research reviewed earlier showing inflated expectations to be a very general problem among job candidates.

The second explanation for recruiting source differences is what has come to be called the "individual differences" hypothesis. Schwab (1982) appears to be the first to state this possibility. The argument is that different sources yield different *types* of recruits.

Unfortunately those who have proposed this explanation have yet to specify exactly what these differences should be, and this has led to considerable confusion among those trying to study this possibility. Without clear guidelines on what differences should be found between inside and outside sources, different researchers have used different types of demographic variables (e.g., age, sex, education). These have not clearly explained the effect that recruiting source has of increasing job survival.

At the present time, the realistic information explanation is the better of the two that have been proposed. However, being the better explanation does not necessarily mean that realistic information is *the* explanation. As has been pointed out previously (Wanous & Colella, 1989), most of the studies on recruiting source differences have not been properly designed to produce unambiguous results. To properly assess whether realistic information is the explanation for increased job survival rates for inside sources, researchers need to do several things that have not yet all been done at the same time. First, they need to make specific and comprehensive measurements of the most important expectations a new recruit has. Second, they need to measure the degree to which these expectations turn out to be realistic. (One way is to ask newcomers to describe their new work climates after entry and compare what they said prior to entry with what they say afterwards.) Third, they need to use proper statistical techniques to "remove" the effects of realistic expectations from the relationship between recruiting source and job survival. (Multiple regression is the preferred technique.) If there *still* is a link between recruiting source and job survival after having done this, some other factor—possibly some differences in types of people—could be an additional explanation.

Sources of effective new organization members are of crucial importance to organizations—so important, in fact, that most businesses do not publish the results of their own surveys. Such information is considered a business secret because it can give a company a competitive edge over its rivals.

The remainder of this chapter is an extended discussion of two different philosophies, or strategies, of how to recruit newcomers to organizations. The nature of the *traditional* versus *realistic* philosophies is explained. This section is the prelude to Chapter 3, which goes into greater detail on the realistic recruitment method.

Contrasting Philosophies of Recruitment

Earlier in this chapter, a model (Fig. 2.1) was shown that outlined a variety of conflicts that occur during organizational entry. One of the four conflicts concerns organizational recruitment philosophy. Those actions taken by organizations to *attract* newcomers are often at odds with the effective *selection* and *retention* of them.

This section explores the roots of this "attraction and selection conflict." However, it will become clear that *this conflict need not occur*. The conflict is, however, quite real and serious for those organizations that recruit newcomers according to the traditional philosophy (Wanous, 1975a,b). Those organizations that have used the realistic recruitment philosophy do *not* experience the conflict between effective attraction on the one hand, and effective selection and retention on the other.

Let's now explore exactly what is meant by traditional and realistic recruitment strategies, or philosophies. Chapter 3 will focus specifically on the methods of realistic recruitment, the results from organizations that have used it, and those theoretical and practical problems that still need to be resolved.

Traditional Recruitment

The traditional philosophy of recruitment can be best summarized as the practice of "selling " the organization to outsiders. Specifically this selling of the organization involves two actions: (a) positive characteristics, rather than those things insiders find dissatisfying about the organization are communicated to outsiders and (b) those features that are advertised may be distorted to make them seem even more positive. The former practice is called presenting *deficient* information (i.e., omitting the negative) to outsiders, and is quite typical of traditional recruitment. The latter practice injects *bias* into the information given out during recruitment and occurs much less often.

Therefore, traditional recruitment is designed to attract as many candidates as possible. Since this is in conflict with the organization's ability to retain newcomers, it is important to analyze the reasons behind such a policy. At least four reasons have been used to justify the traditional approach: (a) the need for a favorable selection ratio, (b) the desire to retain control or initiative in the entry process, (c) the problems of measuring specific employee job wants versus their capabilities, and (d) the concern with job performance rather than job satisfaction.

Need for Favorable Selection Ratio. The selection ratio of an organization is the proportion of job candidates who are hired. For example, if 100 people apply and 10 are actually hired, the selection ratio is .10 (i.e., 10 ÷ 100), or 10 percent of those who applied. The maximum selection ratio that can occur is 1.00, a situation in which every applicant is hired.

Organizations that have personnel departments to do the selecting of newcomers must justify their own budget. A company with a selection ratio of 1.00 has very little need to spend much money on personnel selection. On the other hand, one with a selection ratio of .10 definitely needs to budget money for personnel selection because it must find a way of rejecting 90 percent of the applicants. In this latter case, it is much easier to justify the personnel budget. Therefore, in organizational terms, a "favorable" selection ratio is one that is *low,* i.e., a small proportion of those who apply are actually hired. One way to make the selection ratio favorable is to use the traditional strategy of selling the organization. By attracting a relatively large pool of applicants, the selection ratio can be lowered.

Desire to Retain Initiative and Control Within the Organization. The more an organization sells itself, the more attractive it will appear to outsiders, and the more applicants it will receive. When this occurs, the selection ratio drops to a more favorable level, as discussed earlier. At the same time, however, the degree of control over the influx of newcomers is increased from the organization's perspective. The greater the percentage of "no admittance" decisions, the greater the control the organization has over the input of newcomers. This is an easy way to reduce the risk involved in bringing any newcomer on board.

A Narrow Focus on Matching Capabilities. In Chapter 1, the Matching Model (Fig. 1.1) was shown. The upper portion of that model concerned the match between an individual's capabilities (or potential) and those capabilities required by the organization.

Although this was only one of the two matchings, most organizations have put their strongest efforts toward the capability and job requirements match, rather than toward the individual job wants and organizational climates match. One reason for this difference in emphasis is that tests of human capabilities are not as easy to fake as those that try to measure an individual's job wants. To obtain accurate data on capabilities, the organization must have a valid assessment procedure. (See Chapter 5 for further discussion.) However, to obtain accurate information about job wants, *both* a valid measurement procedure and the willingness of the individual to provide honest answers are needed.[2] A second reason for this is that the impact of a capability and job requirements mismatch falls most directly on job performance, and this is *assumed* to be *more* costly than the low job satisfaction or organizational commitment resulting from the mismatch between an individual's job wants and organizational climates.

This overemphasis on matching capabilities to job requirements is another reason for the traditional selling of the organization to potential new members because the organization obviously wants to obtain the *best* possible (i.e., most capable) newcomers. Since this is the major concern, the best way to do so is to *attract* as many applicants as possible and then *select* those who demonstrate the greatest competence.

Performance Rather than Satisfaction Is the Greater Concern. Job performance, rather than job satisfaction, is of greater concern to most organizations for at least two reasons. First, the dollar costs of poor performance are felt immediately by the organization and are easier to calculate than are those associated with low job satisfaction. Second, the dollar consequences of negative job attitudes have not been as easy to document in the past as they are today. Job satisfaction is related to many other outcomes at work such as quitting, absenteeism, accidents, and mental illness, but satisfaction is not strongly connected to any of these outcomes. The strongest link with job satisfaction appears to be employee turnover (Mobley, 1982; Porter & Steers, 1973), rather than absenteeism (Rhodes & Steers, 1990).

Realistic Recruitment

Rather than "selling" the organization, realistic recruitment presents outsiders with *all pertinent* information *without distortion*. In the remainder of this chapter, the rationale for realistic recruitment

---

2. In research on consumer preferences for certain products, various methods for obtaining valid data have been developed which do *not* depend on the honest cooperation of individuals. These have involved various physiological measures such as how the pupils of one's eyes expand when viewing certain products. In organizational research, no such measures have been developed.

recruitment is presented. In Chapter 3, the practical issues of how to do it, the research results from those organizations that have used realism, and the theoretical issues concerning realistic recruitment are presented. The best way to understand how this philosophy differs from the traditional approach is to contrast the reasons for using realism with those used to justify the traditional method.

The Need for a Favorable Selection Ratio Is a Myopic View. There is nothing logically wrong with an organization wanting to become "more selective," i.e., to have a low selection ratio, because it does provide powerful justification for the budgetary dollars allocated to the personnel selection process. Furthermore, highly selective organizations are able to get better job performance from their newcomers. The problem with using the selection ratio as the rationale for traditional recruitment is that it is too narrow a view of the entire organizational entry process. It is narrow in the sense that it tends to ignore what happens to newcomers *after* they are inside the new organization. A broader perspective includes not only attracting and selecting competent newcomers but also managing to *retain* them as well. Chapter 3 will show that the realistic strategy results in less turnover than the traditional method without any sacrifice in job performance.

The Importance of Self-Selection Is Increasing. A reason for the popularity of traditional recruitment is that it retains initiative and maintains control over who enters the organization. Although we have seen that organizational entry is a two-sided choice process (Fig. 2.1), traditional recruitment does tend to put the final choice initiative more in the control of the organization than that of the individual. This occurs for two reasons. First, the desire of individuals to join the organization is artificially increased by the traditional approach so that relatively few persons are discouraged from considering the organization. Second, by having a low (highly selective) selection ratio, the organization retains control over who gets in and who does not.

With the Civil Rights Act of 1964 and the subsequent guidelines for selection issued by the Equal Employment Opportunity Commission (EEOC) and by the Office of Federal Contract Compliance (OFCC), many organizations, especially business organizations, have found it harder and harder to make selection decisions based on nonjob-related factors. Today, job performance is considered as virtually the only valid basis for selecting new employees. If a particular method of selection cannot be related to subsequent job performance, it is probably illegal. The "burden of proof" now rests on the shoulders of the organization making the selection decisions to justify the decisions to hire and to reject job candidates (Arvey & Faley, 1988).

The net effect has been to decrease the degree of arbitrary control an organization can exert over the input of newcomers. Simultaneously, the importance of the *self*-selection decisions of individuals (see Chapter 4 on Organizational Choice) has increased. Although these self-selection decisions cannot be directly controlled, they can be influenced by the organization.

The issue today is *how* an organization wants to influence the individual's choice of an organization. All types of organizations are going to have an increasing stake in the accuracy of these choices.

Specific Job Wants Can Be Matched to Organizational Climates. One reason for not trying to match individual job wants to climates is the difficulty encountered in trying to do so. Since self-report measures of what individuals want from a job can be easily faked, those who use traditional recruitment can justify their choices in these terms. There is, however, another way in which job wants may be more closely aligned with organizational climates, and it does not have the faking problem. Simply put, realistic recruitment presents the individual with a large amount of valid data about an organization. The more and better the information, the better each person can decide whether or not to try to join. In other words, matching individual job wants and organizational climates can be achieved via the organizational choices made by the individuals themselves.

Low Job Satisfaction Can Be Expensive

The general relationship between job attitudes and job behavior has been a topic of considerable interest to those who study people at work. It is a topic too vast to be reviewed here, except to make two general points. First, attitudes and behavior *cause each other*, i.e., in some cases, attitudes seem to cause behavior, as when low job satisfaction leads to quitting. At other times, behavior causes attitudes to change, as when a newcomer's actions lead to increased organizational commitment (see Chapter 7). Second, the relationship between attitudes and behavior becomes closer or stronger when the organization has relatively few "constraints." For example, when a snow emergency gave employees a good excuse to miss work, the employees with the lowest attitudes were the least likely to come to work (Smith, 1977). For the study of organizational entry, the relationship between initial job satisfaction and turnover among newcomers is particularly important. As newcomers gain more experience in an organization, their commitment to it begins to crystallize and this commitment is also an important factor in turnover (Werbel & Gould, 1984).

In Chapter 1 the costs of replacing bank tellers who leave in their first year of employment was shown to be $4000. A bank can estimate how much can be saved by reducing such early turnover by the type of analysis shown in Figure 2.5. This figure shows how to estimate turnover cost savings by increasing the job satisfaction of newly hired bank tellers.

Assume that this particular bank has 100 branch locations and that turnover at these branches varies somewhat among the branches. On average, the turnover is 5 tellers per branch per year, ranging from a low of 0 (a branch where no one quit) to a high of 10 who left in one year. Assume further that the standard deviation of this distribution of quit rates is 2. Job satisfaction is measured on a 6-point scale, where a 5 represents very high satisfaction and 0 represents the lowest level of satisfaction. Assume that the average satisfaction among new tellers at this particular bank is a 3 on this scale, and that the standard deviation of job satisfaction ratings is 1. Figure 2.5 shows that if job satisfaction were to be increased by one standard deviation up to an average of 4, average turnover would be reduced by .3 standard deviations (i.e., a reduction of .3 x 2 = .6). Thus the new average quit rate would be 4.4, not 5. Because the bank has 100 branches, only 440 tellers would have to be hired in the next year instead of 500. This "savings" of 60 tellers should be worth about $240,000 per year to the bank (60 tellers x $4000 per teller = $240,000).

Two questions have probably occurred to you at this point. First, you might ask where the −.3 correlation between job satisfaction and teller turnover came from. Although this is just an example of how to do an estimate, this is not an unrealistic number for the typical relationship (Mobley, 1982). However, a company who surveyed their own newcomers would be in a better position to determine their own historical relationship between job satisfaction and turnover. For those organizations not having this

Figure 2.5
Translating Increased Job Satisfaction into Dollar Savings

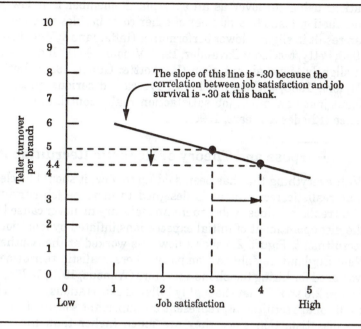

type of information, it is always possible to use the average correlation found in reviews of research from other organizations.

Second, you might ask how this bank would go about increasing job satisfaction since simply waiting for it to go up on its own is not a certainty by any means. The answer is paradoxically both easy and difficult. It is easy because any number of organizational improvements has the potential to increase job satisfaction, e.g., working conditions, supervisory leadership style, pay and benefits, orientation programs (see Chapter 6), or improved socialization tactics (see Chapter 7). The difficult part of this answer is knowing exactly which of these will be most effective in a particular situation—something that is difficult to predict. A safe course of action would be to try to make several improvements, but many organizations might find it difficult to initiate and manage so many changes at the same time.

The main point of this example is to show how to translate job satisfaction among newcomers into dollar costs to an organization, using turnover as an example. Remember that low job satisfaction leads to a number of other costs besides turnover. It can result in slightly lower performance (Iaffaldano & Muchinsky, 1985; Petty, McGee & Cavander, 1984; Vroom, 1964).[3] It can result in slightly lower absenteeism (Hackett & Guion, 1985; Scott & Taylor), 1985, although others have raised serious questions about just how much job satisfaction really contributes to absence (Rhodes & Steers, 1990).

Purpose and Theory of Realistic Recruitment

With everything that has been said up to now, it should be clear that realistic recruitment is designed to increase job survival. Thus realism reduces subsequent unnecessary turnover caused by the disappointment of initial expectations inflated by traditional recruitment. Figure 2.6 shows how this worked at the Southern New England Telephone Company where realistic recruitment was used for hiring telephone operators (Wanous, 1973, 1975a, b). Figure 2.6 shows that the highly inflated expectations, caused by traditional recruitment, represent an important source of initial job dissatisfaction since they are much higher than the level actually found on the job.

Another way to describe the effect of lowering job expectations *before* entering the organization is to call realistic recruitment a "vaccination" (McGuire, 1964) against the negative aspects of real organizational life. The medical concept of a vaccination is to inject a person with a weak dosage of the actual germs that cause a particular disease, for example, smallpox virus. The purpose is to help the human body develop its own resistance and thus *prevent* the disease. The vaccination will *not* cure someone who has already contracted the disease.

Realistic recruitment operates in much the same way as a medical vaccination works because job candidates are given a small dose of organizational reality during the recruitment stage in an attempt to lower initial expectations. (Earlier it was shown

---

3. The average correlation between satisfaction and performance is in the .15 to .20 range; the average correlation between job satisfaction and absenteeism is in the −.10 to −.15 range. See Wanous, Sullivan & Malinak (1989) for a discussion.

Figure 2.6
How Attitudes About Work Change

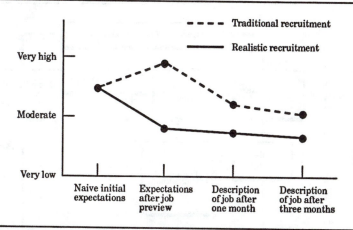

Source: J. P. Wanous, 1975b, Tell it like it is at realistic job previews.
Personnel 52(4): 58. Reprinted by permission of the publisher. Copyright © 1973 by
AMACOM, a division of American Management Associations. All rights reserved.

that inflated expectations are quite common among job candidates). In a manner similar to medical vaccination, realism is *in*effective *after* a person is already inside a new organization since actual job experience provides an ample source of realism.

Besides the "vaccination effect," there are three other ways that realism in recruitment can increase the job survival of new employees: (a) the "self-selection, matching" effect, (b) the "coping" effect, and (c) the "personal commitment" effect. The relationships among all three of these are shown in Figure 2.7.

Besides the vaccination of initial job expectations, turnover can be reduced by a better matching of individual job wants and organizational climates. This relationship is directly derived from the Matching Model. Since people strive to be satisfied, they tend to choose organizations that they believe will lead to personal satisfaction. (See Chapter 4 for the research results on this point.) The better the information job candidates possess, the more effective their own organizational choice can be.

Figure 2.7
Psychological Effects of the Realistic Job Preview (RJP).

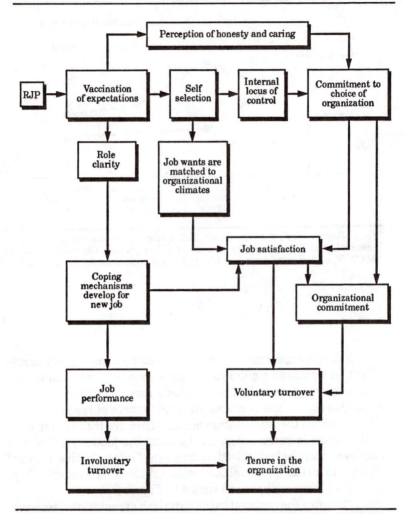

Source: Adapted from J. P. Wanous, 1978, Realistic job previews: Can a procedure to reduce turnover also influence the relationship between abilities and performance? Personnel Psychology *31: 251. Reprinted by permission.*

The "coping" effect is a second way in which realistic expectations can enhance newcomers' entry. Having accurate expectations should clarify the expectations that the organization has for new-comer job performance. This leads newcomers to develop coping strategies so that they will not fail in the new job. Two conse-quences are likely to occur from the development of coping strate-gies. The obvious consequence is that the newcomer is more likely to do a good job and thus less likely to be fired. The less obvious consequence is that the newcomer's coping strategies can "spill over" into job satisfaction because they reduce the anxiety associ-ated with wanting to succeed. In Chapter 6, much more will be said about how organizations can design orientation programs to help in this regard.

Finally, when individuals believe that *they* made a job choice decision without coercion or strong inducements from oth-ers, they tend to be much more *committed* to the decision (Bem, 1970). In situations of coercion or strong external inducements, individuals may comply, but typically do not feel the internal commitment that comes from making their own choices. This is why the research literature on "participation in decision making" has consistently shown that people accept decisions that they have had a hand in making (Vroom, 1969; Vroom & Yetton, 1973; Vroom & Jago, 1988).

The last thing to note here is that these three mechanisms are interlocked. In order for the vaccination effect to occur, the organization must use realistic recruitment. In order for the self-selection matching effect to occur, the vaccination effect must have happened. If expectations have not been "set" at realistic levels, the matching of individual job wants and organizational climates cannot follow. Finally, the personal commitment effect is contingent upon the individual making an organizational choice from among alternative job offers. In some cases, people get only one job offer, so there is no chance to make a meaningful choice.

In some situations the vaccination effect can occur alone without either of the other two. However, the self-selection match-ing effect cannot occur without a prior vaccination. Also, the commitment mechanism is contingent upon a prior vaccination. This interdependency among the psychological mechanisms of realistic recruitment has caused difficult problems for researchers who are interested in determining how realism affects job satis-faction, commitment, performance, and job survival. On the other hand, it has not caused problems for personnel managers because their major concern is with the *degree* of job survival increase due to realism, rather than with the psychological theory of *how* realism acts to increase job survival.

Conclusions

1. The joining process of organizational entry is a *dual* matching process between (a) human capabilities and job requirements, and (b) specific individual job wants and organizational climates.

2. The entry process is also one of *mutual* attraction and selection between individuals and organizations. Traditionally speaking, a number of conflicts are inherent in this view of organizational entry, but they need not occur if realistic recruitment is used instead of the traditional approach.

3. Recruits have inflated expectations about organizations. This happens because recruits cannot easily disentangle their hopes from their expectations. Recruiters also create unrealistic expectations for job candidates.

4. Expectations are most seriously inflated for the most important job factors, with the possible exception of pay.

5. Initially favorable attitudes toward organizations decrease the longer newcomers remain in them—as long as eight or ten years in AT&T or Sears.

6. The best sources of referral for new employees are those from which the recruit will be likely to already have realistic expectations, such as former employees being reemployed or those referred by present employees. Employment agencies and newspaper ads are the worst sources because these recruits have inaccurate expectations.

7. The logical case for realistic recruitment seems more compelling than the case for continued use of traditional methods.

8. The psychology of how realistic recruitment acts to increase job survival is intricate. The "vaccination" of expectations seems to be the cornerstone of this psychological process. A more effective matching between person and organization is also a likely explanation, as is increased commitment to an organizational choice made without much external pressure or coercion.

3

Realistic Recruitment

The focus of this chapter is narrower than that of Chapter 2. One specific aspect of organizational recruitment, the use of *realism*, is examined in four ways: (a) how to diagnose the possible need for realistic recruitment, (b) how to use realistic recruitment, (c) how to develop and provide a realistic job preview during recruitment, and (d) how to evaluate the effects of realistic recruitment. This chapter is addressed to organizations who recruit newcomers rather than to the newcomers themselves. It is designed as a guide for those involved in personnel recruitment for various types of organizations.

Diagnosis of the Need for Realistic Recruitment

Since realistic recruitment is a departure from typical organizational practice, it is necessary to determine whether or not organizational conditions warrant its installation as part of the personnel function. The Matching Model (Fig. 1.1) clearly shows that job satisfaction, organizational commitment, and *voluntary* turnover are the most fertile areas to search for signs of ineffective recruitment. Thus these areas must be monitored during the entry of newcomers. In addition to gathering these data, the organization should also gather information on a variety of specific expectations held by outsiders in order to determine whether or not these expectations are confirmed after entry. Data on *expectation* confirmation (or *disconfirmation*) are important because they can pinpoint areas that are deficient in providing realistic information to recruits.

Presenting realistic information is most typically done *prior to* organizational entry. When this is done, it has been called the Realistic Job Preview (RJP). When realistic information is presented *after* entry, it is part of a newcomer orientation program (see Chapter 6).

Ineffective recruitment may also have an effect on job performance and, consequently, on *in*voluntary turnover. In theory, the *selection* function (see Chapter 5) is designed to screen out those with inappropriate capabilities who may be recruited into an organization. Since selection procedures are far from foolproof, there is no doubt that ineffective recruitment can sometimes create unnecessary involuntary turnover. Although recruitment practices may affect job performance and involuntary turnover, the main impact of recruitment is on the "lower" part of the Matching Model (job satisfaction, organizational commitment, and voluntary turnover).

To monitor an organization for the major symptoms of ineffective recruitment, three types of data from newcomers must be collected: (a) the degree to which initial expectations are confirmed by later experience, (b) satisfaction and commitment, and (c) job survival, especially voluntary turnover rates. Expectation confirmation refers to the comparison of *two* pieces of data: (a) *expectations* reported by *outsiders* to an organization, and (b) *descriptions* of the same job and organization *after* the outsiders have entered the new organization. In contrast, job satisfaction is how one feels about the job itself, and commitment refers to one's attachment to the organization. Organizations need to be able to identify those *specific areas* in which outsiders have inflated expectations, so it is very important that expectation confirmation be measured. Just asking newcomers how satisfied or committed they are does not provide this detailed information.

Measuring voluntary turnover is actually quite complicated. First of all, a job *survival* rate should be calculated for newcomers in specific jobs. This can be calculated in several ways. One is to see how many newcomers are still employed after a certain amount of time has gone by, e.g., six months or a year. When newcomers enter as a group (rather than coming in smaller numbers, but in a steady "trickle"), it is possible to calculate the "half-life" of the group, that is, how long it takes for 50 percent of the group to leave the organization. Both of these methods are preferable to calculating turnover as a percentage of the *total* work force of an organization. This is because the total force contains employees with long tenure in an organization—a group not likely to leave.

After calculating job survival rates or half-life of newcomers, separating voluntary from involuntary turnover is still very difficult. Voluntary turnover refers to the *individual's* decision to leave the organization. Quitting due to dissatisfaction is the most common form, although people resign for other reasons, e.g., to accommodate a marriage partner. In contrast, involuntary turnover refers to actions initiated by the organization, e.g., dismissals, layoffs, or mandatory retirements. The method of categorizing turnover is imperfect because it depends on the quality of the information obtained. Sometimes individuals quit if they know they are going to be fired. Depending on the source of the data (the employee or the organization), a different version of the situation might be obtained.

An important consideration in measuring turnover is to account for the possible effects of performance appraisal on the job survival of newcomers. In many organizations, there is a period in which newcomers are not subject to a job performance appraisal, e.g., students have either a quarter or a semester before course grades are final. In business, the same thing can happen, e.g., new sales personnel may hold a salaried position (during training) for a period of time before going to a commission-on-sales method of payment. As a result, there is usually low turnover during this period, but much higher turnover after the newcomers are put in the field. Similar results have been found with those who sell life insurance. Thus the onset of performance appraisal for newcomers can itself be a cause of turnover for three reasons. First, newcomers may be dismissed for poor performance. Second, newcomers discover for themselves that they are not really qualified to do the new job, and they decide to leave. Third, newcomers may find that the actual job duties are not sufficiently interesting, but this decision is not reached until after the initial training period is completed. The first of these is called involuntary turnover and the latter two are called voluntary.

Since the purpose of this diagnosis is to identify recruitment problems, not other organizational problems, a general rule is that such measurements should be made right after entry and should continue regularly for at least several months. The longer newcomers are inside organizations, the *less* likely are their attitudes and behavior a result of entry, hence the need for early and continuous monitoring of newcomers.

A Case Study of Diagnosis

This case study (Dean & Wanous, 1984) of diagnosing an organization for a possible realistic recruitment program was selected for several reasons. First, the organization was having a difficult time retaining newly hired employees. This bank had to hire about 600 new tellers yearly just to maintain a work force of about 1200. This represented a considerable hiring/replacement cost, and it seemed that an RJP program might be of some help. Second, this was an entry-level job, and unemployment in the labor market for this job was low at the time this study began. (When the study ended two years later, however, unemployment in this labor area had risen dramatically.) Third, two methods were used to conduct the diagnosis: interviews of bank tellers (and other employees) and questionnaires administered to the entire core of employed tellers at this bank.

Using a combination of interviews and questionnaires is probably the most desirable way to conduct such a diagnosis, but it is rarely done because it is so time consuming—in this case, the diagnosis took about one year to complete. The combination of methods is desirable because each approach to diagnosis has its weaknesses. However, the weaknesses of one approach can be the strengths of another. Thus using a combination is ideal because the methods complement each other.

During the interview phase of organizational diagnosis, a variety of employees are asked what it is like to work there. Talking to a cross-section of personnel generally ensures that a variety of experience is represented, i.e., from those who are new at work to those with many years of experience. Interviewing can be relatively easy to do and does not have to take up too much time (Wanous, 1989). In contrast , the more systematic approach of using a questionnaire can be fairly expensive. This is particularly true if you decide to survey a large number of employees because their time away from work can be expensive. (You could avoid this cost by having the employees complete the surveys on their own time, but typically fewer people complete the surveys.)

The interview and questionnaire methods of diagnosis were combined at this large midwestern bank. At the outset about 100 employees were interviewed. These included tellers with varying experience as well as those who supervised tellers and some bank executives familiar with the job. The goal here was to learn the particular language of this job, i.e., its jargon. Being able to speak in the language of the particular organization enhances an outsider's credibility to the organization. When the questionnaire was finally designed using this bank's jargon, its familiar terminology probably enhanced the chances that these employees would fill out the survey and give their honest answers (Alderfer & Brown, 1972).

In conducting these interviews, the interviewer should focus on two questions: (a) which factors in your working environment are most likely to cause you to think about leaving for another job, and (b) of those factors, which ones are most in need of being described realistically to newcomers because the typical newcomer has inflated expectations about them. Those factors in the working climates for bank tellers that meet *both* of these criteria are the ones that *must be* included in an RJP. Inflated expectations that are not important enough to cause quitting can be omitted. Beliefs about very important factors such as pay need not be included if the typical newcomer has accurate expectations for starting pay—which is fairly typical (Wanous, 1972b, 1976).

Following the interview phase of this diagnosis, the next step was to design a questionnaire survey that would measure a wide variety of beliefs about what it was like to be a teller in this bank. The survey was, thus, a combination of questions about factors uncovered in the interviews (the local jargon and the employees' concerns) as well as questions about other elements of the typical organization drawn from previous research on the job characteristics that affect employee satisfaction and motivation (Dawis & Lofquist, 1984; Hackman & Oldham, 1980; Smith, Kendall & Hulin, 1969).

In analyzing the survey data, you should conduct three analyses. First, when the bank tellers are separated into groups based on tenure, do their beliefs about particular organizational climates differ among the groups. Specifically, do the newest tellers say it is a friendly place to work, but the experienced tellers say it is not? Any clear trends from relatively positive beliefs among the most newly hired to more negative beliefs among the most experienced constitute potential material to be included in a realistic recruitment program. So, the first step in analyzing the survey data is to look at the means (averages) for various questions to see if such trends exist.

Looking at trends in means—from high newcomer expectations to lower insider beliefs—is but one type of analysis. The second analysis is to examine the "standard deviations" of these various means. This is a statistical term meaning how much people tended to say the same thing, or whether there was considerable variability among employees in how they answered the survey questions. The greater the standard deviation, the *less* likely are people to be answering in the same way. When this happens, it is difficult to call a particular factor part of an organizational climate (Schneider, 1975a,b). To be an element of an organizational climate, employees must tend to agree among themselves, e.g., almost everyone agrees that it is difficult to get promoted within a year of joining the bank. Organizational climates are *shared beliefs*, i.e., beliefs with *low* standard deviations.

The last analysis to be done on the survey data is to correlate the various questionnaire items with employee job satisfaction and with thoughts of quitting the bank. If particular factors have high correlations, they are probably important enough to be included in an RJP because they could cause job dissatisfaction and could lead newcomers to think about quitting.

The three analyses just discussed can be considered "tests" of which factors to include in a realistic recruitment program. When a survey is done to diagnose an organization, a great many questions are asked. Since each organization is unique to a certain degree, it is often impossible to know what should go into an RJP until after the survey data are analyzed. Those factors that "pass" all three "tests" are the ones that must be included in the RJP.

Table 3.1 shows the particular results we found in this bank. As indicated in the table, we actually constructed two RJPs from interview and survey data. The first RJP was much more specific than the second, although both were realistic. The difference was in the degree of specificity—one RJP simply had more information than the other. This was done to study the effects of increasing detail in an RJP since the RJP research prior to this one had not varied the amount of information given to job candidates.

Table 3.1
Comparison of Realistic Job Preview (RJP) Booklets

Topic	Specific RJP	General RJP
Training	Describes training. Mentions final exam at the end of training. Reports failure rate during training.	Does not mention training content nor failure rate.
Work	Describes banking transactions. Stresses importance of accuracy and warns that it is checked daily. Advises of pressure conditions Mondays & Fridays. States that manager schedules work 1 week in advance. Warns of long periods on your feet. Warns of tendency of work to become routine and repetitive.	Describes banking transactions.
Customers	States that courtesy is always required. Warns of rude customers.	States that courtesy is always required.
Career opportunities	Specifies promotion criteria. Gives average promotion rates for each job. Explains how to move into branch management (college degree needed).	Describes the various teller positions.
Compensation	Specifies pay rates. Describes employee benefits. Explains how pay increases are determined.	Specifies pay rates. Describes employee benefits.
Summary of major points	Includes a summary—1/2 page long, titled "It's not for everyone."	Does not include a summary.

Source: Adapted from Dean & Wanous (1984). The effects of realistic job previews on hiring bank tellers. Journal of Applied Psychology, 69, 61-68. *Copyright 1984 by the American Psychological Association. Adapted by permission.*

Guidelines for When to Use Realistic Recruitment

Diagnosing organizational recruitment problems clearly shows that several conditions must be present in order to justify the use of a realistic job preview (RJP) during recruitment. First, the organization must have a problem retaining newcomers who are effective performers. That is, there must be a problem of the better employees quitting. If only the worst newcomers quit, this would be less of a problem (Dalton & Todor, 1979), but hiring costs still could be significant. Second, the low job survival among the newcomers must be linked to their dissatisfaction resulting from inflated and unfulfilled expectations, and thus to their inability to become committed to the organization. Remember that a great many factors can cause dissatisfaction and low commitment, e.g., low pay, poor leadership, or undesirable working conditions. Realistic recruitment is not designed to solve all the causes of low job survival. Rather, it is designed to address one particular factor: unrealistically inflated expectations, which can cause poor job choices and difficulties in newcomer adjustment.

Even if the problem of inflated expectations among job candidates has been identified, several other factors must be considered prior to installing a realistic recruitment program.

Labor Market Conditions

Over the last several decades, labor economists have shown that the lower the overall level of unemployment in the economy, the higher the quit rates in industry (Eagly, 1965; Gilroy & McIntyre, 1974; Thomas, 1953; Woytinsky, 1942). Two factors seem to account for this: (a) during good economic times, the "marginal worker" is drawn into the labor force, but this type of employee is most likely quit a job, (b) the availability of alternative job opportunities causes employees to reconsider the degree to which they are willing to continue with the same organization (see Hulin, Roznowski & Hachiya, 1985).

The second factor above is of relevance for realistic recruitment. When job candidates have several job opportunities, an RJP can help them make better self-selection decisions and lead to greater job survival. On the other hand, if the candidate has no alternatives to consider, an RJP probably will not affect a candidate's job choice.

The Selection Ratio

Realistic recruitment is best used when the organization has a low selection ratio, i.e., it hires only a small percentage of job candidates. In this situation, the RJP can be used to help screen out job candidates who would not "fit" well with the organization. If an organization must hire almost all of those who apply, the need for realistic recruitment decreases considerably. In this type of situation, the organization should concentrate on helping newcomers succeed through effective training (Wexley & Latham, 1991), orientation (Chapter 6), or socialization (Chapter 7).

The Type of Job

Since realistic recruitment is designed to provide job candidates with valuable information they do not have, some jobs require more of that information than others. For example, an RJP can enhance hiring at the entry level because these individuals are completely new to the organization. In contrast, someone who transfers internally already knows quite a bit about what it is like to be in a particular organization.

A second factor to consider is the "visibility" of the job to an outsider who is a job candidate. Job candidates can observe some jobs—particularly service positions—prior to their actually going to work. A careful observer can get a reasonable idea of what it might be like to be a bank teller, supermarket checkout clerk, or gas station attendant.

The common theme running through both entry-level jobs and those with low visibility is the likely *low* level of accurate information a job candidate has. Thus realistic recruitment can fill this void with both pertinent and accurate information.

Guidelines for Designing RJPs

Chapter 2 presented a theory of how RJPs lead to increased job survival (see Fig. 2.6). A variety of psychological mechanisms were suggested as explanations for the link between realistic recruitment and job survival: (a) preentry expectations are "vaccinated" against on-the-job disappointment, (b) self-selection (one's job choice) is more effective, (c) commitment to job choice is increased as a result of seeing the organization as trustworthy and as a result of feeling free to choose another job instead, and (d) newcomers are able to cope more effectively. The guidelines for designing an RJP described in the following sections are based on this theory, i.e., the principles suggested here are intended to implement these psychological mechanisms.

Encourage Self-Selection Explicitly

The purpose of showing a job preview to job candidate should be made clear at the beginning of an RJP and again at the end. People should be told why they are being given a booklet, shown a video, or told certain things in a job interview. By telling job candidates to consider the realistic job preview information carefully and to make a thoughtful job choice, the organization triggers the psychological mechanism of presenting itself as caring and trustworthy as well as encouraging the candidates to make more effective job choices. This is perhaps best exemplified in one video I have seen (Reilly, Brown, Blood & Malatesta, 1981) in which some job candidates are shown rejecting a job offer by getting up and leaving because they didn't think they would like the job.

Have Message Credibility

It is of paramount importance that job candidates believe what is communicated to them in the RJP. The implementation of this principle differs somewhat depending on the form of the preview, i.e., whether it is a booklet, video, or job interview. A booklet RJP should state that the material was obtained from the employees themselves, e.g., the results of an attitude survey. The more objective the presentation of the information is, the more believable it will be. A video RJP should probably use actual employees rather than actors. They should also speak in their own words, rather than read from a script. The more natural and the less contrived the video is, the more the job candidates will be able to identify with the people they see (Fisher, Ilgen & Hoyer, 1979). An interview RJP should be conducted by an interviewer who has worked in the job. If this is not possible, someone who is currently working in the job could join the job interviewer as a more credible source of information.

The Medium and the Message Must Be Consistent

Two types of inconsistencies are to be avoided here. The first inconsistency occurs when the type of medium used does not match the length of the message. Specifically, if quite a lot of job preview information is to be conveyed, a booklet may be the best medium for communicating with job candidates (Chaiken & Eagly, 1976). Shorter RJPs may lend themselves better to video presentations because videos tend to persuade more effectively than booklets (Eagly & Himmelfarb, 1978; McGuire, 1985).

The second type of inconsistency to be avoided pertains only to video job previews. This inconsistency occurs when the video scenes do not "match" the audio messages. I have seen several instances of videos showing interesting pictures of people at work (lots of action, smiling faces) at the same time that the audio portion was sending a more negative message. Presenting such a conflicting message to job candidates dilutes the impact of an RJP. A more subtle example of this mixed message was observed in my first RJP study (Wanous, 1972a, 1973). In this case, telephone operators were taken on a job visit before they were asked to accept a job offer. This was well intended as a type of job preview. However, in a relatively short visit, job candidates only saw a "high tech" room with well-dressed people in a clean environment. They were not able to ascertain how the people actually felt about the job.

Communicate Feelings as Well as Information

A program of realistic recruitment certainly must include pertinent information in those areas likely to be important to newcomers and also in areas likely to need "deflating." Sometimes we forget that employee feelings about the work itself and the various facets of organizational climates are also important information, too. The RJP should not be composed solely of sterile facts, no matter how pertinent they might be. Having a real employee say in his or her own words what is wrong with the organization will be more persuasive when the person's feelings are also apparent to the listener. In booklet RJPs, this presents more of a problem. One solution is to report results of employee attitude surveys that list those areas that typical employees find to be the most dissatisfying.

RJP Content Should Mirror Organizational Climates

Every attempt should be made to match the "balance" of negative versus positive job factors found in the diagnosis of organizational climates to that in the job preview itself. It is a popular misconception that RJPs contain nothing but "bad news." This is not necessarily true. To the extent that the job has certain satisfying facets, these, too, should be included.

This balancing of negative and positive content is a tough judgment call (Wanous, 1989). Making the preview extremely negative—to the point of being personally threatening—may increase the number of job candidates who decide to go elsewhere, but some of these people may have been satisfied and successful employees. Only a careful diagnosis and analysis of the various organizational climates will enable you to make this judgment call.

Do the Preview Early

One way that realistic information increases job survival among newcomers is in helping them make effective self-selection decisions. For this to happen, job candidates need to consider several job possibilities. If for some reason they become committed to a particular alternative, they may not give serious consideration to the information in an RJP. This can happen if candidates put a lot of their own time and energy into seeking out a job offer. Going to the company, filling out applications, being interviewed, being tested, perhaps being interviewed a second time requiring a second trip, and so on all add up to considerable energy expenditure. For the candidate, this effort easily translates into a feeling of being committed to accepting the job offer in order to justify all of the energy spent in trying to get it. One of the best known findings in psychology is that energy expenditure increases commitment—a finding that has held up over many decades of research (Lewis, 1965; McGuire, 1985). Thus RJPs should be presented to a job candidate early in the hiring process, before the candidate becomes too committed to a particular job.

Realistic Recruitment in Practice

A variety of organizations (business, education, and the military) have all tried realistic recruitment in one form or another. The common element in all these efforts is the attempt to increase the job survival of newcomers. However, the methods used in realistic recruitment are quite different. In this section, several examples show the varieties of realistic recruitment. It should become clear that the use of realism is a *general approach* to recruitment, rather than a specific technique, and that it needs to be tailored for each individual organization. One example is described for each of these types of organizations.

Business Organizations

Studies of realistic recruitment can be found in a variety of jobs: telephone operators, life insurance agents, sewing machine operators, supermarket checkout clerks, and so on.

The first published experimental study of realism was done at the Life and Casualty Insurance Company of Tennessee (Weitz,1956). Following this successful experiment, Prudential Insurance revised the booklet for its own study of life insurance agents (Youngberg, 1963). Although now dated, this example is of historical importance because it launched the concept of creating realistic expectations during recruitment.

Some samples from the Prudential booklet[1] follow:

A Prudential representative finds that a high degree of personal recognition is available. And a successful Prudential Special Agent is recognized in the community as a professional. But there are times when every Special Agent feels discouraged. A career as a Special Agent is not an easy one. It can mean many personal sacrifices; it can mean working four or more nights a week, in the beginning; it can mean postponing a special outing or an evening at home; it can mean having to take extra insurance courses to guarantee a better understanding of life insurance and the needs of clients.

A Special Agent is constantly faced with the challenge of finding the best solution to each new insurance problem encountered. To find this solution, Agents must be willing and able to interpret a client's needs accurately; this often involves several interviews and considerable time. And, of course, time alone does not assure a sale. It is most important for a Special Agent to have the ability to answer objections and accept rejections. It is only through continuous practice that Agents learn to anticipate objections and answer them satisfactorily. But even the "correct approach" cannot guarantee a sale, and it often happens that a prospect's objections cannot be overcome. Each Agent must learn to accept the disappointments and frustrations which are an integral part of insurance selling. The ability to take rejections is of utmost importance for insurance sales.

The booklet also described the company's growth and support given to the agent by home office, agency, and manager. Before concluding with an emphasis on the "painstaking efforts"

---

1. The only changes have been to make this gender neutral.

required, it pointed out a number of specific sources of conflict for every agent under the heading, "The Door to Success Does Not Open Easily."

The situations presented on these pages represent some of the problems that face every Agent. Thinking about what your reaction to them would be should help indicate whether or not you should pursue a life insurance sales career.

1. An Agent spends several hours preparing a sound insurance program for a family . . . only to be turned down during the second interview.

2. An Agent completes the sale of a policy only to have the policyholder allow it to "lapse" by not paying a subsequent premium.

3. An Agent is sincerely interested in helping people plan their futures wisely, but, time after time, people say "No" to these recommendations.

4. An Agent makes the personal sacrifice of making a sales call on a stormy night only to find that the prospect has forgotten the appointment and is not at home.

5. An Agent plans to attend an eagerly anticipated social event . . . but has to postpone it because it is the only night a prospect can meet.

6. An Agent pays a call on a prospect to discuss insurance, only to be subjected to uncomplimentary . . . even though unwarranted . . . remarks about sales personnel.

7. A conscientious Agent wants to qualify prospects carefully and take time to visit policyholders whose insurance is about to lapse . . . but knows that new prospects and new sales are also essential.

8. An Agent realizes that the Home Office tries to provide the best possible service, but cannot help recalling the time an important case was lost because "the prospect cooled off" or "the competition moved in" while an application was being processed.

The Armed Forces

The United States Army funded a project conducted by researchers at the University of South Carolina, which began in

1979, was completed in 1983 (Meglino, DeNisi, Youngblood, Williams, Johnson, Randolph & Laughlin, 1983), and was finally published in 1988 (Meglino, DeNisi, Youngblood & Williams, 1988). Two realistic previews were produced, and they are shown in Figures 3.1 and 3.2. The first preview showed and described a number of events recruits were to go through en route to completing basic training. It emphasized the "content" of what was to be expected during this period.

Figure 3.1
Example of a Military RJP

This preview was titled "I WIN: Basic Training at Ft. Jackson." The major sections of the preview are underlined below, followed by the specific events, which were described in each section.

1. *Preliminary*

    Reception station processing
    First meeting with Drill Sergeant
    Company Commander's welcome
    Living facilities
    Organization of a basic training company
    Inspections
    Hourly schedule of training during typical day
    Overview of four phases of training

2. *Phase I: "I" = Introduction (Weeks 1 and 2)*

    Overview of phase I
    Drill and ceremonies
    Classroom instruction
    Nuclear, biological, and chemical defense
    Physical training
    Obstacle course
    Confidence course
    Victory tower climb

3. *Phase II: "W" = Weapons Training (Weeks 3 and 4)*

    Overview of phase II
    Classroom instruction in M-16 rifle
    Aiming and holding
    Marksmanship training
    Rifle qualification
    Rifle award ceremony

4. *Phase III: "I" = Individual Tactical Training (Weeks 5 and 6)*

    Overview of phase III
    Living in the field

Figure 3.1 Continued
Example of a Military RJP

U.S. weapons training
Defensive training
Hand grenade training
Attack training in teams
Tactical training evaluation
Fifteen mile march

5. *Phase IV: "N" = Necessary Testing (Week 7)*

Overview of phase IV
Commander's inspection
Physical training test
End of cycle test
Graduation from basic training

Source: Meglino et al. (1983). Formulation and analysis of counter attrition strategies in the U.S. Army. *College of Business, University of South Carolina. Reprinted by permission of the author.*

The second preview showed recruits facing particular situations typical of almost all new recruits. This preview went further to show recruits how to cope with these situations, as indicated in Figure 3.2. (More will be said about this second job preview in Chapter 6. I believe that it is really newcomer orientation, although those who developed it call it a job preview.)

Figure 3.2
Example of a Military "Job Coping" Preview

The preview was titled "Adjusting to Basic Training." Trainees were informed that the greatest problem in basic training would be related to their adjustment to Army life rather than to specific events in basic training. They were further told that this presentation would describe the major problems faced by other trainees and suggest methods successful trainees have found helpful in dealing with these problems. Each problem was first described by a Drill Sergeant. The problem was also described by a trainee (actor) who then offered a suggestion for dealing with the problem. (Note: Although these suggestions were given by actors playing the role of trainees, the content of each suggestion was taken from audio tapes of interviews with actual trainees.) The specific problems and suggestions contained in the presentation are as follows:

1. *Problem: Living and Working with New People*

   Suggestions:

   a. Meet other trainees in your unit as soon as possible.

Figure 3.2 Continued
Example of a Military "Job Coping Preview"

---

    b. Help other trainees who are having difficulty.
    c. Get to know one person well—someone you can talk to.

2. *Problem: Leaving Family and Friends Back Home*

    Suggestions:

    a. Talk things over with a close friend in your unit.
    b. Write or call home when you have a chance.
    c. Keep busy and get your mind off it. Concentrate on other things.

3. *Problem: Taking Orders and Being Corrected by a Drill Sergeant*

    Suggestions:

    a. Listen carefully to what is said. Be sure you know what you're supposed to do.
    b. Don't worry about the tone of voice being used.
    c. Do exactly what you are told. Don't question authority.

4. *Problem: Concern Over Inability to Meet Physical Requirements*

    Suggestions:

    a. Encourage yourself. Tell yourself you can handle it.
    b. Set personal goals for yourself and practice when you have time.
    c. Urge fellow trainees to make it by encouraging them.

5. *Problem: Approaching Drill Sergeant About Problem*

    Suggestions:

    If problem requires immediate attention
    a. See Drill Sergeant as soon as possible.
    b. Ask if you can talk about a problem.

    If problem does not require immediate attention
    a. Wait for free time during the evening.
    b. Go to your Drill Sergeant's office.
    c. Ask if you can talk about a problem.

Source: Meglino et al. (1983). Formulation and analysis of counter attrition strategies in the U.S. Army. College of Business, University of South Carolina. Reprinted by permission of the author.

College Students

Two studies of realistic recruitment have been conducted at the United States Military Academy at West Point. Both studies used booklets to describe experiences of typical cadet life. The first study (Macedonia, 1969) used the results from a questionnaire survey of cadets as the basis for realism. This study followed up the entering cadets at the conclusion of their first year at West Point. The second study (Ilgen & Seely, 1974) used a modification of the booklet, with the information limited to the summer period prior to the fall term.

Macedonia (1969, pp. 37–39) has described the booklet as follows:

> It states that the cadet will enter in July and for two months will learn how to be a cadet and a member of the Armed Forces. This period is often referred to as "Beast Barracks." The training is hard and exacting and is designed to develop the qualities of self-discipline and courage—qualities necessary to sustain a leader in combat. And to ensure an orderly adjustment to *Academy* life, it is necessary that the reasons that lie behind training be understood. None of the training at the *Academy* has been instituted to harass or to diminish the cadet's dignity. Its sole purpose is to fully develop leaders . . . .
>
> The second section of the booklet has sketches showing the cadet engaged in each of the various activities available in the fourth class (freshman) year, a brief description of the activity, and the approximate number of hours that each cadet spent in each activity.

Table 3.2 shows the breakdown, included in the booklet, of how cadets spend their time.

Evaluation of Realistic Recruitment

The evaluation of realistic recruitment involves a discussion of what factors should be considered, an analysis of the results accumulated to date, and concludes with an explanation of why realistic recruitment is effective.

Factors to Be Evaluated

A wide variety of criteria is potentially available for use in an evaluation of realistic recruitment. (See Table 3.3.) At one time or another, all of these have been used, although only rarely has a single study used all six of them at the same time.

Table 3.2
Results of Cadet Time Study—"Typical" Day

Activity	Time (hours)
Class	5
Personal	2–3
Athletics	2–3
Eating	2 1/4
Sleeping	6–8
Studying	4–5
Extracurricular	1–2
Fourth-class duties	1 3/4–2 1/2

Also included in section two of the booklet is a copy of the formal schedule of a schoolday:

Activity	Reporting Time
Reveille	0550
Police call	0620
Breakfast	0630
Return to quarters	0715
Class	0745
Dinner	1210
Class	1305
Intramurals (sports)	1535
Supper	1830
Study	1920
Lights out	2300

Source: R. M. Macedonia, 1969. Expectations: Press and survival. Unpublished doctoral dissertation, New York University, p. 39.

The six criteria are arranged in a time sequence running from preentry, through entry, to postentry. The first of these is whether or not realism hampers the organization's ability to attract competent newcomers. This is usually assessed by examining the number of applicants before and after the use of realistic recruitment. Simply examining the raw numbers of applicants is not the best way to evaluate this criterion however. This is because we must take into account the number of *high-quality* applicants, i.e., those who are matched appropriately to the organization. Because of the difficulties involved in making this quality judgment, the usual practice has been to simply analyze the trend in the overall number of applicants.

Table 3.3
*Some Possible Criteria to Use in the Evaluation
of Realistic Recruitment*

Stage of Entry	Evaluation Criteria
Preentry	1. Ability of the organization to recruit newcomers
Entry	2. Initial expectations of newcomers
	3. Choice of organization by the individual, i.e., specific job wants being matched with climates
Postentry	4. Initial job attitudes such as: • satisfaction with the job • commitment to the organization • descriptive statements about the job (to be compared with the expectations held as an outsider) • thoughts about quitting
	5. Job performance
	6. Job survival and voluntary turnover rates

During the entry stage, the impact of realistic recruitment *both* on initial expectations and on the person's organizational choice must be considered. Since the basic purpose of realism is to *deflate* expectations, an assessment should be made to see whether or not this actually happens. One way to do this is to measure the expectations of newcomers both before and after realistic recruitment. Another way is to set up an experiment with two groups, the realistic recruits and the traditional recruits, and then compare their expectations. The second area to be evaluated during entry is the extent to which the newcomer actually chooses an organization consistent with the type of information available at the time of choice. This means that job candidates tend to choose organizations whose *advertised image* is similar to their own specific job wants. When traditional recruitment is used, organizations tend to admit newcomers who are *not* matched well to the various climates of the organization and thus the wrong types of individuals are attracted. Realistic recruitment attracts those newcomers who will be well matched.

Finally, in the postentry period, three other areas need to be evaluated: job attitudes, job performance, and job survival. First, a variety of job attitudes should be measured. Both job satisfaction and organizational commitment data are good indicators of the degree to which the individual's job wants are matched to the organization's climates. Follow-up *descriptions* of the organization should be gathered to be compared with the *expectations* data gathered earlier. When realistic recruitment is used, there should be little difference between the two. When traditional recruitment is practiced, the initial expectations should be inflated with respect to postentry perceptions of the organization. Thoughts about quitting also should be measured. This factor might show a difference between realistic and traditional recruitment practices when there is little or no difference in actual turnover between the two. This is most likely to happen during periods of high unemployment when it is difficult for individuals to leave one organization for another.

The last two areas for evaluation during postentry are job performance and job survival. Both of these are key components of the Matching Model. This model, however, does predict that the effect of realistic recruitment is much more evident on job survival than on job performance because it directly affects the matching of individual job wants and organizational climates. Furthermore, the effect should be stronger on voluntary versus involuntary turnover. Nevertheless, both types of data should be obtained to evaluate realistic versus traditional recruitment.

All of these evaluation criteria are important, but they are important for different purposes. From the more practical viewpoint of a personnel manager, the most important factors are job survival and job performance because they can be easily linked to dollar costs and savings. Because job performance is much less likely to be affected by an RJP, it makes more sense to focus on job survival as the key practical criterion in evaluating realistic recruitment.

An alternative perspective is that the researcher trying to understand *why* realism has the effect of increasing job survival. The researcher must gather data on the other measures of effectiveness as well as on job survival. When this is done, the researcher can assess the various psychological mechanisms that have been proposed (see Fig. 2.6).

The next section, which reviews RJP effectiveness, puts special emphasis on job survival as *the* criterion of effectiveness. There are several reasons for narrowing the focus. First, of all the criteria discussed here, job survival is most commonly measured in the studies. The same cannot be said for the other factors. Thus we can place the most confidence in the accumulated research on job survival. Second, job survival easily translates into cost savings expressed in dollars—the type of "language" that most people understand. We can translate various types of changes in job attitudes (satisfaction, commitment, and so on) into dollar cost savings (as was shown in Chapter 2), but this is a more indirect link to cost savings. Third, job survival is an important factor from *both* the practical and research perspectives.

Evaluating the Impact of Realistic Recruitment

This section is divided into two parts. The first part summarizes the previous reviews of RJPs that have been conducted, and the second part reviews the research that evaluates the impact of realistic recruitment on job survival in particular. The rather dramatic growth in RJP research during the 1980s is noteworthy because the number of previous reviews has also grown rapidly. When this book was originally published in 1980, only one previous review had been written and only 13 studies had been conducted at that time. Today, however, about 40 RJP studies have been written and five reviews have been conducted since the first edition. Thus a simple "review of reviews" can bring readers up to date with the new developments, and then we can focus specifically on job survival.

Conclusions from Previous Reviews

The first known study of RJPs was done in 1956 by the late Joseph Weitz at the Life and Casualty Insurance Company of Tennessee. Years later, Prudential Insurance revised Weitz's booklet to recruit new sales agents (see Youngberg, 1963, a doctoral dissertation supervised by Weitz). With these two studies the idea of realistic recruitment was born.

A decade later I published (Wanous, 1973) my own doctoral dissertation (Wanous, 1972a) and later conducted the first published review (Wanous, 1977). This review plus the review in the first edition of this book seem to have generated considerable interest among researchers of personnel practices because the number of studies and subsequent reviews have increased dramatically. As this has happened, our knowledge of how RJPs affect newcomers has grown. We certainly know more in the early 1990s than we did twenty years ago when I became interested in the topic, but some important questions still remain unanswered.

Wanous (1977). This first review covered only six studies, and the conclusions were necessarily tentative, although somewhat encouraging. It appeared that RJPs did not damage a company's ability to recruit newcomers since there was no evidence of different job acceptance rates when those recruited with an RJP were compared to those recruited in more traditional ways. Initial expectations were lower, initial job attitudes were higher, job survival was longer, and job performance was unaffected for those receiving an RJP. At this time there had been too few studies to indicate *why* realistic recruitment had had these effects. The studies themselves were conducted in quite different types of organizations, so they were somewhat difficult to compare.

Wanous (1980). In the first edition of this book, I was able to locate 13 RJP studies and examined the same factors as in the 1977 review. The additional studies reinforced some conclusions: (a) the ability to recruit was not damaged, (b) initial expectations were lower, and (c) job survival was longer. In other cases, there were modifications: (a) job attitudes were not always more positive, and (b) performance was sometimes greater, sometimes worse, and sometimes unaffected (i.e., it was difficult to predict an RJP's effect on performance.)

Reilly, Brown, Blood & Malatesta (1981). This is the first review to quantify the effect of RJPs on job survival. Based on 11 studies, the authors estimated that survival was 8 percent greater for those being realistically recruited compared to "control" recruits who did not receive an RJP. They went further to conclude that the effect on job survival rates is greater for those types of jobs that are "complex" (i.e., they are *not* entry-level jobs). Without referring to any data, they also concluded that RJPs: (a) have no effect on self-selection, (b) may lead to more positive attitudes, and (c) do not increase met expectations. These latter three "conclusions" are highly suspect because they do not appear to be based on any data reported by Reilly et al. (1981). (Later reviews will show that these three "conclusions" are contradicted by the research data accumulated to date.)

Wanous (1983). In this short review, I calculated the average increase in job survival to be 5 percent, based on 11 studies and over 4000 newly hired job candidates. This estimate was a bit lower than that of Reilly et al. (1981).

McEvoy & Cascio (1985). This review included 15 studies and calculated that job survival would typically increase by 9 percent. What they meant by this is that there would be a 9 *percentage point* difference between job survival rates without an RJP and those with one. They used an example of an increase from 60 to 69 percent. However, 69 percent is actually 15 percent greater than 60 percent, and this has led to some confusion in interpreting what they meant. Despite these results, they concluded that the effect of realistic recruitment was "weak" when compared to alternative methods for increasing job survival such as job enrichment or the use of weighted application blanks in selection.

Premack & Wanous (1985). This review examined a wide variety of effectiveness criteria. The strongest effect of RJPs was the lowering of initial expectations. More modest, but essentially equal, effects were found on increasing the rate of job offer refusal, increasing organizational commitment, and increasing job survival. In the latter case, RJPs were estimated to increase job survival by 12 percent for an organization with a job survival rate of 50 percent for new hires recruited in traditional ways (i.e., from 50 to 56 percent) and by 5 percent for one with an 80 percent survival rate (i.e., from 80 to 84 percent).

This is the first review to suggest that the impact of realistic recruitment on job survival depends on the level of job survival from traditional recruitment, i.e., the level of job survival that existed *prior* to the installation of an RJP. There was no evidence that effectiveness depended on the level of job complexity, however, as had been suggested earlier.

Wanous & Colella (1989). This recent review located 38 studies compared to the Premack and Wanous review, which had 21. However, considering the level of quality of some of the research and that many of the more recent studies are from "laboratory" research simulations, there were only three new studies of job survival in "real" organizations. The Wanous and Colella review concluded that these three studies did not change the estimates of how much job survival would be increased from the Premack and Wanous review done four years earlier.

This review also noted that more than half of the studies placed the RJP *after* the job candidate had made a job choice. This means that the majority of studies cannot measure any effect on self-selection matching nor on commitment to job choice due to feeling free to reject the organization. This elicited a certain amount of dismay because, having accumulated so many more studies, researchers still seemed unable to say conclusively *why* RJPs increase job survival. This topic will be raised again at the end of this chapter.

Effects on Job Survival

Table 3.4 lists 19 studies that measured the impact of realistic recruitment on job survival. This is, of course, only a subset of the 40 studies that have been done. All studies done in simulated organizations (called "lab studies" for short) are excluded because none of them lasted long enough to measure job survival meaningfully. Several other studies with very serious design flaws were excluded (see Wanous & Colella, 1989, for a discussion of these reasons and which ones fall into this category). Table 3.4 is divided into two sections—private industry and the U.S. military—not just because of the differences between these two types of organizations, but because the basic job survival rates for the military are so much higher than those in private industry. The higher the basic rate of job survival with traditional recruitment, the more difficult it is for an RJP to make improvements.

The top half of Table 3.4 shows 13 private industry experiments. (Note that *all* the RJP studies compare one group of job candidates who have been given realistic recruitment to another group of approximately equal size who have not. This type of research is very good at yielding clear conclusions.) The job survival data shown in Table 3.4 were extracted from the various studies as follows. First, if a study reported more than one followup period, e.g., three versus six months, for assessing job survival, the follow-up time period that showed the *greatest difference* was picked. The rationale for this is that there is no particular time period that is always "right" for assessing the impact on job survival. There is, however, most likely an optimal period for affecting job survival that varies considerably among jobs and organizations. It is difficult to predict the optimal period in advance. However, once it is established through research, it can be used as the standard for any subsequent evaluation.

A second decision was made to combine RJP groups when more than one type of preview was being tested. This amounts to a comparison of "realism" versus traditional recruitment. It was done to simplify matters somewhat since some studies compared different methods for doing an RJP. Finally, the data are rounded off to whole number percentages to facilitate interpretation. (This has no effect on the conclusions since rounding up and rounding down canceled each other out.)

The private industry data in Table 3.4 show that RJPs increased job survival in 11 out of 13 experiments. There are two ways to calculate the average increase in job survival. First, when each study is "weighted" by its respective sample size, the average increase is 8 percent (including the two negative results). Second, if the job survival gain is averaged across the 13 studies *without* weighting, the gain is 12 percent. This discrepancy indicates that the larger studies had weaker results. In particular, the largest single study (Reilly et al., 1981) actually had a negative result, and this contributed considerably to the discrepancy between weighted and unweighted average gains.

The military data can be similarly analyzed. When a weighted average is calculated, the job survival gain is only 1 percent. When the average is unweighted the gain is 5 percent. Again, the single largest study in this group (Githens & Zalinski, 1983) had a negative result, which dramatically affected the weighted versus unweighted average gain.

It is somewhat unusual to find the largest sample studies having results so discrepant from all of the rest of the research. In fact, it is usually just the opposite, i.e., the small sample studies tend to depart from the overall group average (Hunter & Schmidt, 1990—see the Appendix). The reader may be advised to consider unweighted averages as more meaningful, since the two largest studies appear to be "outliers." An alternative to using unweighted

Table 3.4
Effects of Realistic Job Previews on Job Survival

Author(s)	Date	Total Sample Size	Job Type	Method Used	Timing of RJP	Percentage Job Survival Control Group	RJP Group	Percentage Gain in Job Survival
Private Industry								
Weitz	1956	474	Insurance agents	Booklet	Preentry	73	81	11
Youngberg	1963	404	Insurance agents	Booklet	Preentry	57	71	25
Wanous	1973	80	Telephone operators	Video	Preentry	50	62	24
Farr, O'Leary & Bartlett	1973	160	Machine operators	Job sample	Preentry	60	89	48
Haccoun	1978	235	Telephone operators	Booklet Narrated slides	Preentry Postentry	73	77	5
Reilly, Tenopyr & Sperling	1979	325	Telephone operators	Booklet	Preentry	85	91	7
Dugoni & Ilgen	1981	320	Supermarket clerks	Interview	Postentry	79	88	11
Zaharia & Baumeister	1981	154	Hospital technicans	Booklet Video	Preentry	46	50	9
Reilly, Brown, Blood & Malatesta	1981	717	Telephone service reps	Video	Preentry	73	71	–3

Table 3.4 Continued
Effects of Realistic Job Previews on Job Survival

Author(s)	Date	Total Sample Size	Job Type	Method Used	Timing of RJP	Percentage Job Survival Control Group	RJP Group	Percentage Gain in Job Survival
Avner, Gusastello & Aderman	1982	325	Gas station attendants	Booklet	Preentry	83	78	-6
Dean & Wanous	1984	249	Bank tellers	Booklet	Preentry	80	85	6
Colarelli	1984	155	Bank tellers	Booklet Interview	Preentry	67	69	3
Hom & Griffeth	1985	158	Nurses	Booklet	Postentry	79	92	16
The U.S. Military								
Macedonia	1969	1260	Cadets	Booklet	Postentry	86	91	6
Ilgen & Seely	1974	468	Cadets	Booklet	Postentry	89	94	6
Horner	1980	678	Basic training	Video	Postentry	67	78	13
Lockman	1980	4658	Basic training	Video	Postentry	89	89	0
Githens & Zalinski	1983	6658	Basic training	Video	Postentry	89	88	-1
Meglino, DeNisi Youngblood & Williams	1988	533	Basic training	Video	Postentry	92	98	6

averages is to recalculate the weighted averages without the larger outlier in each group. When this is done the average gain in job survival is 10.5 percent for business and 2.9 percent for the military.

The usefulness of this amount of increase in job survival depends on several factors. First, the greater the cost of replacing employees, the more useful RJPs will be to an organization. This is because the cost of producing a realistic recruitment program is pretty much the same whether a job has a replacement cost of $4000 (like a bank teller) or $2,000,000 (like a fighter pilot in the U.S. Navy; Morrison, 1990). Second, the utility of RJPs rises when a large number of people are hired in a given year. Again, the cost of producing the preview is fixed regardless of whether a company hires 100 newcomers per year or 1000. Finally, the utility of RJPs is greater when job survival is in the 50 to 60 percent range, compared to the 80 to 90 percent range, as can be clearly seen in Figure 3.3.

Figure 3.3 shows the "plot" of the *percentage gain in job survival using an RJP* against the *job survival rate for traditional recruitment*. There is a strong relationship between the two factors, i.e., the correlation is .57. This clearly indicates that the "usefulness" of RJPs increases when job survival is a greater problem, and it decreases when job survival rates are high. A similar analysis was shown in Chapter 2 where the *percentage gain* in job survival from using "inside" sources was strongly related to the *job survival rate for outside sources*. These two findings are actually typical. (See Steele, Hendrix & Balogh, 1990, for another example of how the "base rate of job survival" affects the relationship between various job attitudes and job survival.) What Figure 3.3 means in practical terms is that you can estimate the expected gain in job survival from using an RJP from this graph, rather than simply taking an overall average.

In theory, the greatest percentage increase in job survival should be found at very low rates of job survival (see Premack & Wanous, 1985, for an explanation), but there have been very few studies of organizations with retention problems of this magnitude. The best example to date is a study of self-service gas station attendants (Avner, Guastello & Aderman, 1982). Of the 325 newly hired attendants, 80 percent left after just two months and all 100 percent were gone by the end of nine months! The first 7 days of employment data from this study in Table 3.4 show that the RJP

Figure 3.3

*How the Job Survival Rate with Traditional Recruitment Affects
the Usefulness of Realistic Recruitment*

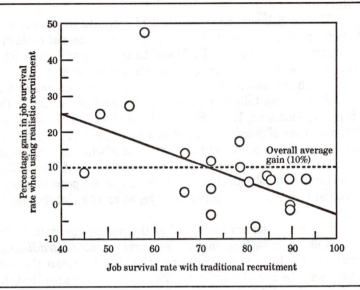

had a *negative* effect on job survival in this particular organization. Until more studies are done of situations like this, the utility of RJPs to increase job survival in very *un*attractive jobs is suspect. The RJP is no substitute for meaningful changes in extremely *un*pleasant working conditions, as this one study clearly shows.

Evaluating the Theory of Realistic Recruitment

In a schematic model form (see Fig. 2.6). Chapter 2 proposed a fairly complicated theory of how realistic recruitment leads to increased job survival. The present chapter has discussed at length the research evidence showing the effects of RJPs on job survival. From a practical viewpoint, solid evidence exists that realistic recruitment "works" because the very best studies in real organizations show improvements in job survival when RJPs are used to recruit newcomers. From a research perspective, however, the reasons for this effect are not completely clear at the present time, despite the rapid increase in research. In some ways, the use of RJPs is like a number of medical procedures. That is, physicians know that certain drugs and procedures can cure, but they aren't sure why. Lack of complete theoretical understanding does not stop medical practice, and it should not stop personnel practice regarding realistic recruitment. Nevertheless, the most probable reasons are considered here in the hope that future researchers will be able to unravel all the psychological factors.

The theory of RJPs (Fig. 2.6) illustrates a number of casual *sequences*. The key word is "sequences" because no single factor, all by itself, is *the* reason why realistic recruitment enhances job survival. Virtually all the researchers who have been concerned with the theory of RJPs have ignored the extreme complexity of these sequences. Instead, they have treated the theory as if it were nothing more than a collection of several separate psychological factors.

The effect of realistic recruitment on initial job expectations is a case in point. This is typically referred to as a "vaccination effect," like a medical vaccination where a weak dose of germs is injected in the hope that the body will develop an immune reaction. Vaccinations cannot cure a disease after it is contracted; they only prevent it. The same has been said of RJPs. That is, they can prevent certain types of early turnover, but they cannot make an unpleasant work organization better.

As the theory of realistic recruitment clearly shows, however, a vaccination all by itself may not be a sufficient reason for RJPs to work. Other psychological mechanisms, e.g., learning to cope, feeling free to reject a job offer, and trusting the organization for being honest, may also need to be triggered. In turn, these psychological mechanisms must affect the newcomers' choice of the organization, initial job satisfaction, commitment to their choice, and so on. Finally, if both job satisfaction and organizational commitment are influenced, voluntary turnover is reduced by an RJP.

Documenting these complex sequences of psychological events is extremely difficult. In fact, there are so many possible connections that searching for *the* explanation is probably a fruitless search (Wanous & Colella, 1989).

If you accept that there is no single reason for the effects of realistic recruitment, does it make sense to try to find data that will support each of the linkages in the theoretical model? There are 18 of them in Figure 2.6! In many, if not most, cases, strong research evidence exists for the validity of these 18 linkages, which is why they have been suggested as reasonable explanations *in this particular context*. The evidence for the linkages, however, comes from similar research in related areas of the psychology of people at work, e.g., turnover (Mobley, 1982), role ambiguity/conflict (Jackson & Schuler, 1985), organizational commitment (Reichers, 1985), and organizational choice (Wanous, Keon & Latack, 1983)—to name just a few of the possibilities.

The accumulated evidence from just those studies of RJPs is somewhat biased because half of them were done *after* job candidates had made a job choice (Wanous & Colella, 1989). Thus it would be impossible in half of the studies to even examine the effects on self-selection, the matching of individual job wants to organizational climates, commitment to job choice, and so on. Since RJPs do have an effect on job survival anyway, the evidence points most clearly at its doing so via the vaccination of expectations and the subsequent effects on role clarity and the ability to cope in a new environment.

Related research on the effects of "met expectations" conducted recently (Wanous, Poland, Premack & Davis, 1991) supports the notion that having accurate expectations leads to increased job satisfaction, greater organizational commitment, a stronger intent to remain in the organization, longer job survival, and slightly improved job performance. This research is actually a compilation of empirical results from 31 studies of over 17,000 people. Although it does not specifically deal with realistic recruitment, the results certainly support one of the central tenets of the realistic recruitment philosophy, i.e., that met expectations are important for newcomers.

Other Applications of Realism

Based on the research conducted thus far, providing realistic preparatory information to job candidates does seem to be useful. Realistic information may also be effective when supplied in other situations, although little or no research has yet been attempted. Nevertheless, it seems a logical extension to expect realistic preparatory information to facilitate other types of employment transitions: (a) the transfer of personnel to new geographical areas, particularly to overseas assignments, and (b) the transfer of employees to new, challenging job assignments. Some transfers, of course, may involve both types of changes—geographical and job duties.

Despite the preceding suggestion, no one has yet developed a realistic preview for job transfer and tested its effectiveness. Some have studied the effect of geographical mobility on health, well being, and various other aspects of life and job satisfaction (Brett, 1982). Others have compared the coping strategies of those who are internal transfers within a company against those of new hires in the same company (Feldman & Brett, 1983). This research suggests that those who are mobile may not be as traumatized as had been assumed. However, the areas of their dissatisfaction are different from those who are less mobile. Similarly, those who do transfer internally have coping strategies that are different from those of newcomers. This suggests that a realistic preview for such transfers should contain different information, and also that it should include more than just information. For example, it should include help in coping with the stress of moving to a new job and new location. (Chapter 6 presents a similar discussion with respect to newcomer orientation, i.e., that orientation involves much more than just the presentation of realistic information.)

An area of increasing concern to large, multinational corporations is the successful transfer of highly paid technicians and executives to foreign countries. The transfer costs are extremely high. They can run well into six figures for an executive who requests a return home after a short, unhappy experience in a foreign country. Despite this obvious need, no one has studied the effectiveness of a realistic preview for international transfers.

In today's business climate, companies are increasingly willing to accept an employee's refusal of geographical transfer. Given this, it is even more crucial that realistic information be provided to personnel as inputs to the decision about accepting or rejecting a transfer. The realistic information can operate in two ways. First, realism may convince an executive to refuse a transfer and thereby save the company money because an error was prevented. Second, realism may induce a reluctant employee to accept a transfer by showing the employee that his or her fears about the move are unrealistic. Given the greater number of transfer refusals today, this latter effect may be quite significant in reducing employee resistance to life-style changes caused by geographical transfers.

Similarly, realistic preparatory information can be used to facilitate the matching of person and job when it is used to decide transfers to a more difficult job assignment within an organization. The only difference between this and realistic recruitment is that the movement is entirely internal, rather than being a shift from outside to inside an organization. Because of this difference in focus, the realistic information provided in an internal transfer concerns new job duties, new co-workers, and new working conditions. Of less concern in preparing someone for internal transfer are those factors that pervade the entire organization; they, of course, are included in the realistic job preview during recruitment.

Conclusions

1. Ineffective recruitment can affect either the job *performance* of newcomers (and thus involuntary turnover) or it can affect the *job satisfaction* and *organizational commitment* of newcomers (and thus voluntary turnover). The primary impact of *recruitment,* however, is on the latter, not the former. Organizational *selection* practices affect the former. (See Conclusion 8.)

2. The diagnosis of the need to use realistic recruitment should include both interviews and questionnaire surveys. A wide variety of data sources should be used, e.g., supervisors, both experienced and inexperienced job-holders, and personal observation.

3. In deciding whether or not to use realistic recruitment, an organization must consider the specific situation: (a) the selection ratio for the job, (b) the type of job, and (c) labor market conditions. The maximum benefits from realistic recruitment occur when it is used for entry-level jobs with low "visibility" to candidates, and with a low selection ratio during times of low unemployment.

4. After the decision to use realistic recruitment has been made, several other factors must be considered: (a) encourage self-selection explicitly, (b) have credible sources communicate the realistic job preview, (c) maintain "consistency" between the medium and the message, (d) communicate feelings as well as information, (e) have the content reflect organizational climates, and (f) do the RJP "early" in the entry process.

5. Realistic recruitment is *not* a specific technique. It is a general philosophy or approach to dealing with newcomers. Several methods of presenting realistic job preview information have included audio-visual techniques (films, videotapes, and automatically narrated slide presentations), booklets, oral presentations, interviews, and realistic work-sample tests.

6. Realistic recruitment does *not* reduce an organization's ability to recruit newcomers.

7. Realistic recruitment deflates the recruits' expectations, which are typically inflated.

8. Realistic recruitment has a small effect on the job performance of newcomers. This is consistent with the Matching Model. (See Conclusion 1.)

9. Realistic recruitment *does*, however, increase the job survival rate for newcomers. The amount of the increase in job survival does depend on the initial level of survival using traditional recruiting methods.

4

Choice of an Organization

Organizational choice is a stage in the entry process that primarily concerns the individual's perspective. Referring to the Matching Model (Fig. 1.1), organizational choice is the primary way in which *specific job wants* are matched to the *climates* of an organization. Chapter 5 on selection of newcomers by the organization will focus on how a person's *capabilities* are matched to the *requirements* of a job; it is a view of entry from the organization's perspective.

This chapter is divided into seven sections. The first section concerns the differences between *organizational* choice and *occupational* entry. Following this, two different views of organizational choice are described. Each of these represents a rather different view of how individuals decide to accept a job offer. The third section reviews research studies in order to evaluate the appropriateness of each view of how organizational choices are made. The fourth section considers the issue of whether or not people *should* be rational in organizational choices. The fifth section is concerned with whether or not people *can* be rational, even if they try. The sixth section explains the connection between recruitment and organizational choice. The seventh section assesses impact of job interviews on the job candidates' choice of an organization. The section reviews research from studies of interviewers and interviewees, and suggests several "guidelines" for job candidates.

Organizational Choice Versus Vocational Choice

Much more research and writing is available on the topic of vocational or occupational entry than is available on organizational choice. The subject of occupational entry is quite broad. For example, it includes the study of how vocational choices are made, how individuals adjust to vocations, what occupational success means, and how satisfied individuals are with their vocation. Theories abound about how vocational choices are made (Crites, 1969). Some theories are exclusively psychological; i.e., they try to explain the hows and whys of individuals' decisions that culminate in vocational entry. Other theories, however, are not so "neatly organized," emphasizing instead the haphazard and accidental way that some people enter particular vocations. Still other theories are sociological, stressing that the *groups* (determined by socioeconomic class, race, or sex) to which an individual belongs influence occupational entry. Thus one important way in which vocational entry differs from organizational choice is that scholars seem to disagree more about how people and vocations are matched to each other than about how people and organizations are matched.

The relationship between organizational choice and vocational entry can be diagrammed as shown in Figure 4.1. This relationship has been called the "exclusion process" (Crites, 1969). It has been so named because the final outcome—a specific job in a particular organization—is the end result of *many choices* made during the individual's growth into adulthood. An example of a general occupational field would be science. An example of a specific occupation would be research chemist. An example of the job choice would be doing research chemistry on the development of a new additive for gasoline. An example of organizational choice would be choosing to work for Exxon instead of Shell Oil Company.

The "flow" of events pictured in Figure 4.1 implies three things about the differences between organizational choice and vocational entry. First, one's choice of an organization typically *follows* the entry into a vocation. Second, entry into a vocation is a long, drawnout *process* composed of many "small" decisions and a few "turning points." In contrast, organizational choice is more a single *event* than a long process. Third, it is probably harder to change one's specific occupation that it is to change organizations,

Figure 4.1
*The Narrowing Down from Occupational Entry
to Organizational Entry*

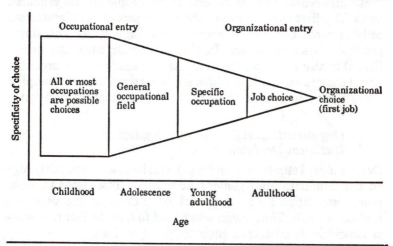

*Source: Adapted from J. O. Crites, 1969, Vocational Psychology, p. 162.
Reprinted by permission of the McGraw-Hill Book Company.*

and it would be even harder to change one's basic occupational field. Thus most people will probably work for several organizations over their working career, few will change jobs, fewer will change to a new occupation, and fewer still will make a radical change to a whole new vocational field.

Two Views of Organizational Choice

Those who have studied how people decide which organizations to enter are not in agreement about how these decisions are made. There are essentially two quite different views on the matter. The first view assumes that individuals are reasonably rational beings, that they seek out information about alternative organizations, and that they try to maximize their potential satisfaction by choosing organizations most likely to meet their important job wants. The second view of organizational choice assumes that individuals *do not* seek out as much information about organizations. Rather they confine themselves to getting data about only the very most important things they are looking for in a new organization. They use less information and fewer criteria to make organizational choices. Only *after* making a choice do they rationalize the choice in terms of a wider variety of factors.

Two hypothetical case studies are presented to highlight these differences in how experts think people choose organizations. The first case examines the choice process as a systematically rational decision, it involves a college senior choosing a graduate business school. In this particular case, the person (Evan) is also participating in a research study of how organizational choices are made in which students were asked to complete a questionnaire detailing how they thought about the decision.

Organizational Choice as a Systematic, Rational Decision

Evan is a good student (A– average), and he also scored fairly high on the Graduate Management Admissions Test (GMAT). However, competition for graduate school is fierce at the very "top ranked" schools. Thus, Evan was forced to face the fact that some of the graduate schools he chose might reject him.

During the latter part of his senior year, Evan was asked to participate in a study of how students select a graduate business school. He was asked to complete a detailed questionnaire about how he considered the alternatives and made his decision. In the months following this initial questionnaire, Evan received a follow-up questionnaire to assess the degree of correspondence between what he said he would do and what he actually did.

Besides asking for personal background data, the questionnaire included items in three areas: (1) *beliefs* about *expected outcomes* for each school considered, (2) the degree of *importance* of each outcome, and (3) Evan's *expectancy of being admitted* to a school *if* he made an effort to apply.

The responses Evan gave to the questions are summarized in Table 4.1. He was asked to name the several schools he had been thinking about, and the four schools Evan listed are shown in Table 4.1. They included a Big Ten school, since it was his own school. The Ivy League college was prestigious and considered a "long shot." The local state college was included as a " fall back" option, should he be rejected at all the others. Finally, the west coast university was considered because it was a good school located in a desirable area.

Table 4.1 shows Evan's answers to the questions asked about each of the schools. The local state college was the only

Table 4.1
Organizational Choice Example : Basic Data

Beliefs about expected outcomes at each college

Measurement	1.0 = A 100 percent chance of this being true at the college
	.9 = A 90 percent chance of this being true at the college
	.8 = An 80 percent chance of this being true at the college
	⋮
	0 = Impossible for this to be true

Results

Questions Asked	Colleges Considered			
	Big Ten	Ivy League	Local State	West Coast University
1. Learn a lot	.9	.9	.4	.8
2. Low cost	.6	0	1.0	.2
3. Good job prospects	.7	1.0	.3	.7
4. Flexible program	.7	.7	.7	.7
5. Desirable geography	.4	.7	.4	.9

Importance of each outcome

Measurement

5 = Extremely important
4 = Very important
3 = Important
2 = Somewhat important
1 = Slightly important
0 = Irrelevant

Results

<u>4</u> 1. Learn a lot
<u>2</u> 2. Low cost
<u>5</u> 3. Good job prospects
<u>1</u> 4. Flexible program
<u>3</u> 5. Desirable geography

Expectancy of being admitted

Measurement

1.0 = A 100% chance of acceptance
.9 = a 90% chance of acceptance
⋮
0 = No chance whatsoever

Results

<u>.8</u> Big Ten school in home state
<u>.2</u> Ivy League college
<u>1.0</u> Local state college
<u>.6</u> West coast university

school he rated low in terms of how much he would probably learn. The cost of the MBA degree varied widely among all four schools, however. Staying close to home would be less expensive than paying for the high tuition (and travel costs) of either the Ivy League school or the out-of-state tuition (and travel costs) at the west coast university. Interestingly, Evan was unable to see many differences in the flexibility of each school's program. Thus he rated them all equally at a moderately high level. Finally, he rated the two local schools lower in terms of desirable location than he did either of the out-of-state alternatives.

Having stated his *beliefs* (or perceptions) about *each school,* Evan rated the *importance of each outcome to him.* In this case, each outcome received a different rating, but all could have received the same one if that's the way he had felt. Evan took a long-range view and rated job prospects as much more important than how much the degree would cost.

Finally, Evan was asked to rate his *expectancy of being admitted* to each school if he applied to it. He saw his chances as pretty slim at the Ivy League school (about 20 percent, or one in five), but excellent at the local state college (no chance for rejection).

Taking the raw data provided in Table 4.1, the researchers conducting the organizational choice study combined the data as shown in Table 4.2.

The way in which these data were combined illustrates a theory of how an organizational choice is made. The theory identifies three components: the *attractiveness* of an organization, the *effort* made to enter one, and the *final choice* of an organization from among those that offer admittance. This theory is called *expectancy theory,* as originally formulated by Vroom (1964). Today it is explained in all textbooks on organizational behavior.

What makes an organization *attractive* to an individual? Two pieces of information are combined in a unique way to indicate the relative attractiveness of the four organizations considered by Evan in the case study: (1) his *beliefs* about *outcomes* associated with each one, and (2) the *importance* of each outcome. As shown in Table 4.2, the attractiveness of an organization can be represented as an algebraic formula:

$$\text{Attractiveness of an organization} = \sum \text{Belief about each outcome} \times \text{Importance of each outcome.}$$

Table 4.2
Organizational Choice Example: How the Model Operates

Calculating the attractiveness of each college

Type of Outcome	Big Ten University Belief X Importance = Attractiveness	Ivy League College Belief X Importance = Attractiveness	Local State College Belief X Importance = Attractiveness	West Coast University Belief X Importance = Attractiveness
1. Learn a lot	.8 X 4 = 3.2	.9 X 4 = 3.6	.4 X 4 = 1.6	.8 X 4 = 3.2
2. Low cost	.6 X 2 = 1.2	0 X 2 = 0	1.0 X 2 = 2.0	.2 X 2 = .4
3. Good job	.7 X 5 = 3.5	1.0 X 5 = 5.0	.3 X 5 = 1.5	.7 X 5 = 3.5
4. Flexible program	.7 X 1 = .7	.7 X 1 = .7	.7 X 1 = .7	.7 X 1 = .7
5. Desirable location	.4 X 3 = 1.2	.7 X 3 = 2.1	.4 X 3 = 1.2	.9 X 3 = 2.7
Total attractiveness	9.8	11.4	7.0	10.5

Calculating the total amount of motivation to apply to each college

	Motivational Components		
School	Total Attractiveness of College	Expectancy of Admittance	Total Motivation
Big Ten university	9.8	X .8 =	7.64
Ivy League college	11.4	X .2 =	2.28
Local state college	7.0	X 1.0 =	7.0
West coast university	10.5	X .6 =	6.3

The *attractiveness* of an organization, often called the *preferred* organization, is an important piece of information, but it is *not sufficient* to indicate the schools to which Evan will actually apply. To understand where he will apply requires information about his *expectancy of being admitted*. At the bottom of Table 4.2, the total attractiveness score for each school is multiplied by the expectancy of admittance to yield Evan's *total motivation to apply to each school*.

$$\begin{array}{c}\text{Total motivation to apply}\\\text{to an organization}\end{array} = \begin{array}{c}\text{Expectancy of}\\\text{being admitted to}\\\text{the organization}\end{array} \times \begin{array}{c}\text{Attractiveness of}\\\text{the organization}\end{array}$$

A comparison of the rank orders of attractiveness and of total motivation shows important differences. The Ivy League college was the most attractive to Evan, but he may not even apply to it! According to expectancy theory, he will certainly apply to the Big Ten university since it is tops in *total* motivation. The local state college and the west coast university, although lower in total motivation, will also probably receive Evan's application. Whether or not he will apply to the Ivy League college is *not clear*. That is, no *minimum level* of motivation has been specified in expectancy theory.

If the total motivational score had been zero, expectancy theory predicts that Evan will definitely *not* apply. The theory, thus, makes predictions at both extremes. That is, any school with a zero score will not be applied to and the one with the highest score will receive an application. However, expectancy theory does not specify *which* of the in-between schools will receive an application.

Expectancy theory also specifies how Evan will make his *final choice* after knowing which schools will accept him. The final choice, of course, depends on which schools actually accept him. If only one does so, there is no choice to be made. If two or more do so, the choice will be based on the *attractiveness* of each school. When a person has already been admitted, the expectancy factor is irrelevant. That is, expectancy = 1.0 for all those schools that accept Evan. Therefore, the differences among such schools are in terms of *attractiveness*.

One point should be remembered about expectancy theory as a model of organizational choice. The theory does *not* say that individuals actually write down all the information contained in

Table 4.1, nor does it say individuals actually write out the calculations shown in Table 4.2. Expectancy theory *does* say that this is the way most people make decisions, whether or not they are consciously aware that all these factors are taken into account as stipulated in the model.

Using the situation in which Evan was participating in a research study was merely a literary convenience so that the various pieces of information could be presented in detailed form. Those who have criticized expectancy theory as being too rational prefer the *unprogrammed* view of decision making (Soelberg, 1967; Power & Aldag, 1985) to be examined in the second case study. Their argument is that researchers who use questionnaires artificially create the appearance of rationality by forcing participants such as Evan into answering according to the prearranged format required by the expectancy theory model of decision making. Those who believe the unprogrammed view is more accurate than expectancy theory tend to avoid the use of structured questionnaires in favor of open-ended interviews with job candidates. It will be seen later that this difference in data-gathering procedure is important because the two methods are extremely hard to compare.

Organizational Choice as an "Unprogrammed" Decision

The procedure just described can be thought of as a highly "programmed" approach to decision making. It is programmed in the sense that a number of factors were considered in the evaluation of different schools. Furthermore, each factor was given only as much "weight" as justified by its *importance* to the person making the choice. By way of contrast with Evan's systematic (and programmed) process, let's now consider the case of another college senior in a similar situation. Arnon was also a senior at the same Big Ten university as Evan, but they were not acquainted. Arnon's decision process was quite different—it was an *un*programmed approach to organizational choice.

Rather than considering five factors,[1] as Evan had, Arnon was primarily concerned with only two, but very *crucial*, outcomes:

---

1. This is a good example of the difference between the two views. The unprogrammed view holds that Evan only considered five factors because he was asked to do so.

(1) the prospects for a job upon graduation, and (2) the geographical location of the school. Regarding the first factor, Arnon wanted to go to a high-prestige school. This seemed to her to be the best route to getting a job with a large, multinational corporation. For the second factor, Arnon wanted to move from the midwest either to the west coast or to New York City. These two factors were absolute. Arnon would not consider a high-prestige school in another area, nor would she consider a weak school in one of the desirable areas. These two criteria severely limited the scope of her search for the ideal MBA program.

The schools that Arnon labeled as "attractive" were thus selected via a different psychological process from the one that Evan used. First, *fewer criteria* were used to judge each school. Second, *the factors were not weighted by importance*—they were either *crucial* or practically irrelevant. There was less room for compromise in Arnon's search than there was in Evan's search.

There were some similarities, however, between Evan's systematic approach and Arnon's unprogrammed procedure. First, both could give a fairly clear description of the ideal school, even though their *process* of coming to this decision differed. Second, both *believed* they were being rational about the decision.

Evan and Arnon also differed in making the decision to apply to schools. Evan considered four schools simultaneously and rated each in terms of the *expectancy* of being admitted. Arnon's process was much less systematic. Rather than considering a number of schools, she began with her ideal choice. She appraised her chances for a successful admission. She then considered another highly attractive school in comparison with the ideal choice. Arnon found it easier to make direct comparisons between two schools at a time, rather than to make the many simultaneous evaluations Evan had made. Rarely did Arnon consider (in an *active* way) more than two or (possibly) three schools. The total number of schools she considered was actually larger than that considered by Evan, but the schools were considered *sequentially* rather than simultaneously.

The unprogrammed approach taken by Arnon is also different from the expectancy theory model in its explanation of how individuals make the "final" choice. Evan chose the school that was the one highest in *attractiveness* of those that had accepted him. It was based on a careful consideration of several factors, each of which was weighted by its importance.

In contrast, the unprogrammed approach taken by Arnon was actually a two-stage process. The first stage was the development of an "implicit choice" (Soelberg, 1967) of which she was not fully aware. In fact, the view of unprogrammed organizational choice stipulates that most individuals are not aware of the direction toward which they are actually leaning. Often it takes the "prodding" of another person to help the individual realize that an implicit decision has been made. The implicit choice is usually based on only a few factors that are not weighted by importance as they are in expectancy theory.

The second stage is called *confirmation* (Soelberg, 1967) and means the type of thinking used to *justify* one's implicit choice. In this stage, there is a great deal of similarity between expectancy theory and the unprogrammed view. During confirmation, the alternative organizations are compared across a much wider spectrum of factors, *and* the factors are weighted by their importance to the individual. However, the crucial difference is that the unprogrammed view stipulates that this occurs only *after* an individual has already made the decision. In contrast, expectancy theory says that this is how the decision was made in the first place.

The final difference between the two views of organizational choice is that the unprogrammed view says that individuals tend to *distort* both their perceptions about organizations *and* the importance they attach to various factors used to make the decision. This distortion is supposed to be a necessary step in the justification, or rationalization, of one's implicit choice. This stems from a common human need to feel that good choices have been made. In this sense, it has been said that most people need to *"feel right"* rather than to actually *"be right"* (Aronson, 1972). In contrast, expectancy theory does not say whether or not distortion occurs.

Evaluating the Two Views of Organizational Choice

In comparing these two cases studies of organizational choice, two questions must be answered: (1) Which of the two better represents the *typical* person? (2) Which is *better* for the welfare of both individuals and organizations? The first question can be discussed by referring to research studies. The second refers to which type of choice process will produce better long-term matches between the individual and the organization.

Research on Expectancy Theory

Studies of how people make job choices, like the case study of Evan, have been done to determine the accuracy of expectancy theory as a model of the *typical* person in that situation. Most of the studies have been of college seniors choosing either their first full-time job or a graduate school to attend. The accumulated research on expectancy has been reviewed by Wanous, Keon, and Latack (1983). Interestingly, no new research on expectancy theory has been conducted since then. Those interested in the details of these studies should consult that review since only the main conclusions will be discussed here.

Remember that expectancy theory makes two basic predictions about how individuals choose organizations. First, it says that the *total amount of effort to join* an organization is the result of (1) the *expectancy of being offered a job* if one were to apply, and (2) the *attractiveness* of the organization. Second, it says that an individual's final choice of a job from among job offers is based on the *attractiveness* of the organization, i.e., people choose the job offer that has the highest attractiveness.

Our review of the accumulated research found the following types of studies. First, we summarized 17 different research projects that used questionnaires to measure the specific components of expectancy theory, as shown earlier in the case study of Evan. A shortcoming of this entire group is that it is very academically oriented. That is, it is mostly of students choosing jobs or other schools. This is precisely the type of person who is most likely to "act rationally" as expectancy theory stipulates.

Second, we reviewed the results for the two major predictions of expectancy theory. Of the 17 projects we found, only 5 of them actually tested the first of the two predictions, although the results are encouraging for the validity of expectancy theory. The major problem in trying to assess the first prediction is coming up with a good way to measure "effort." This concept is tricky to define. The studies we found all used a measurement of effort that was determined by the individuals themselves. This is not necessarily wrong, but it is somewhat limited because it does not account for the types of active steps people take to join organizations, e.g., obtaining information, interviewing, and making trips.

Perhaps the more important prediction is the second one. That is, can data gathered from job candidates at the beginning of the job search process accurately predict which jobs they will actually choose later on. If researchers measure *organizational attractiveness* at one point in time, will this information predict which companies are actually entered later on after the job offers have been made. The test of this aspect of expectancy theory is a "hit rate," that is, a percentage of the time that an individual will choose the organization with the highest attractiveness rating from among those actually offering a job. In the nine studies that calculated this "hit rate," the average was 63 percent. This means that people choose organizations that they had earlier rated as the "logical" or "rational" choice. This is considered to be solid evidence that expectancy theory is a reasonable representation of how the typical person makes such an important decision. Because the hit rate is less than 100 percent, it is also possible that expectancy theory is *too* rational, or that it only applies to some people, whereas other people are best described by the "unprogrammed" model in the case study of Arnon.

Research Assessing the Unprogrammed Model of Organizational Choice

The unprogrammed model of organizational choice developed by Soelberg (1967) is a much broader, more encompassing view compared to expectancy theory. It includes four stages of the process, as shown in Figure 4.2. Expectancy theory is really concerned with actual choice itself, not with phases 1 or 2, and it is not concerned with how people think *after* they have made a choice. The unprogrammed view is concerned with a much larger portion of the entry process. This has also made it extremely difficult to research because it means that job candidates would have to be interviewed (the preferred method of data collection here) a number of times over a considerable period of time. Other than in the original study that launched this particular model of the process (Soelberg, 1967), no one has taken the time to monitor job candidates in the way necessary to study this model. Although it is an intriguing view of organizational choice, it remains to this day more speculation than fact. The few studies to assess this theory are briefly described next.

In Soelberg's original research, he found that 74 percent of the people studied could identify an "acceptable choice" two weeks

Figure 4.2
Soelberg's Job Search and Choice Model

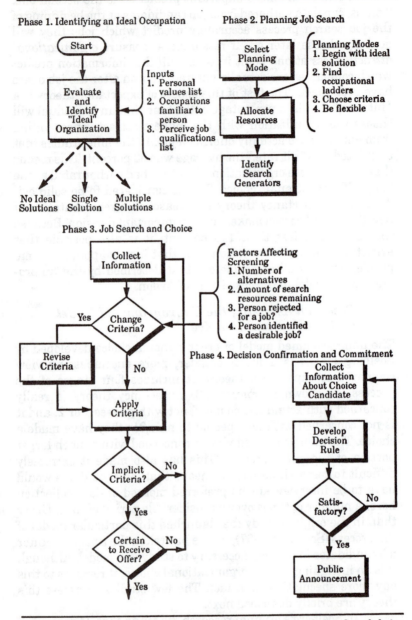

Phase 1. Identifying an Ideal Occupation

Phase 2. Planning Job Search

Start

Evaluate and Identify "Ideal" Organization

Inputs
1. Personal values list
2. Occupations familiar to person
3. Perceive job qualifications list

No Ideal Solutions   Single Solution   Multiple Solutions

Select Planning Mode

Allocate Resources

Identify Search Generators

Planning Modes
1. Begin with ideal solution
2. Find occupational ladders
3. Choose criteria
4. Be flexible

Phase 3. Job Search and Choice

Collect Information

Change Criteria?   Yes   No

Revise Criteria

Apply Criteria

Implicit Criteria?   No   Yes

Certain to Receive Offer?   No   Yes

Factors Affecting Screening
1. Number of alternatives
2. Amount of search resources remaining
3. Person rejected for a job?
4. Person identified a desirable job?

Phase 4. Decision Confirmation and Commitment

Collect Information About Choice Candidate

Develop Decision Rule

Satisfactory?   No   Yes

Public Announcement

Source: D. J. Power & R. J. Aldag, 1985, Soelberg's job search and choice model: A clarification, review, and critique. Academy of Management Review, 10, p. 50. Reprinted by permission.

prior to the end of their search for job offers. Soelberg considered that this finding supported the unprogrammed view. Expectancy theory stipulates that one's organizational choice is made *after* all relevant information has been collected, not *prior* to it, as found by Soelberg.

Three subsequent studies, inspired by Soelberg's original investigation, did *not* find the same degree of "irrational" behavior (Glueck, 1974; Hill, 1974; Sheridan, Richards & Slocum, 1975). For example, 47 percent of the subjects in one study could *not* specify a set of "necessary and sufficient" outcomes that would govern their search for acceptable jobs (Sheridan et al., 1975). Hill (1974) found some evidence that students compared job alternatives *to each other*, rather than to a set of important criteria, as the theory stipulates. Thus the unprogrammed model does not seem to be typical, although it might be accurate for a minority of people.

Should Individuals Make Rational Career and Organizational Choices?

What the typical person does is not the same as what the typical person *should* have done. The data on how organizational choices are made support the rational approach of expectancy theory as the more typical. Yet not everyone is this rational. Some individuals make choices in ways that do *not* involve the search for lots of information and the careful consideration of each alternative. According to the Matching Model, this leads to less than maximum satisfaction with one's choice of organization. The data in Chapter 2 on the "falling satisfaction" of newcomers certainly confirm this.

In the area of *occupational* choices, a step-by-step procedure has been developed to help people think more clearly and systematically about career choices (Janis & Wheeler, 1978). The procedure seems easily transferable to organizational choices.

Janis and Wheeler (1978) have developed the "decision counselor" approach to career decision making. Their efforts have been directed toward this development because they felt that career choices are hard to reverse if they turn out to be wrong.

The main thrust of the decision counselor approach is to have individuals identify all the relevant alternatives and then carefully evaluate each one according to the "balance sheet" approach. Table 4.3 shows an example. Four categories are included: (a) tangible gains and losses for self, (b) tangible gains and losses for others, (c) self-approval or self-disapproval, and (d) social approval or disapproval.

Why all the fuss about helping people behave more rationally? Janis and Mann (1977) identified four ways in which people cope with tough decisions, particularly those in their personal lives: (a) complacency, (b) defensive avoidance, (c) hypervigilance, and (d) vigilance. Only the last "coping style" is rational in the expectancy theory sense. *Complacency* is the coping style used by those who ignore negative information. For example, a new Ph.D. may take a job in a small college rather than in a big university in order to "avoid the publish-or-perish rat race." The person is complacently assuming that job security will be greater in the small college, but the facts may not support this assumption.

Defensive avoidance is a type of denial of the risks involved in making career or organizational choices. People who are defensively avoiding the facts concerning these choices are often quite calm in appearance. They are typically unaware of their defensiveness. There are, however, three tell-tale signs of this coping style. (a) Rationalization, "It can't happen to me."; (b) Procrastination, "Nothing needs to be done now. I can take care of it later."; and (c) Buck Passing, "I'm not the one who needs to do it. Let someone else do it."

Hypervigilance is the coping style used by people who are faced with making a crucial choice under severe time pressure. An extreme form of hypervigilance is panic. The hypervigilant person does not consider a full range of options and may tend to select the first reasonable one that comes along. The person may even display visible signs of stress during the decision process. In a "tight" labor market, some college seniors become hypervigilant.

Vigilant decision making is employed by those who acknowledge that all choices involve risks, who believe that a best solution exists, and who believe they have enough time to make a thoroughly systematic decision. Vigilant decision makers recognize risks and make contingency plans. In contrast, the other three types do not and are emotionally unprepared even for minor setbacks. The balance sheet procedure (Table 4.3) is extremely useful in focusing on the facts of each alternative career or organizational choice. Janis and Wheeler (1978) report that the decision balance sheet was quite well received in four experiments: (1) with Yale seniors deciding what to do the next year, (2) with high school seniors deciding whether or not to attend college, (3) with adults deciding whether or not to diet, and (4) with adults deciding

Table 4.3
A Manager's Balance Sheet

The grid lays out the pros and cons of facing a production manager at a large manufacturing plant who is contemplating a job change: whether or not to remain in the present position. Balance sheets would be filled out as well for all other alternatives, for example, whether or not to seek a lateral transfer within the company.

	Positive Anticipations	Negative Anticipations
Tangible gains and losses for self	1. Satisfactory pay 2. Plenty of opportunities to use my skills and competencies 3. For the present, my status in organization is OK (but it won't be for long if I am not promoted in the next year)	1. Long hours 2. Constant time pressures—deadlines too short 3. Unpleasant paperwork 4. Poor prospects for advancement to a higher level position 5. Repeated reorganizations make my work chaotic 6. Constant disruption from high turnover of other executives I deal with
Tangible gains and losses for others	1. Adequate income for family 2. Spouse and children get special privileges because of my position in the firm	1. Not enough time free to spend with my family 2. Spouse often has to put up with my irritability when I come home after bad days at work

Table 4.3 Continued
A Manager's Balance Sheet

	Positive Anticipations	Negative Anticipations
Self-approval or self-disapproval	1. This position allows me to make full use of my potential 2. Proud of my achievements 3. Proud of the competent team I have shaped up 4. Sense of meaningful accomplishment when I see the products for which we are responsible	1. Sometimes feel I'm a fool to continue putting up with the unreasonable deadlines and other stupid demands made by the top managers
Social approval or disapproval	1. Approval of people on my team, who look up to me as their leader and who are good friends 2. Approval of my superior who is a friend and wants me to stay	1. Very slight skeptical reaction of my spouse who asks me if I might be better off in a different firm 2. A friend in another firm who has been wanting to wangle something for me will be disappointed

Source: I. Janis and D. Wheeler, 1978. Thinking clearly about career choices. Psychology Today (May): 75. Reprinted from Psychology Today magazine. Copyright © 1978 by Ziff-Davis Publishing Company.

whether or not to attend an early morning exercise class for health reasons.

Besides the balance sheet technique, *stress inoculation* is used *after* the decision, but before it is carried out. This is somewhat similar to realistic recruitment, except that Janis believes it is appropriate only *after* a choice (Janis & Mann, 1977; Janis & Wheeler, 1978). Much more will be said about stress inoculation in Chapter 6.

The final technique used to promote vigilant decision making is called *outcome psychodrama*—a type of role-playing exercise. The decision counselor asks the client to assume that a particular career (or organization) has already been chosen and to reflect on what has happened since making the choice (Janis & Wheeler, 1978). The client is asked to repeat and expand upon the scenario until all the potential risks and benefits are considered. The decision counselor keeps a "low profile," relying instead on the client to generate the list of consequences associated with each alternative. Janis and Wheeler report only limited use of outcome psychodrama. Therefore, its effectiveness at the present is unknown. They do caution that a particularly intense session may backfire, causing feelings of hopelessness—just the type of defensive avoidance that we would be trying to overcome with this approach.

Is It Possible for People to Be Rational ?

The theme of this book has been that individuals *can* be rational about organizational choice decisions—at least some people can make such decisions in the way expectancy theory says. Furthermore, the emphasis on realistic recruitment assumes that job candidates are interested in obtaining information about organizations because they will use it in choosing which job offer to accept. Despite all the evidence shown in this book on the rationality of organizational choices and the effectiveness of RJPs in recruitment, there is a considerable body of research on decision making in other contexts. This research strongly suggests that the typical person has several "built-in" biases that make it difficult to make rational choices consistently (see Bazerman, 1990, for a review). This section reviews these biases and discusses their relevance for organizational choice. Those who have researched decision making and identified these biases have done so to increase awareness of them so that individuals will be better able to make rational decisions.

Before reviewing the biases that most people seem to have, let's specify what is meant by a "rational" decision process. This process usually has six components: (1) clearly define the problem, (2) identify the criteria used to make a choice, i.e., what factors are important, (3) weight each of the criteria in terms of its importance, (4) generate alternative solutions, (5) evaluate each solution on each criterion, and (6) compute the "optimal" solution by weighing each criterion rating with its importance weight. This is the same type of decision process implied by the expectancy theory view of organizational choice.

Research on decision making in general has identified three fundamental "rules of thumb" (called heuristics), which can be broken down into eleven more specific forms of nonrational biases (see Table 4.4). These three basic rules of thumb used in decisions have been described as follows (Bazerman, 1990, pp. 6–7):

1. The "Availability" heuristic. An individual assesses the likelihood of something happening (e.g., getting a job offer) based on the degree to which previous experience is "stored" in the individual's memory. People who have been successful at obtaining job offers in the past may actually overrate their chances in the future because their memory of past successes clouds their judgment.

2. The "Representativeness" heuristic. An individual assesses the likelihood of something occurring based on stereotypes developed from previous experience. People may "learn" that a job interviewer who makes very little eye contact with them will not be inviting them to a second interview.

3. "Anchoring and Adjustment" heuristics. Individuals make judgments by starting from some initial value and then adjusting their prediction. A job candidate assesses the reasonableness of a starting salary based on last year's average starting salaries for college graduates.

Readers interested in the specific details of the biases listed and briefly described in Table 4.4 should read Bazerman's book (1990). It is not difficult to see how some of these specific biases can also be found in the organizational entry process. For example, one of the most pervasive findings discussed earlier was that job

Table 4.4
Summary of 13 Biases in Human Judgment

Bias	Description
Biases Emanating from the Availability Heuristic	
1. Ease of recall	Individuals judge events that are more easily recalled from memory, based on vividness or recency, to be more numerous than events of equal frequency whose instances are less easily recalled.
2. Retrievability	Individuals are biased in their assessments of the frequency of events based on how their memory structures affect the search process.
3. Presumed associations	Individuals tend to overestimate the probability of two events co-occurring based on the number of similar associations that are easily recalled, whether from experience or social influence.
Biases Emanating from the Representativeness Heuristic	
4. Insensitivity to base rates	Individuals tend to ignore base rates in assessing the likelihood of events when any other descriptive information is provided—even if it is irrelevant.
5. Insensitivity to sample size	Individuals frequently fail to appreciate the role of sample size in assessing the reliability of sample information.
6. Misconceptions of chance	Individuals expect that a sequence of data generated by a random process will look "random," even when the sequence is too short for those expectations to be statistically valid.
7. Regression to the mean	Individuals tend to ignore the fact that extreme events tend to regress to the mean on subsequent trials.
8. The conjunction fallacy	Individuals falsely judge that conjunctions (two events co-occurring) are more probable than a more global set of occurrences of which conjunction is a subset.

Table 4.4 Continued
Summary of 13 Biases in Human Judgment

Bias	Description
Biases Emanating from Anchoring and Adjustment	
9. Insufficient anchor adjustment	Individuals estimate values based on an initial value (derived from past events, random assignment, or whatever information is available) and typically make insufficient adjustments from that anchor when establishing a final value.
10. Conjunctive and disjunctive events bias	Individuals exhibit a bias toward overestimating the probability of conjunctive events and under-estimating the probability of disjunctive events.
11. Overconfidence	Individuals tend to be overconfi-dent of the infallibility of their judgments when answering moderately to extremely difficult questions.
Two More General Biases	
12. The confirmation trap	Individuals tend to seek con-firmatory information for what they think is true and neglect the search for disconfirmatory evidence.
13. Hindsight	After finding out whether or not an event occurred, individuals tend to overestimate the degree to which they would have predicted the correct outcome.

Source: M. H. Bazerman, 1990. Judgment in managerial decision making (2nd. ed.), pp. 40–41. New York: John Wiley and Sons.

candidates have inflated expectations about the organizations they consider joining. Job candidates may overestimate their chances for obtaining a job offer (their "expectancy" that effort leads to an offer) to the extent that they fall prey to the "conjunc-tive events bias." Job candidates may not realize that to obtain an offer requires success at a number of stages, e.g., the job interview, testing, a second interview, reference check, and drug testing. To the extent that students overgeneralize their chances from casual conversations with other students, they may fall prey to the "sample size insensitivity" bias. If a college graduate ignores the chances for being accepted into medical school, he or she is committing the "insensitivity to base rates" bias—probably because we all like to think we are somehow unusual or unique.

Other biases may lead students to overrate the attractiveness of an organization as a place to work, as was discussed at length in Chapter 2. For example, the "presumed associations" bias might lead students to overestimate the amount of feedback they will get as newcomers on the job because in college they are constantly being given feedback on papers, exams, etc. When thinking about the likelihood of being successful in a new organization, job candidates may overestimate their chances if they fall prey to the "overconfidence" bias.

Finally, after someone has made a job choice, the last two biases listed in Table 4.4 are particularly relevant. The "confirmation trap" clearly implies that newcomers will be more pleased with their job choice *after* they have made it than before. In fact, this tendency was an explicit component of the "unprogrammed" decision model (Soelberg, 1967). The "hindsight" bias can be interpreted as actually helping a newcomer adjust to a new working environment because it implies that the newcomer can rationalize away at least some of the inflated expectations that are unfulfilled. If this were consistently true for all people all the time, there might not be a need for realistic recruitment. Some psychologists have gone further to distinguish between those types of disconfirmed expectations that are more bothersome than others. If a newcomer believes that "I should have known better," they are more likely to be bothered by the disillusionment of inflated expectations. However, if they feel that "nobody's perfect" and "I couldn't have predicted this," they are not as bothered (Carlsmith & Freedman, 1968).

Relationship of Organizational Choice to Recruitment

In Chapters 2 and 3, much was said about the extensive problems related to the inflated expectations held by job candidates as outsiders to organizations. After reading the two accounts of organizational choice, it should be clear that *both* views of the choice process depend heavily on the beliefs and expectations of individuals. The dependence on expectations is probably greater for the expectancy theory model of organizational choice, but the unprogrammed view also contains similar components. In expectancy theory, the accuracy of information obtained by outsiders affects (a) their beliefs about what the organization has to offer and (b) their *expectations* of gaining entry if they apply. You may wonder how expectancy theory could be used as a model of organizational choice when it has already been established that outsider expectations are often incorrectly inflated. This is *not* as serious a problem as it might appear to be. In fact, there is *no* inconsistency between the theme of Chapters 2 and 3 and that of the present one.

The key to understanding the relationship between recruitment and organizational choice is to remember that individuals make choices as *outsiders, prior* to discovering that some of their beliefs were grossly inflated. At the time that most organizational choices are made, outsiders are unaware of organizational realities; i.e., they tend to hold "naive" expectations. Thus it is possible for individuals to act in the way expectancy theory predicts they will. The *long-range* wisdom of organizational choices made with realistic expectations is greater than those decisions made on much less information because people are better able to match their own job wants to an appropriate organization.

To put this another way, the best available research evidence shows that most job candidates are fairly rational when it comes to making a job choice, even though they may make nonrational judgment "errors" in other situations. The best evidence also shows that when people make such choices, they do so with biased information due to inflated expectations. The *process of choice* appears to be rational, but the *information used to make the choice* appears to be biased. In keeping with these basic conclusions, I have recommended realistic recruitment as an *organizational* strategy and also have recommended the use of decision counseling for specific *individuals*.

Organizational Choice and the Job Interview

The interview is used in almost all organizations. As with the other events of organizational entry, the interview can be analyzed both from an individual and an organizational viewpoint. This is because it fulfills two functions during entry—*recruitment* and *selection*. Since the focus here is on organizational choice, this section examines two aspects concerning the recruitment function. First, the impact of an interview on how individuals choose organizations is discussed. Second, the results of research studies on the interpersonal dynamics of the interview are interpreted so that advice can be given to job candidates about to be interviewed for employment. The role of the interview as a *selection* mechanism is discussed in Chapter 5.

Before going into the specifics of what is known about how job interviewers affect job candidates in the entry process, note that there is a surprising *lack* of research from either academic or from industry sources. This is surprising because the interview is uniformly used in the entry process. A recent review of university-based research efforts (Wanous & Colella, 1989) found only eleven studies concerning the effects of job interviews on job candidates. Of these eleven studies, seven were done with real job candidates (the other four were simulations with students), and none of these seven followed the job candidates through their organizational choices right into their early experiences at work. Thus what is known today is based on a few short studies. Nevertheless they do tell us something about the effects on organizational choices, per se.

The results from industry research are no more encouraging. A survey of Fortune 1000 companies about their recruiting practices (Rynes & Boudreau, 1986) only got responses from 145 of the 1000. Only 41 percent of those responding reported that they did recruiter training, and only half of these firms required the training *prior* to sending interviewers out to recruit job candidates.

How the Job Interviewer Affects Organizational Choices of Job Candidates

Studies of the effect of job interviewers on job candidates have been concerned with three questions: (a) How strong is the impact? (b) What causes it? and (c) Is the impact due to the way interviewers treat job candidates (the *process*) or is it due to the information communicated during the interview (the *content*)?

The earliest study was done over 20 years ago at Cornell University (Alderfer & McCord, 1970) with graduating MBA students. The first issue that concerned the researchers was how much job choices are affected by "good" versus "bad" interviewers since most students left the interview having some type of "gut" feeling about how it went. When asked if they would accept a forthcoming job offer after a "good" interview, 57 percent said they would. However, only 23 percent would do the same after a "bad" interview. It seemed clear that students' organizational choices were affected by this initial experience.

The researchers' next issue was what factors cause job candidates to feel that they had "good" or "bad" interviews. Two studies (Alderfer & McCord, 1970; Schmitt & Coyle, 1976) addressed this issue with Cornell and Michigan State students, respectively. The more recent of these two also seems to have been the more influential. Students were asked a great many questions during the campus interview process, but they fell into two basic categories: (a) the *content* of the interview, i.e., the specific things interviewers said, and (b) the *process* of the interview, i.e., the general impression that interviewers created in the minds of job candidates. Table 4.5 organizes the results.

At the present time we simply do not know which of these two basic factors, content or process, has the stronger impact on job candidates. Even if research were to show that one was stronger than the other, it would probably be desirable for organizations to train interviewers in both types of skills. In my opinion it appears much easier to train them in those areas labeled the "content" of the interview because the content factors are much more specific than those in the "process" areas.

The final area of research on job interviewer effects has been to examine the relative strength of the job interviewer's actions as compared to the desirability of the job itself. Put another way, can an effective interviewer motivate candidates to accept a job offer even when the job itself is not particularly attractive? Or the reverse, can an ineffective interviewer drive away candidates from attractive organizations?

The first study to ask this question (Rynes & Miller, 1983) asked University of Minnesota students to watch videotapes of staged interviews and then answer questions about how they might have reacted if they had been in the situation they had just observed. Although both content and process affected the students' reactions to the videotapes, the information about the job itself seemed to have a slightly stronger effect than whether or not the interviewer was attractive or unattractive. Because this study was done with students in a hypothetical situation, a follow-up study

Table 4.5
How Recruiters Affect Job Candidates[1]

Substance of the Interview

How well the interview was organized	The accuracy and precision of the interviewer	The extensiveness of information given
Used appropriate words	Grammatically precise	Stressed variety and change in the job
Did not lose train of thought	Well acquainted with the job	Told about careers of others in the company
Did not use unnecessary detail	Capable of answering questions	Said that high salary was a possibility
Did not repeat questions already answered	Had broad knowledge	Gave information about supervision
Did not interrupt answers	Thought analytically	
Did not interject ums, ahs, or uhs	Asked clear questions	

The Process of the Interview

The interviewer was a nice person	The interviewer was aggressive	The interviewer showed interest in the candidate
Warm personality	Spoke forcefully	Interested in determining my outside interests
Senses other's feelings	Self-confident	Did not slouch
Cooperative	Aggressive	Did not give in to avoid controversy
Thoughtful	Persistent	
Interested in me	Outspoken	
Trustworthy	Used large vocabulary	
	Looked me in the eye	

[1] This is adapted from Schmitt and Coyle (1976).

Source: J. P. Wanous & A. Colella, 1989. Organizational entry research: Current status and future directions. In K. Rowland & G. Ferris (Eds.), Research in Personnel / Human Resource Management *(Vol. 7), p. 95. Reprinted by permission of JAI press.*

with students in actual job interviews at the University of Connecticut was conducted (Powell, 1984). Once again, the information about the job itself (content of the interview) appeared to be the stronger factor. Two more studies following this one also found stronger effects on organizational choices to be descriptions of the job itself rather than the process used by the interviewer (Liden & Parsons, 1986; Taylor & Bergman, 1987). The two most recent studies have found just the reverse (Harris & Fink, 1987; Powell, 1991). That is, there is now some convincing evidence from field studies that recruiting interviewers can affect the attitudes and behavior of job candidates.

Taking all three of these research issues together suggests several general conclusions about organizational entry. First, the job interview does influence job candidates, even though they may have preconceived ideas about the organization. Second, if we dissect the job interview itself into its content and its process, both do influence job candidates, although the content of the interview appears to be the stronger influence. In some ways this is desirable since it is probably easier to train interviewers in content factors than in process factors.

Coping with the Employment Interview

Much of the research on interviews has focused on how the interviewer makes decisions about job candidates. As an outgrowth of this research, some results are relevant for job candidates. Selected conclusions from research on employment interviews are presented in this chapter because of their implications for job candidates (Harris, 1989; Mayfield, 1964; Schmitt, 1976; Ulrich & Trumbo, 1965; Wagner, 1949; and Wright, 1969).

Initial Impressions Are Crucial. Most studies of interviews indicate that the *order* in which information is presented to the interviewer is highly significant. The information obtained *first* has a more significant impact on the decision to hire than that gathered later in the interview. This has been called the "primacy effect," in contrast to the "recency effect." A dramatic example of the primacy effect was revealed in a study that found that the average interviewer reached a conclusion about job candidates after only four minutes of a fifteen-minute interview (Springbett, 1958).

This research finding is important because behavioral scientists have studied the order in which information is presented in a wide variety of situations, e.g., political campaigns and legal proceedings. The primacy effect does *not* occur universally, but it does seem to occur in job interviews. The only time recency effects are found is in the situation in which interviewers are asked to make *two* ratings of candidates, i.e., an initial one and a final one. In this particular situation, the information uncovered last has the greater influence on the hiring decision.

The best explanation for the dominance of early information is that the attention of the interviewer decreases over time. This explains why primacy effects occur with only one rating. It also explains why recency effects occur with repeated ratings because the attention of the interviewer is aroused by having to complete a second formal evaluation. The situation of repeated ratings is typically found in tightly monitored research studies. Outside the context of a research study, however, the interviewer generally makes just one evaluation that is heavily influenced by *initial* impressions and information.

What this means to the job candidate is quite clear: first impressions *do* count heavily. Job candidates are often advised to be "on time" and to "dress appropriately." This advice is usually considered so obvious that no proof is generally offered to substantiate it. However, remember that two of the earliest pieces of information the interviewer gathers concern the punctuality and physical appearance of job candidates.

Negative Information Is Given High Significance. The importance of this research finding is obvious. One study found that a *single* piece of negative information led to a 90 percent chance of a rejection (Springbett, 1958). Virtually all research studies of job interviews show that interviewers give negative information a much higher weight relative to positive information. One or two negatives can far outweigh a much larger number of positive factors. Thus job candidates should be aware that interviewers tend to look for information that leads to a rejection rather than to a selection.

Psychologists have spent quite a lot of time trying to understand why negative information outweighs the positive. At least four reasons have been uncovered. First, most interviewers reflect a corporate strategy of being cost oriented. In most cases it is true that hiring an incompetent person costs more than do the lost opportunities of passing over a qualified person. Therefore, most interviewers try to avoid costly mistakes in hiring, even though they realize an occasional "gem" may be lost. Second, some jobs are easily performed by a large percentage of those interviewed.

Thus the interviewer needs to find some way to reject candidates, hence even a "small" negative fact can lead to the rejection of a job candidate.

The third reason stems from a "figure-ground" contrast. Consider the following situation. A tall tree seems to "stand-out" among a much larger cluster of shorter trees. In this case, the tall tree is the "figure" and the others form the "ground" (or background). The typical interview presents a similar situation. When the majority of information is positive, a small number of negatives easily diverts the interviewer's attention. The fourth reason is that interviewers are typically more familiar with failures than successes. This is because they are quite likely to be criticized for unsuccessful hires since they contributed to the decision. Thus interviewers tend to know more specifics about who failed than they do about who succeeded.

Other Ways to Cope: Knowing What Questions to Expect and Managing Your Own Impression. Job interviewers ask a wide variety of questions, as we are told in self-help books on job finding (e.g., Strasser & Sena, 1990). Questions can be loosely categorized as follows. First, some questions are "open-ended" or general. For example, they ask you to discuss your strengths and weaknesses, your experience, why you want this job in this company, or where you want your career to be in 5 to 10 years. Second, some questions can be general, too, but more hypothetical. For example, you might be asked to describe your leadership style or the type of leadership style you look for in a boss. Third, some questions can be illegal, or border on illegality. For example, they can ask about your marital status, your spouse's plans, your child care responsibilities, and other personal, non–job-related information. Finally, some questions may be more specific and job related than the previous types. For example, you might be asked to describe a specific project or job assignment that you succeeded or failed at and then say what you learned as a result. This last category is discussed next.

One trend in job interviewing is to move away from "unstructured" interviews to those with specific "structured" objectives. (See Chapter 5 for details on this procedure and its effectiveness.) Since the best predictor of someone's future job performance is their past performance, these structured interview approaches (Janz, 1982; Latham & Saari, 1980) attempt to assess a job candidate's likely performance based on two slightly different methods. The first approach to this (Latham & Saari, 1980) uses *hypothetical* situations that might be likely to occur on the job. Job candidates are asked how they *might* respond in such a situation were they ever to face it. Answers to these situations are quantitatively scored based on what managers say are good-mediocre-poor responses. This is a type of simulation, but it is carried out in an interview situation. The second approach (Janz, 1982) asks job candidates to *give examples from their own experience* that might be relevant to a future job. For example, if a student is being considered for a sales job but has no sales experience, the interviewer might ask about situations where he or she has exercised successful persuasion in the past.

The best advice for coping with these two interview techniques is to thoroughly research the type of job for which you are being considered. Then ask yourself what crucial elements of human judgment or knowledge might be asked. Continuing with the sales job example mentioned earlier, job candidates might also be expected to be asked about how they go about planning a typical day. Being highly organized is a "good" answer if you use daily "to do" lists, set objectives, and generally can demonstrate that you provide your own motivation. Questions about favorite leisure activities might also reveal a pattern of individual (versus group) activity (like jogging) in which you set goals (time and distance). Such a person is likely to be rated fairly highly in the "need for achievement" category (McClelland, 1961) and thus would make a fairly good "outside" salesperson who could work alone making customer calls.

An entirely different approach to coping with the interview is to learn from those social psychologists who study "impression management," so you could try to present yourself as positively to the interviewer as possible. (Although I personally believe this can easily lead to a poor fit with the organization, I recognize that many readers are sufficiently anxious about getting a job that they might not want to mirror my advice to organizations, i.e., present yourself honestly.) Several impression management "techniques" have been recently summarized as relevant for the job interview (Fletcher, 1989):

1. **Ingratiation.** People like those who make them "feel good," so anything that compliments the interviewer or the organization may have this effect.

2. **Self-Promotion.** Emphasize your accomplishments and basic skills.
3. **Basking in Reflected Glory.** By claiming an association with high-status people or organizations, an interviewer might assume a high degree of competence.
4. **Nonverbal Behavior.** Making eye contact and dressing the way an interviewer expects you to dress both send strong nonverbal signals.
5. **Assertiveness.** Some research shows that it is better to try to justify past failures rather than try to explain them. This is a subtle difference, but it may be more persuasive.

Fletcher (1989) has also cautioned against being overly manipulative in one's self-presentation. This is because most job candidates have insufficient information about the job interviewer to make ingratiation very effective, and the result could backfire on the candidate's being seen quite negatively. (See Baron, 1989, for research evidence on the likelihood of having one's efforts backfire).

Conclusions

1. Organizational choice is a more limited topic than is the vocational entry process. Organizational choices typically follow occupational choices and are usually easier to reverse.
2. Organizational choice has been described in two alternative ways: as a systematic, rational choice by expectancy theory and as an unprogrammed decision. These two views differ in the amount of information considered in the decision, the number of criteria used, and in how individuals process the information that is obtained.
3. Both views of organizational choices have received some research support due to the different research designs used to study each one. More studies of expectancy theory have been done, and the evidence supporting expectancy theory is stronger than that for the unprogrammed view of organizational choice.
4. Decision counseling is a new approach to help individuals be "vigilant" decision makers in a way similar to

expectancy theory. Such counseling includes: balance sheets, stress inoculation, and outcome psychodrama.

5. Research on decision making in general has uncovered several fairly basic rules of thumb that cause people to be less than rational. These basic heuristics can be further broken down into eleven more specific biases that plague the efforts of individual decision makers to be rational.

6. The pervasive problem of incorrect (inflated) expectations does *not* directly affect the degree to which individuals try to be rational in making an organizational choice. However, the long-term wisdom of organizational choices is impaired by inflated expectations.

7. Relatively little research has concerned how the job interview affects someone's organizational choice. That which has been done suggests that the content or substance of the interview is more important than the process by which it is conducted, although both influence job choices.

8. To cope effectively with the job interview, you need to recognize that the early portion of the interview is crucial and that negative information can be particularly damaging to your chance for a job offer.

9. Anticipating the types of questions that will be asked is one way to cope with job interviews, as is managing the impression you create when being interviewed.

5

Selection of Newcomers by an Organization

The topic of selection is extremely vast, even if it were only to be summarized. Not only have entire books been written on the topic of selection (e.g., Cook, 1988; Gatewood & Feild, 1987; Schneider & Schmitt, 1986), but there are also entire books devoted to specific aspects of selection, for example, fairness within legal guidelines (e.g., Arvey & Faley, 1988), interviewing (e.g., Eder & Ferris, 1989; Janz, Hellervick & Gilmore, 1986), selecting college graduates (Herriot, 1984), and even the rather unique process of "selecting elites" at Harvard (Klitgaard, 1985). The two most important American research journals in the field of industrial and organizational psychology (the *Journal of Applied Psychology* and *Personnel Psychology*) publish a great many papers on the topic, as is also the case for Great Britain's *Journal of Occupational Psychology*. There is much discussion in the press about the validity and fairness of various selection techniques such as ability testing, drug testing, honesty testing, letters of reference, and so on.

Due to the breadth of personnel selection as a topic, choices had to be made about how to focus the topic here. Consistent with the Matching Model presented in Chapter 1 (Fig. 1.1), this chapter is concerned with selection procedures that facilitate each of the two match-ups. That is, the Matching Model shows that individuals and organizations can be matched as follows: (a) individual/potential capabilities to organizationally required capabilities, and (b) specific individual job wants for a working environment to the various climates in an organization. Up to now, this book has emphasized the latter of these two match-ups, as in earlier discussions of realistic recruitment, how job candidates choose organizations, and how candidates are affected by interviewers. These topics are all related to the self-selection process, which is most relevant for the individual job wants–organizational climates match.

One solution is to focus on those selection methods that are likely to facilitate *both* match-ups, rather than just the capabilities–job requirements match. This narrows the discussion considerably because only a subset of all possible selection procedures are then relevant. The rationale for this strategy is that one main theme in the book is the dual matching process, with an emphasis on realistic recruitment. It will be seen that those selection methods which facilitate *both* match-ups are also those that communicate the most realistic information to a job candidate, thereby helping that candidate make an effective self-selection decision to enter a particular organization. A second solution is to include those selection techniques that are primarily designed to facilitate the match between individual job wants and organizational climates, e.g., personality tests and motivation/need tests. Personnel testing experts have generally ignored these types of tests in favor of mental and physical ability tests. Because this book's main theme is the dual matching process, however, it is important that they be included here.

This chapter is, thus, divided into two sections. The first section concerns those selection methods that are primarily designed to facilitate the individual capabilities–organizational job requirements match, but which may secondarily facilitate the match between individual job wants and organizational climates. This section is called "Realistic Selection Methods." These realistic selection methods are primarily aimed at assessing individual capabilities, but they also may communicate realistic information about job duties to candidates. The second section concerns those methods primarily used to assess the latter match-up. This section is called "Selection for Organizational Climates."

Realistic Selection Methods

Table 5.1 illustrates a "hierarchy" of selection methods based on "job relatedness." (See Guion, 1974. I have split the job interview into two types: structured and unstructured. At the time Guion

Table 5.1
The Job Relatedness of Selection Methods

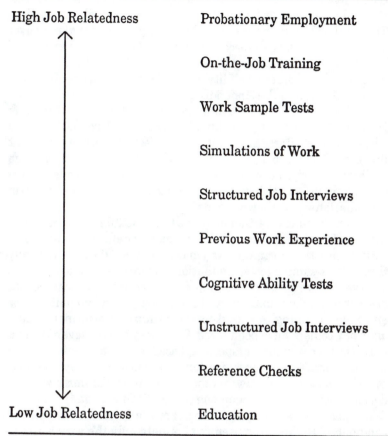

High Job Relatedness   Probationary Employment

On-the-Job Training

Work Sample Tests

Simulations of Work

Structured Job Interviews

Previous Work Experience

Cognitive Ability Tests

Unstructured Job Interviews

Reference Checks

Low Job Relatedness   Education

Source: Adapted from R. M. Guion, 1974. Open a new window: Validities and values in psychological measurement. American Psychologist, 29, p. 291. *Copyright 1974 by the American Psychological Association. Reprinted by permission.*

suggested this hierarchy, structured job interviews had not been invented. As will be seen later, they are much more effective than unstructured interviews.) Assessing job relatedness is basically a judgment of how similar the selection method is to the actual job situation. The methods that are the closest to the actual job can communicate realistic information about job duties, which helps job candidates make more effective job choices. The methods that are "farther away" from the actual job conditions may effectively assess a job candidate's capabilities/potential, but they do not communicate realistic information that candidates can use to make an organizational choice. Probably the best example of this latter type is ability testing. These types of tests have enjoyed a resurgence in popularity over the last decade largely because they can be used in a variety of situations *without* having to be revalidated each time they are used (see the work on "validity generalization" such as Hunter & Hunter, 1984, and the Appendix here).

Reviews of the personnel selection literature (Hunter & Hunter, 1984; Schmitt, Gooding, Noe & Kirsh, 1984) confirm the job relatedness hierarchy. That is, the selection methods shown at the top of Table 5.1 are the best ways to predict future job performance of job candidates; those at the bottom are less accurate in doing so, although they can be useful, particularly in combination with other methods.

Of the nine selection methods listed in Table 5.1, the five at the top of the list appear to have the most potential for communicating realistic information to job candidates. Of these five, only three (work sample tests, simulations of work, and structured job interviews) are selection techniques used to assess job candidates *prior* to organizational entry. Probationary employment and/or on-the-job training are used to assess future performance only *after* newcomers have been hired. Thus they are irrelevant from a realistic recruitment perspective because the newcomers have already entered the organization. Furthermore, they are not, strictly speaking, *selection* methods, which we define as ways to decide whom to hire from among job applicants. Finally, in many cases, probationary employment is not really used to screen out candidates. Rather, it is used to eliminate only the very worst of the new hires, who were hired on the basis of some other selection method. Probationary employment is rarely used as the primary selection method. Likewise, on-the-job training typically *follows* a selection decision, rather than being the sole, or even primary, selection method. Therefore, probationary employment and on-the-job training are not discussed in this chapter.

Work Sample Tests and Simulations

Work sample tests and simulations are commonly thought of as "mini-replicas" of important tasks that are part of a job (Asher & Sciarinno, 1974). One way to categorize them is "motor" versus "verbal" tests. Examples of the former are typing tests, tests requiring candidates to sew on a sewing machine or to weigh meat on a scale, the road test portion of a driver's license test, and so on. Examples of the latter are tests of legal facts for lawyers, language proficiency tests for foreign teaching assistants in U.S. universities or for Peace Corps volunteers, writing a business letter, and so on. An alternative way to categorize them is as follows (Robertson & Kandola, 1982): (a) psychomotor—the manipulation of objects, (b) individual situational decision making, e.g., the in-basket exercise, (c) job-related information—tests of knowledge of work behavior, and (d) group discussion/decision exercises. The latter three of these four categories were all combined into the "verbal" type of work sample test mentioned earlier.

Since the dividing line between a *work sample test* and a *simulation* is not always clear, the two are combined in this section. In principle, a simulation should be an "approximation" of what is done on the job, rather than a replica. For example, a popular classroom exercise to assess interpersonal skills and emergent leadership is the "Lost in the Desert (or—in the Arctic, or—at Sea, or—on a Mountain, or—on the Moon)," leaderless, group discussion problem. No manager would face such a contrived situation, yet some of the skills involved in successfully solving these "lost somewhere" problems are similar to those that managers use in actual job situations. In contrast, a group discussion problem based on actual job-related problems (e.g., whom to hire, promote, fire, or how to allocate a 10 percent cutback among personnel) would qualify as a work sample. Although these examples show how work samples and simulations *could* differ, many other examples are difficult to categorize. Thus the researchers concerned with these types of selection procedures (e.g., Asher & Sciarinno, 1974; Robertson & Kandola, 1982) have combined them for the purpose of reviewing their effectiveness.

Effectiveness. The most common way to evaluate the effectiveness of any personnel selection method is to *correlate* scores from the method with subsequent measure of job performance. Various work sample tests and simulations, have been reviewed and the reviews are summarized here. The first review to focus specifically on these types of selection methods (Asher & Sciarinno, 1974) used the raw data published in an earlier review of all types of personnel selection methods (Ghiselli, 1966). It concluded that motor work sample tests were better than verbal ones, but that both were among the very best ways to select job candidates. It reported that 78 percent of the validity coefficients (correlations between the work sample and job performance) were at least .30 or above for motor type tests. Verbal work sample or simulations had 60 percent of the validities above .30. Unfortunately no average correlations were reported, so that comparisons to the most recent reviews cannot be made since they all report averages.

The second review to focus specifically on these methods (Robertson & Kandola, 1982) reported the average correlation with future success on the job (job performance, performance in training, or getting promoted). The specific types of work sample or simulation and their average validities are as follows: psychomotor (.39), job-related information (.40), situational decision making (.28), and group decision/discussion (.34).

The third and fourth reviews concerned all types of selection methods, rather than just focusing on work samples or simulations. One of these (Hunter & Hunter, 1984) reported high average correlations (validities) for work samples (.54) and for job knowledge tests (.51). These validities are about as high as can be found for *any* selection method. In fact, most selection experts agree that correlations of around .50 for a selection method are probably the ceiling, i.e., being able to predict future job performance with any greater accuracy is beyond current—or likely future—technology. The fourth review (Schmitt et al., 1984) also compared alternative selection methods. Work sample tests averaged .38 for their validity. Although these two most recent reviews differ, they both concluded that work samples were among the most valid methods to use in selection. These strong results should not be surprising because work samples and simulations are "close" to actual job conditions. The more job related a selection method is, the more likely it is to be an accurate predictor of the future, and this is borne out by the accumulated research conducted over the last decade.

There is a glaring omission in the reviews of validation research, however. Very few—almost none—of the studies considered work sample tests or simulations as having an effect on factors other than job performance. The reviews all failed to consider the possibility that these methods are sufficiently realistic as to have an effect on the match-up between an individual's specific job wants and organizational climates through their effect on self-selection. Although these methods obviously do not communicate the same breadth of information as an RJP, they do communicate realistic information about the specific nature of the tasks an employee is expected to perform. Until further evidence is gathered—or uncovered by scrutinizing previous studies—the following example can serve to suggest what can be possible.

Sewing Machine Operators. A rather unique study of sewing machine operator job candidates in Great Britain was conducted in the mid 1970s and reported later (Downs, Farr & Colbeck, 1978). Unfortunately others have not followed this model. Nevertheless it serves as an excellent example of how *self*-selection can be influenced by a work sample test. Briefly, the study involved 1134 job candidates in 50 different companies. All of these candidates had been previously screened, and some rejected, based on a job interview and other tests. Thus they are not completely representative of the applicant pool, which would have included those with the lowest potential to be a successful operator. Nevertheless there was quite a wide range in the skills of those in this group.

A work sample simulation was designed that could be completed in approximately 30 minutes. It involved two phases, each of which was under the direct supervision of a trained tester. In phase one, the tester gave the applicant two pieces of cloth and then gave verbal instructions on how to sew three seams together to make a small open bag. Next, the candidate sewed the bag together with full assistance from the tester. In phase two, the candidate was to make three bags without further assistance. During this phase, the tester observed the behavior of each person and recorded the number and types of errors committed during this work sample. Figure 5.1 shows the checklist and rating form that the testers used. At the bottom of the form is the overall rating that the tester made at the end of the session. It is important to note that *the tester did not communicate the results of the formal assessment to the job candidate.* Whatever impression the job candidates formed was entirely from their own experience and impression of this work sample and how well they thought they had performed.

After the work sample was completed, all job candidates were offered a job, regardless of how well they had done on the

Figure 5.1
Assessment of Performance in a Realistic Work Sample Test for Sewing Machine Operators

OVERLOCK TRAINABILITY ASSESSMENT FORM

Factory_____ Assessor_____

Name_____ Age_____ Date_____

Country of Birth_____ Experienced / Inexperienced_____

	Seam 1 Bag 1	Seam 1 Bag 2	Seam 1 Bag 3
Aligns wrong seam first			
Presents incorrect corner			
Forgets to position cloth correctly			
Forgets to align seam			
Puts thumb on top			
Does not use fingers of left hand correctly			
Does not use fingers of right hand correctly			
Seam not completed in one sew			
Does not remember cutting method *on last seam*			

Other errors (please describe)_____

Total errors_____

Overall ratings

Positioning of hands good: Always____ generally____ sometimes____ rarely____

Positioning of feet good: Always____ generally____ sometimes____ rarely____

Notices errors and subsequently corrects:

Always____ generally____ sometimes____ rarely____

Please circle appropriate letter.

A Extremely good. The assessor would expect her to become a very good machinist in a short time.

B Fairly good without being outstanding. The assessor would expect her to reach 100 performances in a reasonable time.

C Good enough for simple work. The assessor would expect her to become a steady worker on a simple machine, or task.

D Would have difficulty training. The assessor would expect her to take longer training, and to perform a simple task.

E Would not be trainable. Even with a great deal of attention she would not make the grade, even on an easy operation.

Source: S. R. Downs, R. M. Farr & L. Colbeck, 1976. Self-appraisal: A convergence of selection and guidance. Journal of Occupational Psychology, 51.

work sample test. This may seem strange at first, but the purpose of the study was to see if job candidates could accurately assess their own performance on the work sample and whether or not they would then make self-selection decisions accordingly. Were the companies to have taken only the very best performers, there would have been no way to assess how the low performers made self-selection decisions. Thus this type of procedure is necessary when *initially* assessing the effectiveness of a new selection procedure.

The results were rather dramatic. There was a very clear relationship between how well the job candidates had done (according to the tester) and how likely they were to accept or reject the job offer. The percentage of candidates who *declined* the job offer for each of the tester's performance grades was as follows:

Work Sample "Grade"	Percentage Declining Offer
A (highest)	9%
B	19%
C	24%
D	45%
E (lowest)	77%

Assessment Centers/Large-Scale Simulations

Simulations of future work situations can be found in two other methods, the assessment center and large-scale simulations (Thornton, 1992; Thornton & Cleveland, 1990). Since these are somewhat unique methods, they are treated separately from work samples. Assessment centers are different because they involve a *combination* of assessment methods, including simulations, but they are not limited only to simulations. Large-scale simulations are different because they are vastly more complex than the typical simulation, i.e., they are designed to be so realistic that they encompass almost the entire spectrum of managerial skills.

Assessment Centers. The assessment center method grew out of efforts in World War II to select intelligence officers for the Office of Strategic Services (OSS, 1948). During the late 1950s and early 1960s, American Telephone & Telegraph (AT&T) developed the first assessment center for managerial personnel (Bray, Campbell & Grant, 1974). The success of this effort at AT&T led others in industry to follow. Today over 2000 companies use assessment centers (Gaugler, Rosenthal, Thornton & Bentson, 1987).

An assessment center combines a host of assessment methods such as the leaderless group discussion, an in-basket exercise, oral presentations, written cases, one-on-one interview simulations, and small business games. Trained assessors, who may be professional psychologists or trained high-level managers, observe the individuals throughout. These assessors classify their observations by specific factors of job performance (e.g., judgment, interpersonal sensitivity, and effort/energy). They rate the observations as to the degree of effectiveness on each of the job performance factors and make an overall rating of potential. Figure 5.2 shows an example of how different assessment methods provide opportunities to observe different factors in job performance. Note that no single exercise affords the opportunity to assess all of the skills; only the *combination* of exercises can do this.

For more than thirty years, assessment centers have been employed in industry to select job candidates for hire, to determine future management potential among current employees, and to identify specific areas of skill weakness that would be targets for training and development. The trend in use today is more on development than selection, which is a reverse in emphasis from the 1970s (Hollenbeck, 1990). Another trend is to do away with the original idea that the center is a concentrated 2–3 day experience in a particular physical location. Today the assessment exercises do not necessarily have to be so concentrated, and thus the term "center" is becoming somewhat anachronistic (Hollenbeck, 1990).

Assessment centers are quite effective, as revealed by summaries of the research conducted on them over the last 30 years. In the most comprehensive summary to date, a total of 50 studies were located in which 107 separate analyses were done correlating assessment center predictions with subsequent job performance as rated by the individual's boss (Gaugler et al., 1987). The average

Figure 5.2
Assessment Center Exercises and Factors
in Management Performance

Assessment Center Exercises

Factors in Management Performance	One-on-one Interview	In-Basket Exercise	Leaderless Group Discussion
Oral Communication		✕	
Listening Skills		✕	
Initiative	✕		
Problem Analysis			
Written Communication	✕		✕

correlation found was .36, which is considered a strong relationship. Earlier reviews covering fewer studies came to much the same conclusion. For example, both Hunter and Hunter (1984) and Schmitt et al. (1984) reported average correlations of .43 with job performance ratings. A recent book on assessment centers (Thornton, 1992) concluded that their average validity is about .40.

None of the research reviews of assessment centers has reported any correlations with job satisfaction; furthermore, there is no research on job survival. Thus we have no hard data that shows assessment centers can also function as job previews by communicating information to job candidates about the type of work that they will encounter. In the first edition of this book, I noted the same fact and called on others to gather this type of information. At that time it seemed logical that the types of simulations used in assessment centers could easily lead job candidates to make personal judgments about how successful they were likely to be. Although this is only part of the information that would be included in a program of realistic recruitment, it seemed to me that it would be an important component. Nevertheless there are still no systematic data to support my belief that assessment centers can and do operate in this way. However, the dramatic example of self-selection seen earlier among sewing machine operators strongly suggests that assessment centers have the potential to also influence self-selection decisions.

Large-Scale Simulations. In the late 1970s, a complex simulation of a manufacturing organization (called "Looking Glass") was developed at the Center for Creative Leadership in Greensboro, NC (McCall & Lombardo, 1979). This simulation includes 20 different senior management roles across four levels of hierarchy. Each person has his or her own role description and in-basket of materials. Since the amount of information is overwhelming, participants must assess and select what they will actually use. Most uses of this simulation include realistic "props," e.g., a telephone system, various offices and meeting rooms, a mail delivery system, and an information system from which participants can request additional information beyond that given out initially. The simulation has both long and short versions, but the long one can run for two days. (The short version, developed for university classroom situations, can be run in a few hours.) Table 5.2 shows the key elements and procedures typical of such a large-scale simulation.

I was a participant in a session conducted for business school professors at the Center for Creative Leadership and can personally attest to the complexity and realism of the simulation. It embodies the wide array of intellectual and interpersonal skills typically found in a management position. This is not surprising since the developers were careful to build in all of the most crucial, generic management skills. (See McCall, 1983, for a summary of research on what managers actually do with their time during the work day.)

Table 5.3 lists all the large-scale simulations that have been developed, including Looking Glass. These are products of the 1980s and are likely to be in increasing use during the 1990s. The

Table 5.2
Key Elements of Large-Scale Simulations

- Each involves an intensive, interactive experience which re-creates a day in the life of top management.

- Each generates managerial behaviors which are observed by trained staff and reviewed by participants as part of the feedback process.

- Each contains multiple problems and opportunities ranging from tactical to strategic. The situations cover several areas, including sales and marketing, personnel, research and development, finance, and operations.

- Each has many distinct roles, which contain extensive information on past business decisions, current issues, problem symptoms, and decision situations.

- None requires past knowledge or experience in the specific industries simulated (i.e., consumer goods, glass manufacturing, information and financial services, banking, securities brokerage, insurance or arts organizations).

- Each allows the participants to control the simulation outcomes. Depending on the styles, actions, and goals of the participants involved, different problems may become important or different solutions may be found for the same problem.

- At the end of each simulation, participants fill out questionnaires that uncover information on organizational goals, decision making, the use of power, work group climate, and how each participant viewed the other participants with whom he or she worked. Combined with the observations of professional staff, this information forms the basis for diagnostic feedback on individual performance.

Source: S. A. Stumpf, 1990. Using the next generation of assessment centre technology for skill diagnosis. International Journal of Career Management, *2, p. 4.*

major use of these simulations has been for the assessment of individual managerial skills (particularly strategic management skills) and the assessment of teamwork among an existing management team. They have yet to be used for the selection of

Table 5.3
Specific Large-Scale Simulations

Foodcorp International

Foodcorp International, a food manufacturing organization, simulates 13 senior management roles, three levels of hierarchy, two product groups, and two subsidiaries (Sonny's Restaurants and Farm Fresh Yogurt).

Foodcorp's products (dry goods and frozen foods) are sold to distributors and retail supermarkets throughout the US and in 60 other countries through 30 manufacturing plants, 15 marketing affiliates, seven licenses, and six regional export sales organizations. Foodcorp is a fairly large firm within its industry with 25,000 employees and $2.7 billion in sales.

Foodcorp uses a matrix organizational structure and has several committees to augment this structure. New product development activity, internal corporate venturing, and diversification/consolidation activities are integral to Foodcorp and the food processing industry. Consumer marketing (including brand development and advertising) and production quality are key issues domestically and internationally.

Looking Glass Inc. (LGI)

LGI is a glass manufacturing company that simulates 20 senior management roles, four levels of hierarchy, and three product divisions. Its eight product lines extend from conventional lightbulb casings to high-tech optical fibers. All products are manufactured by LGI and sold to other organizations, not individual consumers or distributors. LGI is a mid-sized firm with 4,000 employees and $200 million in sales.

The three product divisions of LGI (Advanced Products, Commercial Glass, Industrial Glass) experience substantially different market environments and tend to function as autonomous entities within LGI. While several issues and capital expansion proposals require collaboration among the divisions, each division is debriefed separately. Skills related to the management of interdivision rivalry, sharing information across formal corporate boundaries, networking, and the management of a diversified portfolio of products are easily diagnosed.

Globalcorp

Globalcorp is a diversified international conglomerate of $27 billion in assets. Each of its 13 senior management roles has corporate strategy development and business portfolio management responsibilities. The banking services sector is comprised of a consumer banking group, business and personal group, and consumer credit group. The advisory services sector includes a management consulting group and a travel services group. The investment services sector is comprised of an insurance group, broker/dealer group, and capital markets group. Each group has two or three lines of business that offer a full array of products or services and has profit-center responsibility.

Table 5.3 Continued
Specific Large-Scale Simulations

Unlike the autonomous divisional activity common to LGI, Globalcorp involves active coordination and competition across lines of business. The three levels of Globalcorp hierarchy are augmented by a committee structure that encourages cross-sector and cross-business discussions of new business ventures, acquisitions, mergers, divestitures, and strategic direction.

Metrobank

Metrobank is one of three simulated companies in the financial services industry (see Investcorp and Landmark Insurance Company). These simulations each have 12 or 13 senior management positions across three levels of hierarchy and two major product-service areas (individual and corporate/institutional services). These financial service firms are typically debriefed as full companies to permit all participants to experience the firm as an entity. They are used separately, in multiples, and in various combinations.

Metrobank is part of Metrobank Holding Company, which includes a regional bank with $1.5 billion in assets and a medium-sized regional finance company offering mortgages and installment loans, Leading Finance. Business activities include savings and loan products for consumers, commercial lending, and corporate banking.

As a bank, Metrobank confronts a variety of regulatory constraints to its market initiatives, as well as a rapidly intensifying competitive environment. Merger and acquisition activity is common within the industry, as well as rapid technological improvements in operations, data processing, and delivery systems. In addition to managerial and strategic management skills, questions of customer service, cross-selling products to customers, responding to changing competitive pressures, target marketing, and the consistency of business goals and participant actions are easily diagnosed.

Investcorp

Investcorp is part of Investcorp Holding Company, which includes a large securities firm with $108 million in capital and a regional life insurance company, Rolley Insurance. Services offered range from investment banking to retail and institutional sales of stocks, bonds, options, etc., to specialized customer services. The three selling entities of Investcorp (Capital/Markets, Institutional Sales, Retail Sales) experience different customers, markets, and competitors—yet they need to collaborate extensively on a day-to-day basis.

The securities industry is highly time and transaction oriented. Minutes in the trading area can mean thousands of dollars in profits or losses. Participants must ensure that Investcorp is organized for and operationally ready for this challenge. In addition to managerial and strategic management skills, questions of support for new product introductions, a rapid and flexible response to the marketplace, internal

Table 5.3 Continued
Specific Large-Scale Simulations

---

coordination and control, and the consistency of business goals with participant actions are easily diagnosed.

Landmark Insurance Company
Landmark is among the top twenty mutual life insurance companies in the United States. Operated for the benefit of its more than one million policyholders, Landmark has assets of over $15 billion, life insurance in force of over $69 billion, and paid dividends and benefits of over $2.17 billion last year. The services offered range from individual insurance and investment products to group life and health insurance, to group pension plans. Landmark affiliated companies include Realty Management, Securities, and Research Services.

As a mutual life insurance company, Landmark's goals may differ from companies owned by stockholders. Landmark's responsibilities are to its policyholders (there are no stockholders). Long-term stability in a rapidly changing environment is essential. This raises questions of how to respond effectively to changes within the industry. What new products, services, lines of business, and channels of distribution should Landmark pursue? To facilitate these issues being addressed by participants, Landmark has a matrixed committee structure within its formal hierarchical structure. Managerial skills related to questions of open information sharing, identifying goals and formulating strategies, and addressing change are easily diagnosed.

Northwood Arts Center
The Northwood Arts Center (NAC) is a not-for-profit arts organization composed of three units: The Crandall Museum, the New Horizons Theater, and the NAC staff and support services. NAC's expenses last year exceeded $3 million, leaving a shortfall of $31,000. NAC is managed by seven directors. The Crandall Museum has over 2,500 members and 100,000 visitors each year. New Horizons has about 14,000 subscribers and 116,000 customers annually.

As with most not-for-profits, NAC has many constituencies that it must satisfy—each placing different demands on what NAC does. On the funding side, the state, local, and federal government grants and charitable contributions often have strings attached. For earned income, different consumers want different types of performances and different art forms displayed. Community groups want to influence NAC's activities to support their concerns. Board members often have their own views of what performances should be done—and they are often art donors and financial supporters of NAC. In addition to managerial and strategic management skills, questions of accommodating diverse constituencies, establishing a viable programming policy, and managing people who bring strong but differing values to an organization are key areas for diagnosis.

Source: S. A. Stumpf, 1990. Using the next generation of assessment centre technology for skill diagnosis. International Journal of Career Management, 2, 8–9.

newcomers, however, because the cost of conducting a simulation is quite high (according to Stumpf, 1990, it is $500–600 per participant, with a minimum of 13 participants). To conduct a truly complex simulation, we could combine Metrobank, Investcorp, and Landmark Insurance Company for a simulation of the financial services *industry*. This would require 36–39 participants, however, and a number of trained observers to provide feedback to participants.

The large-scale simulation is discussed last because it has yet to be used for selection. The potential for its being effective is probably high because it bears similarity to the assessment center method. Its potential as a realistic job preview has also been untapped. Because the simulations focus on generic management skills, they do not communicate any of the uniqueness about a *particular* organization's climates. One possibility for their use as a job preview would be among college students contemplating careers in management. These simulations would appear to be quite useful as a *career* preview.

Structured Job Interviews

The job interview has been the single most frequently used method for personnel selection in business, despite decades of academic research and criticism that shows that interviews are of low validity. Beginning over 40 years ago, professional personnel psychologists looking at job interview research have repeatedly concluded that its popularity is simply not justified by its actual validity for predicting the future performance of job candidates (Arvey & Campion, 1982; Mayfield, 1964; Schmitt, 1976; Ulrich & Trumbo, 1965; Wagner, 1949; Wright, 1969). One influential review of the job interview calculated that the average validity (correlation between interviewer ratings and subsequent job performance) is just .14 (Hunter & Hunter, 1984). Furthermore, the interview also can be the cause of unfair discrimination against racial minorities (Arvey & Faley, 1988).

The most recent evidence (see Harris, 1989, for a comprehensive review of interviews) suggests that there may be hope for the job interview, however. Remember that Table 5.1 distinguished between "structured" and "unstructured" job interviews. It now appears that the "old fashioned" (unstructured) interview has been the culprit in the poor track record for predicting future job performance.

Distinguishing between structured and unstructured interviews is easier if the newer, structured approach is described first because all other interview methods are, by definition, *un*structured. The key to the difference between the two types is that *structured interviews are based on a thorough job analysis that specifies critical factors in success and the assessment of these areas is "scored" quantitatively according to predetermined, organizationally correct answers.* The interviewer "scores" applicant responses to questions during the interview so that the *combination* of scores determines the overall score—*not* a subjective impression. In contrast, an *un*structured interview is usually *not* based on a job analysis. It may lack the predetermined set of questions, may not use rating scales, or may allow interviewers to make an overall rating in a subjective manner.

Two variations of structured interviews have been developed during the 1980s: (a) the "situational interview" (Latham, Saari, Pursell & Campion, 1980), and (b) the "patterned behavior description interview" (Janz, 1982; Janz et al.,1986). The essential difference between these two types of interviews is that in the former, interviewers ask job candidates how they *would respond to job-relevant, but hypothetical situations,* whereas in the latter, candidates are asked how they *have responded to job-relevant situations in the past.*

Before describing each of these types of structured interviews, let's see just how effective they are. Two reviews of structured interviews have been conducted. The first, and larger of the two, calculated that the average validity of structured interviews is .34 for the prediction of future job performance. This is considerably higher than the validity of unstructured interviews, whose average correlation with future job performance was found to be .17 (Wiesner & Cronshaw, 1988). This review appears to be extensive because it compared the results from 47 structured interview studies versus 38 studies of unstructured interviews. (The definition of "structured" in this review is broader than it is in the two specific types of structured interviews that are the focus in this chapter.) The second review (Wright, Lichtenfels & Pursell, 1989) reported the results from 13 studies of 870 people who went through situational interviews in particular. The average correlation of interviewer scores and subsequent job performance was reported as .29, a result quite close to that in the first review. Only a few published studies of the patterned behavior description

interview have been reported (Janz, 1982, 1989; Orpen, 1985).
Two of these studies (Janz, 1982; Orpen, 1985) found validities
above .50, which is quite high. This approach is clearly promising,
but more research needs to be conducted to see if this high level
of predictive accuracy can be maintained. Thus it appears that
the validity of the structured job interview is around the .30 (or
better) level, which is considered to be high and certainly useful
in making predictions about whom to hire.

The Situational Interview. The situational interview
approach was developed over ten years ago to overcome two major
problems with job interviews. First, interviewers rarely ask exactly the same questions in the same way. Thus is it difficult to
compare two job candidates, and interviewers frequently disagree
among themselves. Second, even when the same questions are
asked, interviewers frequently disagree about the desirability of
the answers. As a result of these problems, interviewers do not
agree in their assessments of job candidates. Accurate predictions
about future job performance are difficult to make in light of this
disagreement.

To "standardize" the format of the interview, the situational interview was developed (Latham et al., 1980; see also
Robertson, Gratton & Rout, 1990, for a good description of how
to develop this type of interview). The development of a situational interview has three stages: (a) generate a list of basic
"dimensions" of job performance, e.g., 8–12 factors that, taken
together, comprise all of the most important things an individual should do on the job, (b) get specific, "critical incidents" of
what people do that are the best examples of both good *and* poor
performance, and (c) rate the degree of effectiveness of each
critical incident on a scale, e.g., a 5-point scale from poor to
excellent. At each stage, the input of current employees and
their supervisors is critical to the development of a situational
interview. Professional personnel psychologists have conducted
numerous interviews to elicit this type of information.

The originators of this technique (Latham et al., 1980, p. 424)
provided an example of an interview question: "Your spouse and two
teenage children are sick in bed with a cold. There are no relatives or
friends available to look in on them. Your shift starts in three hours.
What would you do in this situation?" The "benchmarks" for rating
answers were defined as follows for the interviewers: 5 = since they only

have colds, I'd come to work, 3 = I'd phone my supervisor and explain my situation, and 1 = I'd stay home—my spouse and family come first. The preceding example is a hypothetical, but typical, work situation. It is the type of question used to hire newcomers unfamiliar with the job itself. Another type of question used to hire newcomers could pertain to an applicant's willingness to perform certain tasks under certain circumstances, e.g., be willing to work on weekends or holidays. When using interviews to hire for technical positions or to promote personnel internally to a more technically complex job, interviewers may ask questions about job knowledge. For example, candidates may be asked how they know that a particular machine needs repair or maintenance, or they may be asked specific questions about the names and functions of certain components of equipment used. In these cases, as in the hypothetical work situation, interviewers have benchmark answers so that their scoring of the applicant's answers has clear and consistent guidelines.

Situational interviews have been developed for a variety of jobs (Latham, 1989): unionized sawmill workers, supervisors in the sawmill, pulp mill workers (Latham et al., 1980), clerical staff and general "utility" workers in a paper mill (Latham & Saari, 1984), sales personnel (Weekley & Gier, 1987), and white collar administrative positions in the financial services industry (Robertson et al., 1990).

Patterned Behavior Description Interview. Janz (1982) developed the patterned behavior description interview technique for exactly the same reasons that led to the development of the situational interview. In fact, the two share a great deal in terms of the methods used to develop scoring guidelines for interviewers. Specifically the same "critical incident methodology" is used to develop basic job dimensions and the examples that illustrate the range of excellent to poor performance. However, the interviewer using this technique probes the applicant's own background and experience for specific examples of how that person in the past has handled situations similar to those he or she might face in the position that is currently open. For example, if the position were that of a salesperson, the interviewer would ask the job candidate to give examples of times when successful persuasion had been exercised, when strangers had been approached on the phone or in person and asked to do something, when the person had worked alone without direct supervision, and so on. As with the

Table 5.4
Example of a Patterned Behavior Description Interview

◆ Bank Teller

◆ Behavior Dimensions

1. Is pleasant, courteous, and helpful to all customers *versus* is curt, rude, or insulting to difficult customers.
2. Works steadily, is timely *versus* wastes time, is tardy.
3. Checks for errors, omissions *versus* makes mistakes.
4. Contributes to pleasant, cooperative relations with peers *versus* argues, bickers, or causes resentment and dissension.
5. Reports problems or difficulties to the supervisor promptly *versus* hides problems or blames others.

◆ Interview Questions

0.1 Let's begin by having you fill me in on your duties and responsibilities at your most recent job that are related to our opening for a teller position.

1.1 I'm sure you realize how important it is to serve customers cheerfully and pleasantly. Tell me about the nicest compliment you received when serving a customer.

- ◆ What did the customer want?
- ◆ Do you remember what you said at the time?
- ◆ What did the customer say when he or she complimented you?
- ◆ Did the customer tell anyone else?
- ◆ How often did this type of event come up last year?
- ◆ Tell me about another one. [repeat probes]

1.2 Not all customers are that nice. Sometimes customers are irritating or rude. Tell me about the most irritating customer you have had to deal with.

- ◆ When did this happen?
- ◆ What did the person do that was irritating?
- ◆ What did you say in response?
- ◆ How did you overcome the person's rudeness?
- ◆ Was the person satisfied when he or she left?
- ◆ Did the person say anything to your boss? What?

Table 5.4 Continued

Example of a Patterned Behavior Description Interview

    ◆ How often did this kind of customer show up?

    ◆ Tell me about another one. [repeat probes]

1.3 Everyone has said something to a customer, especially the difficult ones, that they wish they hadn't said. What is the thing you most regretted saying to a customer?

    ◆ What led up to this particular event?

    ◆ What happened after that?

    ◆ Did you take any steps to make sure it didn't happen again?

    ◆ What were they? Was it effective?

0.2 Let's move on from your customer relations. Now I'd like to find out a bit about your success in catching errors. What do you do that helps you pick out mistakes?

3.1 Can you think of the mistake you picked out on your last job that saved the company the most money?

    ◆ When did that happen?

    ◆ What was the mistake? Who was responsible?

    ◆ Was the mistake avoidable? How?

    ◆ What did you do to correct the mistake?

    ◆ What did you do to avoid it in the future?

    ◆ When was the next time this kind of mistake came up?

3.2 We can all think of the one that got away—the mistake we would most like the chance to do over. Tell me about the mistake you would most like to do over.

    ◆ What was your responsibility in this instance?

    ◆ What actually happened? For how long?

    ◆ What did your boss say about this mistake?

    ◆ What did you do to avoid this in the future?

    ◆ Did this kind of mistake ever happen again?

5.1 Another important quality of a bank teller is pointing out problems and difficulties promptly to your supervisor. Tell me about a time when pointing out a problem or difficulty you were having helped you and your company a lot.

Table 5.4 Continued
Example of a Patterned Behavior Description Interview

- When did you go to your supervisor?
- What did you say about the problem?
- What did the supervisor do that was helpful?
- What kinds of problems did this prevent?
- How often did this kind of situation come up last year?

5.2 We all have one story about a time when we put off talking to our boss about something. Tell me about the time you were most reluctant to go and talk with your supervisor, even though you knew you should?

- What were the circumstances surrounding this event?
- What restrained you from talking with your supervisor?
- When did you actually talk to your boss?
- When did you first conclude that you should check this out with your supervisor?
- What were the consequences of waiting?

0.3 One thing in the banking business that is common to many jobs is that customer demand has its ups and downs. Sometimes you are very busy and other times it slacks off. How did you generally prepare for the peak rushes on your last job?

2.1 Tell me about the busiest time you had on your last job.

- What did you do to prepare yourself for the onslaught?
- How did you know what to expect?
- How did your preparations pay off during the rush?
- Did your boss ever mention anything about your ability to handle a rush? What was said?

2.2 Just as there are busy times, there are also slack times. Tell me about the most recent slack time you faced.

- When did this happen?
- How slack was it compared to a normal flow?
- What did you do during this period?
- What were your peers doing during this time?
- Did you ever ask for assignments during slack times?
- [If yes] Tell me about a time when you did.

Table 5.4 Continued
Example of a Patterned Behavior Description Interview

0.4 I'd like to close by asking a few questions about how well you got along with your co-workers. What are some of your strengths in dealing with your co-workers?

4.1 Tell me about the last time you used one of those strengths to smooth over an argument you had with a co-worker.

◆ What was the problem about?
◆ What did you say when you approached the co-worker?
◆ When did you approach the co-worker about the problem?
◆ How did the co-worker respond to you?
◆ What was the eventual resolution of the problem?
◆ When was the next time this problem surfaced again?

4.2 Tell me about a time when you helped a co-worker with learning a new task or solving a problem.

◆ What was the task you helped the co-worker with?
◆ How did you learn that the co-worker needed help?
◆ How did you explain the answer?
◆ What did the co-worker do?
◆ How did the co-worker feel about your help?
◆ How do you know the co-worker felt that way?

4.3 Tell me about the most trying time you have had with a co-worker. We all experience some unpleasant times with our peers.

◆ What led up to this event?
◆ How did you approach the situation?
◆ What did you say?
◆ What did the co-worker say in response?

Source: T. Janz, L. Hellervick & D. C. Gilmore, 1986. Behavior description interviewing. *Boston: Allyn & Bacon, pp. 122–125.*

situational interview, the interviewer would score the applicant's responses according to the scales derived for the specific job.

Table 5.4 shows a specific example of how to conduct a patterned behavior description interview for a bank teller (Janz et al., 1986). The various interview questions are geared to elicit information about each of the five job behavior dimensions listed at the top of the table. The first digit of the number refers to the specific dimension; the second digit refers to the number of the question pertaining to that dimension. Questions that begin with a "0" simply introduce a new topic area. Questions prefaced with the diamond-shaped "bullet" are the "probes" designed to get people talking. This is but one example described in Janz et al. (1986). Other jobs with similar guidelines include cashier supervisor, computer programmer, computer science engineer, government laborer, life insurance administrative consultant, middle manager in the petroleum industry, nurse, part-time lab worker, personnel officer, probation officer, regional sales representative, secretary/office clerk, small business manager, staff accountant, and systems analyst. Needless to say, these examples take up 100 pages in a book (Janz et al., 1986).

Advocates of the patterned behavior description interview approach argue that it may be superior to the situational interview because it carefully measures what the job candidate has actually done in the past, rather than what the candidate might do in a hypothetical situation. Since past behavior is the best predictor of future behavior in a similar situation, proponents of this method believe that it may be more "job related" than the situational interview. On the other hand, advocates of the situational interview approach respond by saying that the extensive literature on goal setting (e.g., Locke & Latham, 1990) clearly shows that people *do* what they say they will do. It is too early to say whether one method is superior to the other. There is also no reason why they cannot be combined (Campion, Pursell & Brown, 1988). However, it is clear that both of these "structured" interviews produce much better predictions about future job performance than does the "traditional" unstructured approach.

What about the use of structured interviews to facilitate the match-up between individual job wants and organizational climates? Are there any data on newcomer job satisfaction, organizational commitment, or job survival that suggest that these interviews can serve a dual purpose? Unfortunately none of the reviews of these interviews reported any correlations with these factors, probably because the authors of the original studies did not gather this information. This is somewhat curious since the originators of the situational interview method explicitly state that it is consistent with the realistic job preview approach to recruiting (Latham & Saari, 1894).

The "Low-Fidelity" Simulation.

A variation of the situational interview was recently developed (Motowidlo, Dunnette & Carter, 1990). It is named a "low-fidelity" simulation because it bears no physical resemblance to a real job situation—or even a simulation of a job situation. It is at the opposite end of some type of "realism scale" that would have the large-scale simulations (e.g., Tables 5.2 and 5.3) at the *other* end exemplifying the most realistic of all simulations.

The low-fidelity simulation is actually quite similar to the situational interview, except that the job candidates answer multiple choice questions about how they might respond to a hypothetical situation. Almost exactly the same method is used to develop the test questions and answers as is used in the situational interview. Table 5.5 describes the procedure used, shows a sample question, and explains the scoring procedure.

The initial results with this approach are quite encouraging. When scores from the 55-item test were correlated with ratings by bosses of overall effectiveness, the result was a correlation of .30, similar to other simulations and to structured interviews. (It is particularly similar to the validity of the situational interview upon which it is based.) It is also encouraging that this test is equally valid for both whites and blacks, and for both men and women. The only drawback the authors noted is that it took the average person about 1 1/2 hours to complete the test. By selecting the 30 (out of 55) items that had the highest correlations with job performance ratings, they were able to reduce testing time to 45 minutes. Also, by picking only the best items, the overall validity of the 30-item test battery improved to over .40. However, future research needs to recheck this last result.

The developers of low-fidelity simulation believe it to be a viable substitute for the situational interview because it achieves the same level of validity without the cost of having an interviewer present to conduct one-on-one job interviews. They believe it is simply more efficient with no sacrifice in predictive accuracy. The developers further note that this should be used in combination with the patterned behavior description interview since virtually no company will hire someone without an interview. In this way, the combination would be able to assess job-relevant information

Table 5.5
Designing a Low-Fidelity Simulation

Method

This was a nationwide project supported by a consortium of seven companies in the telecommunications industry. The companies provided research sites and research participants.

Simulation Development

Our objective was to develop a low-fidelity simulation to sample behaviors from the domain of general management performance. This was not an effort to develop a measure of any particular predispositional sign or construct, although it might be interesting eventually to discover what constructs are associated with behaviors sampled by the simulation.

Management positions in this study included functional specialties in administration, engineering, marketing and sales, programming, and supervision. A preliminary review of several job analyses that had already been done for these positions indicated that although they differ in necessary technical skills, the five functional areas share a core of necessary managerial skills in communication, problem-solving and interpersonal areas. For the simulation, we focused only on the problem-solving and interpersonal areas. The problem-solving area was defined in terms of four performance elements—organization, thoroughness, drive, and resourcefulness. The interpersonal area was defined in terms of four other performance elements—leadership, assertiveness, flexibility, and sensitivity.

We developed the simulation in three stages. At each stage, persons representing all seven participating companies were included. First, we met with 78 incumbents and 61 supervisors in small groups to collect critical incidents of managerial effectiveness and ineffectiveness, especially in the problem-solving, interpersonal, and communication areas. They provided approximately 1,200 written critical incidents, which we used to write brief descriptions of task situations for managers. In doing this, we looked for critical incidents that seemed to represent specific elements in interpersonal and problem-solving aspects of management performance. Thus, we wrote descriptions of 42 task situations designed to reflect interpersonal elements (leadership, assertiveness, flexibility, and sensitivity) and 22 task situations designed to reflect problem-solving elements (organization, thoroughness, drive, and resourcefulness), for a total of 64 management-task situations.

Second, we met with 150 other incumbent managers in small groups and asked them to write a few sentences to describe how they would handle each problem situation. These managers were instructed to write only what they thought would be the best thing to do in each sitution. We did not ask them to describe responses that would be seen as ineffective.

Table 5.5 Continued
Designing a Low-Fidelity Simulation

On the basis of their responses, we prepared five to seven general strategies for each task situation. Thus, at this point we had 64 problem situations and five to seven alternative strategies for handling each one.

Third, we asked a group of very experienced, senior managers to evaluate the effectiveness of the alternative strategies for each task situation. Twenty-five managers rated all 64 problems, 9 rated half of the problems, and 8 rated the other half. Therefore, response alternatives for each situation were rated by a total of 33 or 34 very experienced managers. They identified the best and worst alternative strategy for each situation and rated all alternatives for their effectiveness in dealing with the situation. We dropped 6 situational questions at this point because managers did not agree sufficiently in their evaluations of response alternatives or because alternatives did not differ sufficiently in judged effectiveness for us to identify either a best or a worst response for the situation.

A total of 58 situational questions survived this process. Intraclass correlations for the ratings of effectiveness that the experienced managers assigned to response alternatives ranged from .85 to .99; the mean (across 58 items) was .95. As a check on the behavioral content represented by the task situations and their response alternatives, Stephan J. Motowidlo and Marvin D. Dunnette independently judged whether each item reflected primarily interpersonal elements or primarily problem-solving elements. They agreed on 51 of the 58 items ($\emptyset$ = .76) and, after some discussion, agreed on 4 of the remaining 7 items. The set of 55 items on which they agreed includes 33 task situations judged as primarily interpersonal and 22 task situations judged as primarily problem solving.

On the basis of the experienced managers' effectiveness ratings of response alternatives, we identified the most and least effective alternatives for each task situation. The decision rules for accomplishing this were rather complicated, but the result, finally, was that for most items, one or more alternatives were classified as the best ones and one or more alternatives were classified as the worst ones.

In its final form, the simulation asks applicants to pick one alternative they would most likely take and one alternative they would least likely take in each task situation. An illustrative item follows:

You and someone from another department are jointly responsible for coordinating a project involving both departments. This other person is not carrying out his share of the responsibilities. You would . . .

____Most Likely ____Least Likely

1. Discuss the situation with your manager and ask him to take it up with the other person's manager.
2. Remind him that you need his help and that the project won't

Table 5.5 Continued
Designing a Low-Fidelity Simulation

be completed effectively without a full team effort from both of you.

3. Tell him that he is not doing his share of the work, that you will not do it all yourself, and that if he doesn't start doing more, you'll be forced to take the matter to his manager.
4. Try to find out why he is not doing his share and explain to him that this creates more work for you and makes it harder to finish the project.
5. Get someone else from his department to help with the project.

Each of the two alternatives chosen by an applicant was scored either 1, 0, or –1 according to the following scoring rule: The alternative chosen by an applicant as his or her most likely response was scored 1 if it was one of the best ones, –1 if it was one of the worst ones, or 0 if it was neither best nor worst. The alternative chosen by an applicant as his or her least likely response was scored 1 if it was one of the worst alternatives, –1 if it was one of the best ones, or 0 if it was neither. Scores for alternatives chosen as most and least likely were then summed; the final score for an item could range from –2 to 2. A score of –2 means that an applicant indicated he or she would most likely perform one of the worst alternatives and would least likely perform one of the best ones. A score of 2 means that an applicant indicated he or she would most likely perform one of the best alternatives and would least likely perform one of the worst ones.

Source: S. J. Motowidlo, M. D. Dunnette & G. W. Carter, 1990. An alternative selection procedure: The low-fidelity simulation. Journal of Applied Psychology, *75, pp. 641–642. Copyright 1990 by the American Psychological Association. Reprinted by permission.*

from candidates about what they *would be likely to do* as well as *what they actually have done*. It will be interesting to see how this combination works when it is put to the test.

The developers of the low-fidelity simulation do not mention the possibility that it can communicate realistic job information to job candidates. It certainly seems likely that the *questions* communicate the types of general situations likely to be encountered on the job, even if the *answers* are not obvious to candidates. After reading 55 (or even 30) hypothetical situation questions, most job candidates will have some notion of the range of management activity to be expected at work. The test does not appear to communicate unique information about a particular organization, and it does not go beyond job duties, as would an RJP. Only future research will be able to assess its impact on job satisfaction, organizational commitment, and job survival, but I certainly hope those who do use this in the future will remember to consider these factors in their research on this type of simulation.

Selection for Organizational Climates

This section discusses the selection methods that have the potential to facilitate the match-up between an individual's specific job wants and organizational climates (see Fig. 1.1). These selection methods are designed to affect this match-up *directly*, whereas the realistic selection method discussed in the previous section can have only *indirect* effects. The difference lies in the amount of job information they communicate. The methods discussed here communicate no job information at all to candidates. Instead, the organization uses these methods to select from among job candidates. Thus, the methods here are similar to traditional personnel selection in that the organization does the choosing. Conversely, the realistic methods discussed in the previous section relied on *self*-selection to facilitate the match-up between specific job wants and organizational climates. In other words, realistic selection makes the job candidate responsible for the choice. Although the selection methods for organizational climates and those for realistic recruitment have the same objective, they differ substantially different in their approach.

A quick review of the Matching Model (Fig 1.1) shows two "levels" of match-ups that could be targets for these selection methods: (a) *human needs* to organizational *culture* and (b) specific individual *job wants* to organizational *climates*. As discussed in Chapter 1, the latter match-up is preferred because it more directly influences job satisfaction, organizational commitment, and job survival. Despite this preference, the search for methods used to do this type of selection was not limited only to such methods. Any method that purported to assess the "fit" of the person to the organization was considered, regardless of whether it concerned needs versus job wants, or culture versus climate.

Types of Methods Used

Figure 5.3 shows a continuum of the types of methods used to facilitate the "fit" of job candidates to an organization. Only the methods at the right-hand side of the scale ("organization specific")

Figure 5.3
Matching Job Candidates to Organizations

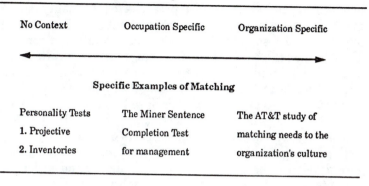

No Context	Occupation Specific	Organization Specific

Specific Examples of Matching

Personality Tests	The Miner Sentence	The AT&T study of
1. Projective	Completion Test	matching needs to the
2. Inventories	for management	organization's culture

are implied by the Matching Model because they involve gathering information about the organizational culture or its various climates and then assessing the job candidate's fit with the organization. The methods labeled "occupation specific" are geared to assess an individual's fit with a type of *job,* e.g., being a manager. They do not attempt to assess the person's fit with a particular organization, e.g., being a manager at IBM as opposed to Apple Computer. Finally, the methods on the far left end of the continuum ("context free") were developed without any type of context in mind. Note that the examples shown in Figure 5.3 are not intended to represent all the possibilities.

After reviewing all of the methods shown in Figure 5.3, it became clear that the number of attempts at using these to select newcomers is in *reverse order to their desirability for accomplishing the match-up.* That is, the greatest number of studies are of those from the "context free" category, followed by those in the "occupation specific" category. By comparison, there are hardly any published efforts to match job candidates to either organizational cultures or specific climates. This is just the opposite from what we would hope.

Of the selection methods shown in Figure 5.3, the most popular is the "personality test." This is a category of tests that includes two rather different approaches to personality measurement: projective tests and personality inventories. Projective tests ask people to respond to an *ambiguous* "stimulus" of some sort. The stimulus can be a series of inkblots, a picture, a cartoon, or an incomplete sentence. In each case, the person taking the test can *respond freely* to the particular stimulus. Thus the purpose of taking the test clearly must be "disguised" to the person taking it.

The theory behind a projective test is that the individuals responding will reveal important aspects of personality by "projecting" their own personality into the response. Clinical psychologists developed these tests to help them understand each of their patients as a whole person. For the most part, they were not developed for personnel selection, which is why they are labeled "context free" in Figure 5.3. Projective tests have two underlying assumptions: (a) people are often unaware of their own motives or psychological states and cannot give accurate reports about them, and (b) even when people are aware, they tend to give distorted or exaggerated reports about themselves (Cornelius, 1983).

Personality inventories are tests with "structured" response formats. Typically the test takers are asked to agree or disagree with certain statements, or are asked to say whether or not a statement is true or false about themselves. Because of this difference, personality inventories can be easily scored, whereas projective tests are scored by expert judgment about the likely "meaning" of a person's responses to the ambiguous stimulus. Examples of personality factors (see Hough, Eaton, Dunnette, Kamp & McCoy, 1990) that can be measured on such inventories include: (a) energy level—a person high in energy is enthusiastic, active, vital, optimistic, cheerful, zesty, and gets things done, (b) adjustment—a well-adjusted person is calm, displays an even mood, is not overly distraught by stress, remains composed, thinks clearly, as compared to someone who is nervous, moody, easily irritated, and cannot handle stress, (c) dependability—a highly dependable person is well organized, planful, prefers order, thinks before acting, holds himself or herself accountable, accepts and respects authority, abides by rules, avoids trouble, and can be trusted.

Occupation-specific tests come closer to the "matching" concept because they are designed to assess the fit between a person's stated interests and the characteristics of specific occupations. They measure the *motivational fit* between person and occupation, so they predict whether or not a person will select an occupation in the first place, the length of time someone will spend in an occupation, and the person's satisfaction with that occupation. However, they do not necessarily predict how well the person will perform. Probably the most relevant example of this category for organizational entry is the Miner Sentence Completion Scale (Miner, 1978) used to assess a person's motivation to be a manager. The test itself is "projective" in that people are asked to finish incomplete sentences, e.g., "Presenting a report at a staff meeting . . . ." Because the incomplete sentence test items were developed to measure motivation in six managerial roles, this test is an excellent example of measuring motivational fit with this type of occupation.

Miner uses six managerial roles:

1. Managers must generally have positive attitudes about authority and must be willing to behave in ways that do not provoke negative reactions from superiors.

2. Managers must have positive attitudes toward competition and must be willing to compete for available rewards, both for themselves and the group.

3. Managers must behave in an assertive way.

4. Managers cannot find it difficult or emotionally disturbing to exercise power over subordinates and must direct their behavior in a manner consistent with organizational objectives.

5. Managers must be willing to deviate from the immediate group and assume a position of high visibility.

6. Managers must be responsible in dealing with routine administrative demands and ideally gain some satisfaction from it.

The final category of organizationally specific tests has by far the fewest examples. In fact, I could find no cases that attempted to match either needs or job wants to organizational culture or to specific climates *for the purpose of personnel selection.* The only available evidence for either of these two types of organizational match-ups is that found in research on the Matching Model (see Chapter 1), but that research used data gathered *after* people had been hired. Furthermore, the data gathered were for research purposes only. Because of these two factors, the people had no incentive to "fake" their answers, which would be much more likely to occur among job applicants.

One area of research on matching of specific individual job wants to organizational climates comes from the effects of job characteristics on employee performance and satisfaction (see Hackman & Oldham, 1980, for a summary of this work). In this particular context, it has been argued that jobs that have been "enriched" with variety, autonomy, feedback, significance, and a "wholeness" will motivate employees best when the employees themselves desire exactly these kinds of jobs (Wanous, 1976b). When employees do *not* want such enriched jobs, their perfor-mance and satisfaction do not increase as much as when they do desire them. The evidence gathered over the last 20 years (since Hackman & Lawler, 1971, proposed this theory) has generally supported the matching concept (see Fried & Ferris, 1987, for a review). For example, the correlation between enriching job characteristics and job performance is .14 when employees do not want job enrichment, but it is .45 when they do want enrichment (Fried & Ferris, 1987, p. 308). This is precisely the type of matching between specific individual job wants and organizational climates that the Matching Model of Chapter 1 implies. Although these results are quite encouraging, they too come from a context other than personnel selection, i.e., one in which research was being conducted.

One example of person-organization matching conducted at AT&T (McClelland & Boyatzis, 1982) does show the *potential* of selecting newcomers for organizational climates. This is a study of newly hired, male, college graduates entering the managerial ranks of one of the world's largest bureaucracies (it was done prior to the break-up of the Bell System). Projective measures were taken of the job candidate's power and affiliation motives (McClelland, 1975). The results of this test were, however, *not* used in selection. Therefore, after the candidates began working, researchers could follow up on those who scored high and low on the various measures. The authors argued that AT&T represented a very bureaucratic type of organization in which a particular type of leadership style called the Leadership Motive Pattern (LMP), would be most likely to succeed. This style is represented by persons who have moderate to high power motivation *and* whose power motivation is higher than their affiliation motivation. Furthermore, an appropriate LMP would also have to have a high level of "activity inhibition," which meant that such individuals would be unlikely to express their high level of power needs *personally*. Rather, the managers would seek to satisfy their power needs through *group* success. Finally, the authors of this study separated those who managed technical units versus those who were in such nontechnical areas as customer service, marketing, operations, general administration, and personnel. They argued that AT&T had two subcultures—technical and bureaucratic—such that the appropriate match between the leadership motive profile and the organization only was relevant for the nontechnical (bureaucratic) areas of leadership.

The AT&T study is probably more representative of matching human *needs* to organizational *culture* than of matching specific job wants to organizational climates because the projective method used to measure affiliation and power motives is a classical approach to identifying important, basic human needs. The method is *not* used to identify very specific job wants, such as a person who likes to have lunch with co-workers, but maintains a private social life after the workday is over. In one sense, such a person could be considered high in affiliation, but in another sense, there is a limit to how close interpersonal relationships will actually get at work. Furthermore, the AT&T study did not actually gather data from an organizational diagnosis to specify what types of climates existed, as has been advocated here. Rather, they *assumed* that there were two major subcultures (technical and bureaucratic). If this were a study of organizational climates, more factors would have to be considered, e.g., the climate for providing service to customers, the climate for cooperation among employees, and the climate for getting promotions.

Even though the AT&T study exemplifies a "higher level" of person-organization matching, it is a good illustration of how matching specific job wants to organizational climates *could* be done for personnel selection. The next section reviews the effectiveness of the selection methods for organizational climates. The final section presents guidelines for how the matching process *should* be conducted.

Effectiveness of Methods

Since most of the research on the methods illustrated in Figure 5.3 comes from those in the "context free" category, this section focuses on using "personality" measures to predict future behavior of job candidates. The effectiveness of the Miner Sentence Completion Scale for predicting managerial fit follows. Finally, the least studied area, "organization specific" matching, is discussed last, using the results from the AT&T study, which are probably the best estimate of what might be found if more attempts were made to do this type of selection.

Personality Testing. Over the last 25 years there have been many reviews of personality tests for selecting newcomers (Barrick & Mount, 1991; Cornelius, 1983; Ghiselli, 1966, 1973; Guion & Gottier, 1965; Hunter & Hunter, 1984; Kinslinger, 1966; Korman, 1968; Reilly & Chao, 1982; Schmitt et al., 1984). The "conventional wisdom" has been that these types of tests are *not* good at predicting future behavior at work, particularly when compared to alternative methods for selection.

It is easy to see how the conventional wisdom developed over the years in response to the conclusions of these reviews. The earliest reviews were not enthusiastic about the accuracy of personality tests, whether they were projective tests or personality inventories. Even the most recent reviews that make specific comparisons among alternative types of selection methods have found that personality tests generally are the least accurate of all predictors. For example, Hunter and Hunter (1984) report an average correlation with job performance of .11 for what they label "interest" tests; Reilly and Chao (1982) report an average of .18 for projective tests; Schmitt et al. (1984) report an average correlation of .15 for personality tests; and Barrick and Mount (1991) report average correlations between .00 and .15. The strength of these average correlations is much lower than those found in the realistic selection methods discussed earlier in this chapter.

Despite the conventional wisdom, various people are taking a "hard second look" at the accumulated evidence and coming to more optimistic conclusions (Barrick & Mount, 1991; Cornelius, 1983; Guion, 1987; Hollenbeck & Whitener, 1988; Hough et al., 1990; Nathan, Ledford, Bowen & Cummings, 1990; Schneider & Schmitt, 1986). There are two basic reasons for this optimism.

The first basic reason is that the bad reputation of personality tests has been based largely on research in which the *wrong criterion of effectiveness was applied.* Personality tests have been used to predict future job performance, rather than to predict the criteria suggested by the Matching Model (satisfaction, commitment, or job survival). Thus it should not be surprising to see that *ability tests* or the *realistic selection methods* reviewed earlier do a better job of predicting future job performance. These types of tests are primarily designed to do precisely that, whereas personality tests were *never* designed to predict job performance. Most of them were designed for use in the diagnosis of patients for general use by clinical psychologists. The one example of a test being developed exclusively for management (the Miner Sentence Completion Scale) was developed to predict *motivation or interest* in being a manager, not necessarily how well a person would perform on the job as a manager.

The second basic reason for today's current optimism is that some companies are using personnel selection to assess a more complex set of employee skills than in the past. Today interpersonal skills are considered to be very important in the more participative designs of both manufacturing and service organizations (Lawler, 1986; Bowen, Chase & Cummings, 1990). In the past, many companies focused more narrowly on the types of mental and physical abilities necessary to perform a job. This, however, is changing with the current trend toward using autonomous work groups, self-management, quality circles, and so on. Employees must be able to work effectively in teams, and some team members must be able to provide effective leadership for their peers.

Two reviews of personality tests (Cornelius, 1983; Schneider & Schmitt, 1986) and a recent study of personality tests in the military (Hough et al., 1990) show the potential of these tests. Cornelius (1983) reviewed the *projective* type of personality test and found a number of encouraging studies. For example, 10 of 14 studies reported statistically significant correlations between these tests and various measures of effectiveness. The only drawback Cornelius noted was that projective tests require scoring by a professional psychologist, so that using them for large-scale selection would not be practical.

Schneider and Schmitt (1986) agree with Cornelius's conclusions regarding projective tests and go further to argue that there is convincing evidence that personality *inventories* can also predict future on-the-job behavior. Despite the low average correlations mentioned earlier, the reason for the optimism is that in those studies where personality tests were selected with the particular job in mind, better than average results were obtained. The key seems to be in carefully analyzing the necessary skills and then selecting a personality inventory that measures those skills.

A recent study of personality inventories in the U.S. Army (Hough et al., 1990) illustrates how the potential can be realized. First, the authors reviewed available personality inventories and their predictive accuracy. Based on this review, they selected several basic types of personality components that seemed common across the various tests, e.g., achievement, adjustment, agreeableness, dependability, and "surgency" (dominance and energy level). Second, personality inventory items were developed for each of the components. Third, the inventory was given to several groups of Army enlisted personnel in order to evaluate its relationship to various aspects of military performance. For example over 9000 personnel took the test, and their scores on the personality factors were correlated with various aspects of their effectiveness such as ratings by peers and superiors, results of performance tests, and grades in military classes. Another study was done of how much "faking" would affect the scores on this test.

The authors considered the results of these tests very encouraging. Specifically, components of personality were correlated above .20 for several of the effectiveness measures, although not for all of them. The types of effectiveness associated with this test were effort and leadership, personal discipline, and physical fitness and military bearing. The types of effectiveness *not* related to personality were technical proficiency and general soldiering proficiency. This pattern is about what might be expected. That is, the personality test was not related to "job" performance in the narrow sense of being able to do the physical and mental aspects of soldiering. However, it was related to broader aspects of effectiveness that probably reflect more on a person's "motivation" than on abilities.

One prominent aspect of the Army study was how it handled the issue of faking when taking a personality test. This has been considered a serious limitation in using such tests for personnel selection. However, the results of several tests show that the Army recruits could affect their scores when instructed to "fake a bad score," but not when instructed to "fake a good score." It is the "fake a good score" problem that has caused some people to avoid personality inventories, yet this extensive research shows it is relatively insignificant. They recommend that a stern warning against faking may be all that is needed to remove the possibility of bias due to faking.

Occupation-Specific Tests: The Miner Sentence Completion Scale. The main source of information about the Miner Sentence Completion Scale is a review conducted by the author/originator (Miner, 1978). His review included 33 studies, but only 21 of them were conducted in "relevant" organizations, i.e., bureaucracies. The other 12 were done in situations *not* relevant to managerial motivation, e.g., research and development laboratories or small school districts. In all of the 21 studies in large bureaucratic organizations, significant results were obtained. However, no average correlation between test scores and measures of effectiveness was reported, so the results of research on this test cannot be directly compared to those from other tests. In the 12 tests outside the relevant type of organization, none of the test scores was significantly correlated with measures of effectiveness. Based on Miner's review of his own test, others have concluded that it shows good promise (e.g., Cornelius, 1983; Schneider & Schmitt, 1986).

Organization Specific Tests: The AT&T Study. The design of the AT&T study was described earlier. The results are actually quite dramatic when you examine those who were promoted within the hierarchy compared to those who were not. Those managers who scored *high* on the Leadership Motive Pattern described earlier made it to "middle" management much more often than those who scored *low:* 66 percent versus 36 percent. What is so interesting about this is that the researchers gathered the LMP data at the point of entry into AT&T, but promotion rates were not assessed until *eight* years later! Considering that the LMP is primarily a measure of motivational fit with the bureaucratic nature of AT&T, rather than a measure of ability, this is quite impressive.

The results of using the LMP on managers in technical jobs were quite different, but as expected. The LMP was largely *irrelevant* in predicting who would or would not get promoted in these types of jobs. Only 16 percent of those *high* in LMP were promoted to middle manager in eight years compared to 19 percent of those who were *low*. Thus high versus low LMP scores did not make a difference in rate of promotion. The combination of LMP "fit" being very significant in promotion for one subculture at AT&T versus the other subculture is an excellent example of the matching concept reiterated throughout this book. The striking results are somewhat amazing because they are based entirely on a relatively small sample of a person's writing in response to some ambiguous pictures. Furthermore, a great many factors can affect a person's promotion beyond the fit of that person's needs to the culture of the organization.

How Should Selection for Climates Be Done?

The obvious answer to the question posed for this final section is to use *both* types of selection methods discussed in this chapter. First, conduct a thorough analysis of both job requirements and organizational climates, as shown in the Matching Model (Figure 1.1). Second, choose the *realistic selection* method best suited to assessing job candidate capabilities for effective job performance. Since a realistic selection method also communicates pertinent information about the job to candidates, some self-selection will take place. Because the amount of self-selection that takes place is likely to be *in*sufficient for a complete matching to organizational climates, consider using a more *direct* approach to selection.

Thus the third element of selection for climates is to choose an existing personality test *if one can be found that is relevant for the particular organization.* If one cannot be found that measures the types of climates (or even culture), an alternative may have to be developed for the organization itself. Research on existing tests has been sufficiently encouraging that it is probably not necessary to invent new tests. This assumes, however, that a thorough diagnosis was done, so that the selection of a personality test really is "relevant" for the organization. The final element in this process is to discourage faking by admonishing job candidates to "be honest" in their answers. Research has shown this to be an effective strategy (Hough et al., 1990).

When this type of selection strategy is in place, it must be evaluated appropriately. Too many evaluations in the past have used job performance as the criterion for judging the predictive power of personality tests. Such tests must be judged against other criteria as well, particularly initial job satisfaction, commitment to the organization, and job survival. When job performance is evaluated, it is important to focus on those aspects of performance that are likely to be relevant for the matching of an individual's job wants to organizational climates. This will most likely involve certain such interpersonal factors as cooperation, team spirit, and willingness to work without supervision, which are typical of "newer," more participative organizational cultures.

Conclusions

1. Personnel selection has been primarily concerned with the matching of individual capabilities with organizational job requirements. Among those methods designed for this purpose, several also communicate realistic job information to candidates. This information can be used to help candidates make more effective self-selection job choices.

2. Realistic work sample tests and simulations can be categorized in several ways, e.g., verbal versus motor skills. Reviews of their effectiveness indicate that they predict future job performance quite well—as well as any other selection method. They have potential to influence self-selection, as evidenced in an important study of sewing machine operators.

3. Assessment centers and large-scale simulations are among the most complex and expensive of all methods. The predictive accuracy of assessment centers is also very high, but large-scale simulations have yet to be used for selection. Both of these have the potential to influence self-selection, although it is not clear at this time if they can affect occupational self-selection (e.g., choosing management versus a technical job) or organizational self-selection.

4. Structured interviews can be divided into the situational interview and the patterned behavior description interview.

The former asks job candidates to respond to hypothetical, but job-related, situations. The latter asks job candidates to provide specific job-related examples from their own experience. The predictive accuracy of these methods is approximately equal and substantially better than unstructured interviews. Their accuracy is, however, a bit lower than that of realistic work samples, simulations, or assessment centers.

5. The low-fidelity simulation is a blend of the situational interview and a realistic work sample. As a new technique it needs further testing, but its predictive accuracy is as good as that of structured interviews. The per-person cost to administer this technique is much less than that for an interview or for more elaborate simulations, however.

6. Selection methods that attempt to match the job candidate's needs or job wants to the organizational culture or climate have most typically used projective tests and personality inventories. Unless these tests are carefully selected to match the organization, their predictive accuracy is quite low.

7. When personality tests are matched to the organization, they can predict future behavior, particularly future motivation, interpersonal effectiveness, and promotions. Recent studies conducted in the U.S. Army and at AT&T show the potential for these methods.

8. Concerns about job candidates "faking" answers to personality tests appear to be exaggerated. This fear should not prevent an organization from using personality tests.

6

Newcomer Orientation

This is the first of two chapters concerning the *post*entry period for newcomers to organizations. In one sense of the term, everything that happens after entry can be defined as "socialization" (Van Maanen & Schein, 1979). However, there are good reasons for separating the period that *immediately* follows organizational entry and calling it orientation. Personnel experts have recognized the importance of newcomer orientation as a separate entity (see Feldman, 1988; Lubliner, 1978; McGarrell, 1984; St. John, 1980). Academic researchers have yet to focus much attention on this immediate postentry period. I hope this chapter and other recent writing (e.g., Wanous, 1992) will encourage more thinking and research into this topic.

This chapter begins with a definition of newcomer orientation. A critical element in this definition is the emphasis on helping newcomers cope with "entry stress." Thus, the second section concerns methods for *coping* with stress. After describing several general methods for coping, a special emphasis is placed on programs that prepare medical patients for hospitalization and invasive diagnostic procedures. Although this may seem to be an odd choice of topics, the psychological preparation of medical patients is directly applicable to organizational entry. The next section describes and evaluates the few existing studies of newcomer orientation programs. Recommendations for the design of newcomer orientation programs conclude the chapter.

What Is Newcomer Orientation?

Newcomer orientation is one of those terms that almost everyone uses, but there is no consensus as to what it means. That is, there is no agreed-upon definition that includes: (a) *when* orientation occurs, (b) the *objectives* of an orientation, and (c) the *methods* used to conduct the orientation. Despite this lack of agreement in precisely what is meant, many organizations have some sort of orientation program for newcomers. For example, a survey found that 64 percent of university graduates on the East and West coasts said they had gone through an orientation program upon entry (Louis, Posner & Powell, 1983).

The first element of a definition is to identify when newcomer orientation begins and ends. Since orientation concerns the immediate postentry period, the real questions are: How long after entry does orientation continue, and when does socialization begin? The answers are purely arbitrary. None of the published research describes orientation programs that lasted any longer than the first day, and some were only part of the first day. Here at The Ohio State University there is a 1 1/2-day orientation for new freshmen, (Fieley, 1991) and there are unpublished examples of colleges and graduate schools that have new students report as much as a week prior to the beginning of classes. Thus I will define the newcomer orientation period as extending as long as the first week after entry, although in many cases it is, practically speaking, simply the first day.

The second element of a definition is the objectives of newcomer orientation. In keeping with the Matching Model used throughout this book, the objectives of orientation are to facilitate *both* of the match-ups shown in the model. In achieving these dual match-ups the key focus should be on the *stress* associated with each of them. That is, stress is likely to be associated with unrealistically high expectations that simply cannot possibly be fulfilled, as has been discussed at length in previous chapters. Stress is also associated with the individual's concerns about being *capable* of meeting organizationally defined job requirements. Because of this, newcomer orientation programs have their primary focus on *both* match-ups. This is in contrast to the other entry topics discussed already, which primarily focused on one or the other of the match-ups. Newcomer orientation has a broader focus than either recruitment or selection techniques, even if it is of fairly short duration.

The final element of our definition concerns how the organization handles newcomer stress. The key to this is what are called "coping strategies" (Latack, 1984) or "stress management interventions" (Ivancevich, Matteson, Freedman & Phillips, 1990). Regardless of which term is used, there is general agreement that stress coping methods fall into one of three categories, depending on the focus of the coping activity: (a) the causes of stress, (b) the way people think about their stress, and (c) the way people react to the symptoms of stress.

Orientation Versus Recruitment

Orientation programs for newcomers are *not* the same thing as realistic job previews applied at a later point in time. There are important differences. Orientation programs are aimed at helping newcomers cope with stress, whereas the RJP can increase stress by communicating negative information to job candidates. Thus the emphasis in newcomer orientation is more on encouragement than on discouragement. This difference seems logical since by the time a person has joined an organization, an appropriate self-selection decision has been made. There is no further need to increase self selection with discouraging negative (even though realistic) information.

To solidify the difference between orientation and recruitment programs, I have developed an acronym for orientation: ROPES, which stands for Realistic Orientation Programs for new Employee Stress. You can think of ROPES as a way to help newcomers "learn the ropes" by starting their first day on the job with help from the organization on how to deal with present and upcoming stress. ROPES should be more complex than simply the presentation of information, which is typical of the RJP.

Why the Emphasis on Stress?

There is evidence that newcomers experience more stress right after entry than before entry as a job candidate and more than after entry as they gain experience. Furthermore, the levels of stress are sufficiently high to warrant immediate attention.

Consider the following study as evidence of just how serious newcomer stress can be.

A study of Army recruits entering basic training found that reported stress levels peaked on the first day (Bourne, 1967). This same study also found that blood and urine samples taken at that time showed levels of certain chemicals associated with extremely high stress, and that the levels were comparable to those found among hospitalized mental patients!

One reason why stress levels are so high at this time is that the newcomer has just undergone multiple role transitions (Latack, 1984) and has experienced considerable changes in his or her life outside of work. For example, the typical college graduate moving into a first full-time job experiences a dramatic "role change" from being a student to becoming a full-time employee. The newcomer will probably move geographically, will have a change in income, will lose some friends but gain others, and so on. Each of these changes has what can be called a "stress value," i.e., a point value that roughly indicates the severity of the stress associated with the type of change. Table 6.1 shows how two researchers (Cochrane & Robertson, 1973) revised the scoring system of the originators (Holmes & Rahe, 1967) of the idea that stressful events can be quantified. When reading this table, you should consider *all* the changes that a newcomer will likely experience. The latest stress research shows that simply adding up multiple stressful events *overstates* the degree of experienced stress. This is because there is the tendency for each event added to other events to have less impact than it would have had if it were the only event experienced (Birnbaum & Sotoodeh, 1991). Nevertheless, each additional stressful event experienced by a newcomer does add something to the total stress level.

Decades of research on stress and human performance have revealed the existence of an *optimal level of stress,* known as the "inverted-U shaped function," in which both low and high stress are associated with low performance. Only moderate levels of stress lead to maximum performance. Consider Figure 6.1 as an example of the relationship between stress and performance. The most recent evidence today (Anderson, 1990) continues to support the inverted-U relationship.

Figure 6.2 shows the likely relationship between stress levels and the stage of organizational entry. The curve is drawn to show that stress peaks at the point of entry into a new organization. Since we already know that high levels of stress

Table 6.1
*Weights Obtained from Several Groups for Items
on the Life Events Inventory*

	Psychiatrists $N = 60$	Patients $N = 42$	Students $N = 75$	Total $N = 177$
Section 1. All				
1. Unemployment (of head of household)	67	73	66	68
2. Trouble with superiors at work*	35	48	39	40
3. New job in same line of work	23	39	29	31
4. New job in new line of work	40	47	50	46
5. Change in hours or conditions in present job	20	40	28	31
6. Promotion or change of responsibilities at work*	32	43	40	39
7. Retirement*	62	45	52	54
8. Moving house	36	46	41	42
9. Purchasing own house (taking out mortgage)	26	58	40	40
10. New neighbors	18	23	16	18
11. Quarrel with neighbors	25	32	23	26
12. Income increased substantially (25%)	25	39	35	35
13. Income decreased substantially (25%)	61	65	60	62
14. Getting into debt beyond means of repayment	58	74	67	66
15. Going on holiday*	14	35	27	29
16. Conviction for minor violation (e.g., speeding or drunkenness)*	23	37	20	34
17. Jail sentence*	81	72	72	75
18. Involvement in fight	30	47	31	38
19. Immediate family member starts drinking heavily	63	70	63	65

Table 6.1 Continued
Weights Obtained from Several Groups for Items
on the Life Events Inventory

	Psychiatrists $N = 60$	Patients $N = 42$	Students $N = 75$	Total $N = 177$
Section 1. All				
20. Immediate family member attempts suicide	62	73	66	66
21. Immediate family member sent to prison	66	62	56	61
22. Death of immediate family member*	68	73	67	69
23. Death of close friend*	46	69	54	55
24. Immediate family member seriously ill	56	71	55	59
25. Gain of new family member (immediate)*	37	50	42	43
26. (Problems related to alcohol or drugs)				59
27. Serious restriction of social life	40	60	45	49
28. (Period of homelessness (hostel or sleeping rough))				51
29. (Serious physical illness or injury requiring hospital treatment	71	59	63	65
30. (Prolonged ill health requiring treatment by own doctor)				48
31. Sudden and serious impairment of vision or hearing	63	56	58	59
32. (Unwanted pregnancy)				70
33. (Miscarriage)				65
34. (Abortion)				63
35. Sex difficulties*	52	62	58	57

Table 6.1 Continued
Weights Obtained from Several Groups for Items on the Life Events Inventory

	Psychiatrists N = 60	Patients N = 42	Students N = 75	Total N = 177
Section 2. Ever-married only				
36. Marriage*	50	50	50	50
37. Pregnancy (or of wife)*	43	50	49	49
38. Increase in number of arguments with spouse	44	67	52	55
39. (Increase in number of arguments with other immediate family members (e.g., children)				43
40. Trouble with other relatives (e.g., in-laws)	35	45	28	38
41. Son or daughter left home*	44	59	46	44
42. (Children in care of others)				54
43. (Trouble or behavior problems in own children)				49
44. Death of spouse*	89	82	83	86
45. Divorce*	78	73	70	75
46. Marital separation*	72	73	65	70
47. Extra-marital sexual affair	54	66	56	61
48. (Break up of affair)				47
49. Infidelity of spouse	62	67	70	68
50. Marital reconciliation*	44	60	53	53
51. Wife begins or stops work*	25	42	31	34
Section 3. Never-married only				
52. (Break up with steady boy or girl friend				51

Table 6.1 Continued
Weights Obtained from Several Groups for Items
on the Life Events Inventory

	Psychiatrists N = 60	Patients N = 42	Students N = 75	Total N = 177
Section 3. Never-married only				
53. (Problems related to sexual relationship)				54
54. (Increase in number of family arguments (e.g., with parents))				43
55. (Break up of family)				77

*Item derived from Schedule of Recent Experiences. Items in parentheses were added after the main study. Weights obtained from a second group of students (N = 60).

Source: R. Cochrane & A. Robertson, 1973. The life events inventory: A measure of the relative severity of psycho-social stressors. Journal of Psychosomatic Research, 17, 135–139.

reduce performance and are linked to a whole host of undesirable symptoms, it is clear that organizations need different strategies for stress management, depending on the stage of entry. Chapter 3 described the realistic job preview as providing "bad news" to job candidates about the job and organization they were considering joining. Thus the RJP can be thought of as a technique that *increases* stress for job candidates. Since job candidates can benefit from this, it is an appropriate organizational strategy for this particular stage of entry. However, after newcomers enter an organization, their stress levels peak and thus a different strategy needs to be developed. For this reason, ROPES are targeted to *reduce* the stress of newcomers. The next section discusses the three main approaches to stress management and then describes more specific approaches for stress coping in the context of medical patients facing upcoming hospitalization.

Figure 6.1
Relationship Between Stress and Performance

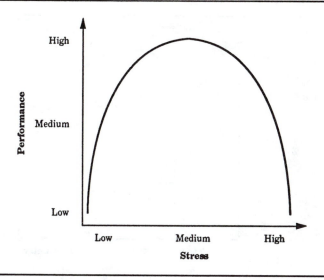

Ways to Manage Stress

Basic Approaches

Many specific actions can be taken to reduce stress, but they all fall into one of three basic categories. First, one approach is to take direct action on whatever is causing the stress—confront the very cause of stress directly. For example, if an unsatisfactory interpersonal relationship has caused the stress, the stressed person should deal directly with the other person rather than avoiding contact. If the person feels overburdened by things to do, he or she could make out a "to do" list and then *do* the things on the list. A second approach to stress management is to reappraise the situation. This approach avoids action directed to the cause of the stress. Rather, it encourages the person to engage in some type of "self-talk" in order to diminish the threat. For example, some people experience stress at making mistakes, but they can ease the stress if they realize that "nobody's perfect." The third approach to stress management is to deal only with the symptoms of stress. Thus this category includes such activities as exercise,

Figure 6.2
*Relationship Between Stage of Organizational Entry
and Level of Stress*

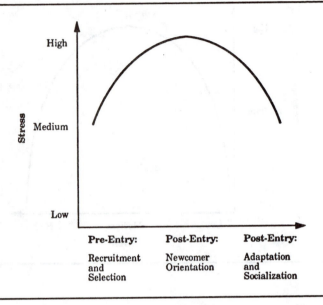

relaxation techniques, and the use of alcohol or drugs to relieve
the symptoms of high stress.

Stress Coping for Medical Patients

You might wonder why this particular area of stress coping has
been selected as relevant for organizational entry. There are
several reasons. First, medical patients experience a *level* of stress
that is quite high (see Table 6.1) and similar to that experienced
by newcomers. Second, the programs developed here are designed
to *anticipate forthcoming stress* rather than to deal with stress
after it has occurred, which is comparable to organizational entry.
A classic example of dealing with stress after it has occurred is
helping soldiers to cope with the "post-traumatic stress

syndrome," as has been found among Vietnam veterans (Druck-man & Swets, 1988). Third, the methods for coping with antici-pated stress are presented to medical patients as part of a *formal program upon entry into the hospital.*

The research on preparing medical patients has spanned a fairly wide variety of situations—from life threatening to more routine procedures. The situations include: (a) management of chronic pain, (b) invasive diagnostic medical and dental proce-dures, (c) childbirth, and (d) surgery. In almost all cases, hospi-talization was also involved.

Specific Programs for Stress Preparation of Medical Patients

A considerable body of psychological research conducted in medi-cal situations is relatively unknown to those outside the medical field. The number of studies done to prepare medical patients for upcoming stress associated with their particular problems is in excess of 50, which is a lot of research by anyone's standards. This research has been reviewed eight times, and these reviews form the basis for this section (Anderson & Masur, 1983; Auerbach & Kilman, 1977; Ludwick-Rosenthal & Neufeld, 1988; MacDonald & Kuiper, 1983; Mumford, Schlesinger & Glass, 1982; Posavac, 1980; Tan, 1982; Wilson-Barnett, 1984).

Medical patients have been psychologically prepared in five ways: (a) presenting information, (b) showing models, (c) doing stress inoculation, (d) conducting short psychotherapy, and (e) teaching self-control of thoughts and/or feelings.

Presenting Information. One of the most popular meth-ods for preparing medical patients for upcoming stress is to pro-vide them with information. One type of preparation is to convey realistic information about what will happen, e.g., what will be done, when it will begin, how long it will take, and so on. This has been called "what kind of event." A second type of information concerns "how you will feel" about upcoming physical and emo-tional sensations (Miller, 1981).

Modeling. Modeling (based on Bandura, 1977) is a tech-nique used in various types of business training programs (e.g., Goldstein & Sorcher, 1974). The same principles are used in medical research. That is, patients are first shown a model coping with the situation, followed by a discussion of what was observed and a practice or rehearsal of what was observed. Both live and videotaped models have been used, as have puppets for children.

Stress Inoculation. Stress inoculation has three essential steps (Janis, 1958; 1983): (a) call attention to upcoming events—both gains and losses, (b) encourage the person to engage in self-reassurance and other coping techniques, and (c) give help in practicing the coping methods. The first step essentially provides information. The second step can include a rather wide variety of specific actions, e.g., various imagination strategies, "self-talk" about coping and even physical actions to cope with pain such as deep breathing and relaxation exercises. During the third step, patients can test out their newly acquired coping skills in various ways, e.g., talking, imagining, role-playing, and even experiencing mild forms of pain under controlled conditions.

Short Psychotherapy. This type of therapy has been done both individually and in groups, ranging in duration from a 1-hour session to several sessions of 1/2–1 hour in length. Generally speaking, patients are encouraged to express their expectations, feelings, and coping plans. The therapy provider typically gives general reassurance and emotional support and may even provide information to make expectations more accurate (Mumford et al., 1982). Some therapists have even used hypnosis. Of all the categories, this one is the most diverse because it includes interventions aimed at thoughts (e.g., the Rational-Emotive Therapy of Ellis, 1962, 1970), feelings, and the unconscious (i.e., the use of hypnosis).

Self-Control: Thoughts and Feelings. Tan (1977) describes six variations for cognitive coping with pain: (a) imaginative inattention (think about being at the beach), (b) imaginative transformation of pain (acknowledge it, but minimize it as either trivial or unreal), (c) imaginative transformation of context (acknowledge the pain, but pretend it was caused by something else, e.g., a championship football game), (d) external attention-diversion (e.g., count ceiling tiles), (e) internal attention-diversion (e.g., do mental arithmetic), and (f) somatization (focus on the pain area in a detailed manner as if you were observing yourself).

A second form of self-control has focused on feelings rather than on thoughts. Two techniques have been used. The first is relaxation as a way to cope with stress, e.g., exercises in muscle flexing and breathing (Jacobson, 1970). The second is desensitization, a clinical technique for overcoming fear where the patient approaches the fearful situation in a series of increasingly realistic approximations (Machen & Johnson, 1974). For example, a surgery patient might first be shown a hospital room and then the other areas where he or she might be during the course of the stay (e.g., preoperation preparation, an operating room, x-ray lab). Showing these locations prior to hospitalization can reduce some of the fear people have.

Effectiveness of Patient Stress Preparation

The main factor in evaluating the success of stress coping preparation programs has been the length of stay in the hospital. This is a criterion with considerable consequences for the financial health of hospitals. Many insurance plans (and all of Medicare) pay medical providers a fixed amount for certain procedures or for certain types of diagnoses (e.g., a broken arm). This means that the hospital loses money if the actual costs exceed the allowed amount, and, of course, they make money if the costs are less. Thus anything that can reduce the number of days spent in the hospital has the potential to increase revenue.

The programs to help patients cope are quite effective in reducing hospital stays. One study quantified the average reduction as *two full days for stress-prepared patients* as compared to "control" groups of patients who did not receive such preparation (Mumford et al., 1982). The authors who came to this conclusion were quite enthusiastic about the practical usefulness of stress preparation programs because they are usually quite inexpensive to conduct, yet they have a significant payback for such a small investment. They went further to suggest that incredibly expensive machines do not have the same impact, and, even if they did, they would not be as cost effective.

All of the reviewers of these studies come to essentially the same conclusion: The more complex the method used to teach coping, the more effective the results. This means that the simple provision of information—which is analogous to the

RJP—is not as effective as stress inoculation training or modeling. This is because stress inoculation training and modeling begin with realistic information, but they go further to show people what to do with the information, and then they incorporate some type of practice. Stress inoculation training goes further than modeling to include explicit reassurance and emotional support as part of the program. The self-control of thoughts and feelings is also a fairly simple technique that is generally less effective than modeling or stress inoculation training. Short psychotherapy has been effective, although it has been used much less frequently than the other techniques.

Based on the effectiveness of the various techniques and their possible applicability to newcomer orientation, it appears that stress inoculation training and modeling should be the approaches "borrowed" from the medical arena and used in business, education, and military organizations. The next section describes three newcomer orientation experiments. These three come closest to what should be done in orientation, although each has its own weaknesses. The chapter concludes with guidelines for the more effective development of newcomer orientation programs.

Three Studies of Newcomer Orientation

Gomersall and Myers (1966) developed an "anxiety reduction" orientation program for assemblers of electronic equipment at Texas Instruments in order to increase the rate at which newcomers learned their jobs. They determined which areas where highly stressful for typical newcomers by interviewing employees, their supervisors, and middle management. As a result, they developed a 6-hour program for the first day at work, which would follow the existing 2-hour orientation conducted by the personnel department. To test this program, they randomly assigned new hires to attend either the 2-hour personnel program or to attend both programs. The personnel program was a typical orientation program that focused on the hours of work, insurance programs, parking, work rules, and employee services. It also included warnings about the consequences of not living up to company expectations.

The experimental stress coping orientation program emphasized four main points: (a) opportunities to succeed are actually very good because only less than 1 percent of newcomers fail to perform satisfactorily; (b) "hall talk" should be disregarded because "old timers" liked to "play games" with the newcomers and exaggerated problems; (c) people should take the initiative in communication, particularly with their supervisors; (d) newcomers were told something unique about their own supervisor, e.g., "Joe is strict, but friendly. His hobbies are fishing and ham radio operation. He tends to be shy sometimes, but he really likes to talk to you if you want to. He would like you to check with him before you go on a personal break, just so he knows where you are" (Gomersall & Myers, 1966, p. 67). These four points were communicated to newcomers in small groups composed of those who would be assigned to the same supervisor. The groups were given an opportunity to discuss these points.

Approximately 100 newcomers were assigned to each of the two orientations (traditional versus stress coping). The authors report that training time was greatly reduced, productivity increased, and absenteeism reduced for those who received the stress coping orientation.

This orientation program is similar to stress inoculation, but it is not a complete stress inoculation program. It did include some realistic information about upcoming stressors that the newcomers would encounter on the job. It did provide ways to deal with these stressors and some discussion of how to implement the advice given. However, it did not allow newcomers to rehearse what was being taught, and it did not offer any general supportive or emotional reassurance that they would be able to cope as newcomers.

The second stress coping orientation program (Novaco, Cook & Sarason, 1983) showed "behavioral models" coping with the rigors of military basic training during a 35-minute video (appropriately called "Making It"). The video began with a short segment of realistic preview information, but then it focused largely on two themes for the remainder: (a) self-control regulation of emotions and (b) effective performance of tasks. These two themes were intertwined throughout the video since focusing on effective task performance is one of the recommended ways to control emotions. The video first provided recruits with general reassurance by acknowledging that they were probably feeling distressed, and then it quickly offered an explanation for why they were feeling this way. The video showed specific examples of things that make newcomers anxious, e.g., drill instructors who yell at them all the time. It was explained that the drill instructor is just doing a job and that none of the yelling was directed at them personally. To facilitate effective performance, scenes were shown of recruits making a bed properly, while "under the close and highly energetic supervision of a drill instructor" (Novaco et al., 1983, p. 410).

A total of 530 new recruits were randomly assigned to see either this "Making It" stress coping orientation video, or they were assigned to a traditional RJP video, which had previously been used in the military (Horner, 1980). This test comparison was done to see if the stress coping approach to newcomer orientation would, in fact, be superior to the RJP (which, of course, only presented information without any stress coping material). Their description of the results indicates that the stress coping video was superior at increasing the recruits' self-confidence, and it reduced the number of problems they had adjusting to drill instructors. (No data on attrition differences between these two groups were reported, however, and this is unfortunate.)

This orientation program combined elements of both modeling and stress inoculation. That is, it gave realistic information, showed models who were coping successfully, and offered general support and reassurance. However, the program did not have explicit discussion among recruits about the models' behavior and what was to be learned. There was no rehearsal either.

The third experimental study of newcomer orientation was also conducted for military recruits about to begin basic training (see Meglino, DeNisi, Youngblood, Williams, Johnson, Randolph & Laughlin, 1983, for the original report, and Meglino, DeNisi, Youngblood & Williams, 1988, for the published version). Two videos were produced with professional actors taking the parts of recruit "behavioral models." One of the videos is a typical RJP in that it presents realistic, but mostly negative, information about what is in store for the new recruits. The authors originally called this a "content preview" and later called it a "reduction preview." It is a typical RJP and will be referred to in this way. The second video is a stress coping orientation. (It was originally called a "coping preview," but later it was called an "enhancement preview."). This is a coping orientation video, as originally labeled and will be referred to in this way. Tables 3.2 and 3.3 previously showed the topics covered in these videos, when this study was first mentioned in Chapter 3.

A total of 533 new recruits were randomly assigned to one of four groups: (a) RJP video only, (b) coping orientation video only, (c) both videos (RJP first, then coping), and (d) neither video. Those who saw *both* videos had the lowest attrition from basic training of any of the four groups. There was no difference in attrition between those who saw one or the other of the two videos. The strongest results for attrition were found for those recruits whose commitment to the Army was in the top 50 percent of their group. For these more committed personnel, seeing either one of the videos reduced attrition compared to not seeing a video. For those with the lowest commitment, however, the use of either type of video had little effect on attrition.

This stress coping video has some, but not all, of the elements of a modeling program. That is, behavioral models are shown coping with various stressful situations, but the orientation program had no group discussion nor any rehearsal. The coping orientation video had elements of stress inoculation in that it showed realistic information and suggested coping methods. However, the recruits were given neither explicit emotional support nor general support.

These three studies are the best examples of newcomer orientation programs that attempt to do more than the traditional type, which usually focuses on filling out various forms, and so on. All three addressed the issue of newcomer stress and tried to teach coping methods to the newcomers. Despite their good intentions, the accumulated results from these three are modest. There are two plausible reasons for the lack of stronger results. First, a mere three studies is insufficient to "prove" anything. Thus more studies perhaps would reveal a trend that has not yet been detected. Statisticians call this a "type II error," which is the error in thinking that something is *not* true, when it actually is true. In this case, the error would be in concluding that newcomer orientation programs have only modest effects because these three studies do not all show strong results. Three studies is too few.

The second reason for these modest results is that none of the studies had an orientation program that was sufficiently complex. Not one of these programs had all of the critical elements of either stress inoculation or modeling. They all had some of the elements, but the missing elements were noted in each case. Thus these programs perhaps were themselves deficient. This, of course, raises the issue of how newcomer orientation programs *should* be designed. The final section addresses this issue.

Design Guidelines for ROPES

The ROPES guidelines developed here are based in part on the types of stress coping programs developed for medical patients as well as on those that have been tried in the context of organizational entry. Since there is little research in the latter context, these guidelines are based on the assumption that research work with medical patients can be applied to newcomers.

1. **Include realistic information.** An effective newcomer orientation program includes much of what is contained in a realistic job preview. The type of information should be obtained in the same careful way as when constructing an RJP. Differences in content might occur because a ROPES program would be specifically tailored at those factors causing stress for new employees. That is, once the newcomer "gets over" the entry shock of disconfirmed expectations, the enduring problems causing stress need to be identified. The diagnostic methods will be the same for RJPs and for ROPES.

2. **Provide general support and reassurance.** General support and reassurance is a critical element since the objective is to help people cope and succeed. This can be done in several ways. First, the organization can directly express support and reassurance to the newcomers, as was the case in the second example of newcomer orientation programs. In that video, the voice commentary reassured recruits that their feelings of fear and anxiety were "normal" and that they would not always feel that way. Second, the mere presence of other newcomers in the same situation can be supportive and reassuring, as was seen in the small groups of new electronics assemblers from the first example discussed earlier. Large groups of newcomers, as seen in the two military examples, are not conducive to providing this type of support. It is best done in smaller groups, particularly when all of the newcomers will be facing the same situation—like all having the same supervisor. Third, supportive bosses can provide reas-

surance, too, although none of the studies examined this possibility.

3. **Use models to show coping skills.** It is insufficient to just talk about how to cope. Newcomers must see some sort of "model" actually performing the recommended actions to solve or prevent certain organizational stressors. The medical research findings suggest that live models are preferable to video models, but not that many studies actually compared the two directly. Newcomers can engage in a dialogue with a live model, which is not possible with a video model. On the other hand, video models are still useful and much more cost effective when large cohorts of newcomers enter, as is found in the military or in educational organizations.

4. **The model's actions should be discussed.** This is one of the cornerstones of the behavioral modeling technique, but one that was not applied in either of the military studies discussed earlier. No matter how explicit the instructions from a video model are, more learning takes place when newcomers actively participate in a discussion, rather than passively viewing a video.

5. **Rehearsal is necessary.** The most glaring weakness in all three of the newcomer orientation programs discussed earlier is their lack of rehearsal. Once again, this is a cornerstone of both the behavioral modeling and the stress inoculation training programs (Goldstein & Sorcher, 1974; Janis, 1958).

6. **Teach self-control of thoughts and feelings.** No program of newcomer stress coping can anticipate all the situations people may face, so something needs to be done for those times when the training cannot be applied. Teaching general relaxation skills, as is more frequently done for medical patients facing physical pain, may have a place in organizational entry, too. Given that the research shows newcomer stress is high, some fairly general self-help skills seem warranted as part of a complete ROPES program.

7. **Specific stressors should be targeted to specific newcomers.** The Texas Instruments program discussed

cussed earlier used this principle with respect to what was said about a new boss. It seems reasonable to be concerned with a blend of general stressors that will affect most new recruits, and then those that will affect some, but not others. This obviously adds to the complexity of designing and executing a ROPES program, but it probably will increase its impact. It may also have the effect of increasing its credibility in the eyes of the newcomers, since it will be obvious to the newcomers, that a great deal of care and energy has gone into the program.

Conclusions

1. Newcomer orientation refers to the immediate postentry period, up to about the end of the first week at work. The objectives of newcomer entry programs should be to develop stress coping skills. Methods used to help newcomers cope can deal directly with the causes of stress, the ways people think about stress, or with how they manage the symptoms of stress.

2. Realistic Orientation Programs for new Employee Stress (ROPES) are different from realistic recruitment in that the latter encourages job candidates to drop out from further consideration, whereas ROPES encourage them to stay in the organization.

3. The stress associated with organizational entry seems to peak for newcomers, as compared to job candidates or to more experienced employees. Thus the emphasis on stress coping is the essence of newcomer orientation.

4. Quite a lot of research on stress coping has been done for medical patients, and it has greatly reduced the length of hospital stays for those who received this type of psychological preparation.

5. Five types of stress coping programs have been tried for medical patients: presenting realistic information, behavioral modeling, stress inoculation, short psychotherapy, and the self-control of thoughts and feelings.

6. Only three good examples of ROPES could be found in the accumulated research on organizational entry.

The results of these three show some promise, but the overall results are modest.

7. None of the existing studies of ROPES was of a program that meets all of the criteria for success, and this may be one reason why the results are not stronger.

8. The guidelines for developing ROPES are: (a) present realistic information, (b) provide general support and reassurance, (c) use models to show coping skills, (d) discuss the model's actions, (e) rehearse coping skills, (e) teach self-control of thoughts and feelings, and (g) target specific stressors for specific newcomers.

7

Organizational Socialization

Compared to the other phases of organizational entry, socialization certainly is the longest and most complex. Socialization concerns the ways in which newcomers change and adapt to the organization. The types of changes are learning new roles, norms, and values. In other words, learning what is "acceptable" behavior (Van Maanen, 1976a). In terms of the Matching Model used in this book, the changes that occur pertain to both types of match-ups, but primarily to that between organizational climates and individual job wants. Training programs are the primary influence on the individual capabilities and organizational job requirements match-up, although some socialization activities also affect how individuals are expected to perform a job. Thus socialization efforts are best judged by the levels of job satisfaction, organizational commitment, and job survival of newcomers.

Organizational socialization concerns how newcomers change, but "personalization" is how the *organization* changes as a result of the newcomers who join it (Bakke, 1953). In contrast to socialization, personalization has received almost no attention from scholars. There are two reasons for this imbalance. First, in most organizations, newcomers enter in small numbers, rather than in large cohorts. As they enter the ongoing system, they tend to be overwhelmed by the momentum of the existing climates with their respective norms and values. Thus it is much more likely that the newcomers will change rather than the organization. Second, when trying to examine changes, it is easier to observe them in newcomers than in the organization as a whole. The larger the organization is, the harder it is to detect changes in it. Related to this is the basic problem of trying to define what is meant by he " the organization." If you were looking for organizational changes caused by newcomers, where would you begin to look—the immediate work group, a department, a division? For these two reasons, then, most academic scholars have paid attention to the socialization of newly hired individuals rather than the personalization of organizations.

Six topics are covered in this chapter. First, distinctions are drawn between newcomer orientation and organizational socialization that justify their being treated separately. Second, the basic objective of socialization is defined as maintaining organizational control over newcomers. Both socialization and personnel selection are ways to achieve this control, and they can be substituted for each other. Third, an overall framework of change and adaptation is developed. The particular emphasis of the framework is to distinguish socialization effects on newcomers from those changes that occur in the work groups they join. Fourth, the types of changes that occur are discussed in terms of "stage models" of socialization. These models all attempt to depict the sequence of events that typical newcomers experience. An "integrative" model of these stages is offered as a way of summarizing the various proposals. Fifth, the basic psychological principles of persuasion are explained because they form the basis for specific tactics used to socialize newcomers. Sixth, the tactics for organizational socialization are discussed, and several case study examples of socialization "dynamics" are described.

Socialization Versus Orientation

In contrast to newcomer orientation, organizational socialization is a very broad topic. Although some experts consider socialization to be so broad a topic that it includes newcomer orientation (Van Maanen & Schein, 1979), this is not the position I have taken.

There are some important differences between orientation and socialization, which is why each is considered in a separate chapter. First, the fundamental purpose of newcomer orientation is to help newcomers cope with entry stress. In one sense, the coping methods previously discussed tend to make the newcomer *resilient* to change, whereas socialization typically concerns the conformity of newcomers to important organizational norms and values (Schein, 1968).

Second, newcomer orientation refers to specific *programs,* whereas socialization is a term used to describe a *process of change* rather than any specific action to accomplish the change. Because of this, newcomer orientation was defined as pertaining to the first day, and possibly the first week, at work. Socialization refers to a much longer period of time after someone enters the organization. There is no agreed upon length of time that is considered to be *the* period of organizational socialization, although the first year is certainly included. As will be seen later, some of the views of socialization extend into the first several years. In fact, one viewpoint of socialization (Schein, 1971) is that it continues throughout a career in an organization because it becomes relevant each time a person makes some type of internal change (e.g., change in job function, geographical location, or promotion).

Third, the number of people who conduct a newcomer's orientation is usually less than the number who influence the newcomer's socialization. In fact, those conducting the orientation might not be the individual's peers, co-workers, nor even the boss. In contrast, the two main sources of socializing influence are conformity to peer group pressure and obedience to authority.

Organizational Control Is the Basic Objective

Organizational socialization is one way to ensure that newcomers will adhere to the important values of the organization. Socialization is, thus, a type of "control mechanism" to maintain the status quo in an organization (Etzioni, 1964). What is meant by "important values," and what happens if newcomers deviate from them. Furthermore, can there be too much conformity?

One scholar of organizational socialization has proposed that there are two basic types of organizational values: pivotal and relevant (Schein, 1968). Pivotal values are absolutely essential to the survival of the organization; they define its essence. For example, a strong belief in the profit motive is essential for business organizations; a belief in God is central to most religious organizations; the acquisition and dissemination of knowledge is the crux of educational organizations, particularly universities. These are by no means the only examples of pivotal values. In business organizations, a belief in the free enterprise system might be pivotal, although some organizations try to create monopoly or oligopolistic markets in order to increase profits.

The "relevant" values of an organization are important, but they are not *absolutely* necessary for membership. Examples of these types of values include such things as dress codes, standards for public behavior, expectations about where employees should live, desirable political views, or the types of clubs or churches to join.

Figure 7.1 shows what might happen when newcomers accept or reject either or both types of organizational values. The key outcome is the degree of "innovation" in an organization. When newcomers conform to *all* values, both pivotal and relevant, the chances for innovation or change in the organization are low. If newcomers reject the pivotal values, chaos is likely to result. There may be "change," but it will *not* be innovative; it will be counterproductive to the existence of the organization itself. Finally, if newcomers accept the pivotal values, but reject some of the relevant values, they may be catalysts for innovation by challenging some of the "accepted" ways of doing business while avoiding a threat to the essence of the organization.

Figure 7.1
Possible Relationship Between Newcomer Conformity and Innovation

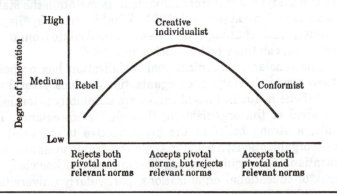

Source: *Based on E. H. Schein, 1968. Organizational Socialization and the profession of management.* Industrial Management Review, 9, 1–16.

The relationship shown in Figure 7.1 is logically appealing, but it has not been subjected to much scrutiny by researchers. Perhaps the best example of its validity can be found in a pair of studies done at a New England bank. The original study of the bank (Argyris, 1954) found that the bank hired new managers who fit into the "conformist" category in Figure 7.1. In fact, they were called the "right type" employee: quiet, slightly nervous, very willing to take orders, and relatively unwilling to give orders. They preferred security, stability, and isolation, and they avoided conflict or aggression.

Years later, a former student of the original investigator went back to the same bank to see what changes had occurred as a result of a new program to bring in personnel more like "creative individualists" and to socialize them differently (Alderfer, 1971). The major change in hiring was to have a wider group of bank executives interview potential candidates for management training than had previously been involved. The major change in socialization was to provide a 33-week program for newcomer management trainees that included a formal mentor ("big brother" to the newcomer) and rotation through a series of jobs in the bank. These changes seem to account for a somewhat "newer breed" of manager—at least they were not as conformist as their predecessors had been a generation earlier. In one sense, the program had some success. In another sense, new conflicts were created internally. The bank now had three groups of managers: (a) the older conformists, (b) the newer, creative individualists, and (c) those whose careers had peaked and who were not on the same "fast track" as the new hires in this program. The friction among these groups led the older managers to resist change and those whose careers were "plateaued" to resent the newer managers. This friction dampened the degree of change that the newer, creative individualists could initiate.

Some scholars of the staffing process (Schneider, 1983, 1987) have gone so far as to assert that *all* organizations have the tendency toward conformity as in the preceding example of the New England bank. Through the process of "attraction-selection-attrition," organizations tend to maintain a high degree of homogeneity and resist the types of internal changes that could come from a creative individualist. The argument is that such individualists are not attracted to organizations with which they have a poor " fit," that they are less likely to be selected by such organizations, and that, if hired, they tend to quit more frequently than those who conform to the organization.

The argument that all organizations tend to perpetuate themselves is reasonably persuasive, although it has not been directly tested in a real organization. The only research to evaluate it directly has been a laboratory study using college students as subjects (Bretz, Ash & Dreher, 1989). This particular study, however, did *not* support the idea of homogeneity among organization members. Other studies of nurses (Alutto, Hrebiniak & Alonso, 1971) and of medical students (Shuval & Adler, 1977) found that the diversity in newcomer values and commitment actually *increased* after entry, rather than decreased. The direction of these changes is, of course, contrary to the self-perpetuating conformity viewpoint of Schneider's attraction-selection-attrition framework.

Clearly we need a careful analysis of the attraction-selection-attrition effect in an organization that permits outside researchers to monitor the entry of newcomers for a substantial period of time.

Socialization and Selection

An alternative to using socialization is to rely heavily on *selection* to screen out those who would be likely to deviate from pivotal organizational values. Figure 7.2 graphically shows how the need for socialization increases as the degree of selectivity in personnel selection decreases. One way to think about this is with the formula: $a + b = c$, where a refers to the degree of selectivity in selection, b refers to the amount of socialization activity, and c refers to the *total* "control" that the organization exercises over newcomers from the combination of selection and socialization.

Despite the logical appeal of this view, relatively little research has been designed to test it. One exception is a study of civil defense organizations in Minnesota, Georgia, and Massachusetts (Mulford, Klonglan, Beal & Bohlen, 1968).

Civil defense is, on average, *moderate* in terms of its control over the selection of newcomers. Although the average degree of selectivity is moderate, there were differences among the various ($N = 240$) local organizations. Some organizations had high selectivity, and others had low selectivity.

The degree of selectivity was measured using the *selection ratio* for each local organization, and the results were divided into

Figure 7.2
Achieving Control Over Newcomers via Personnel Selection and Organizational Socialization

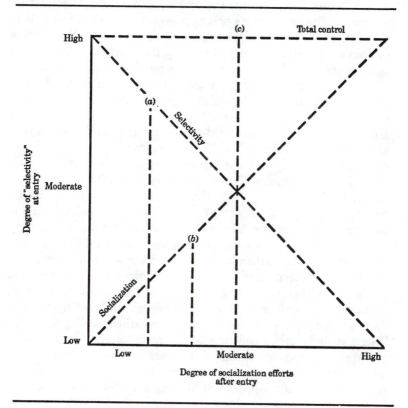

three groups (high, medium, and low selectivity) for further analysis. The authors found that

- In general, both selectivity and socialization efforts increase performance.
- The effects of socialization on performance is "zero" for those organizations that were highly selective in the entry of newcomers.

- Socialization efforts increased performance for both the medium and low selective organizations.

The final way in which selectivity and socialization interact is through the newcomer's *preentry* experiences. One example of this is the way some newcomers are socialized by the type of professional training received in school, and another is the way newcomers self-select themselves into particular occupations.

Much has been written about the entry of professionally trained newcomers into organizations and the issue of where the loyalties of these newcomers ultimately lie. The issue is whether a professional will be able to closely identify with the employing organization (and be a "local"), or whether a professional will continue to identify with the larger group of similar professionals (and be a "cosmopolitan"), as originally discussed by Gouldner (1957, 1958). For many years the need to socialize professionals has been considered important. Socialization of professionals is sometimes seen as the "antidote" to extensive preentry, *professional* socialization. However, others have taken a different view. This view is that socialization in a person's profession is primarily reflected in that person's *self-selection* into an organization. A study of 390 aerospace engineers found that those with PhDs gravitated toward basic research, whereas those with master's degrees went into applied research units (Miller & Wager, 1971). These authors argue that the basic "cosmopolitan versus local" orientation is set *prior* to entry during professional training. Then, when newcomers self-select into particular jobs, they choose matching parts of the organization. The net effects of this self-selection process are to reduce the potential for individual versus organization conflict and to reduce the need for the organization to attempt extensive socialization.

Who and What Changes During Socialization?

At its most basic level, organizational socialization is the transmission of important norms and values to the newcomer by the "insiders" in the organization. Socialization is an *interpersonal* process (Reichers, 1987). Interpersonal behavior can be analyzed and categorized at two levels (Argyris, 1971): (a) statements made about oneself or directed to another person, and (b) the group norms that are implied by the actions taken in (a). Furthermore, interpersonal behavior can be categorized as concerning either ideas, or feelings. Table 7.1 shows

Table 7.1

Analyzing and Coding Interpersonal Behavior and Its Implication for Group Norms

Level I			Level II	
Individual		**Interpersonal**	**Norms**	
Experimenting	i	Help others to	i	Trust	i
	f	experiment	f		f
Openness	i	Help others to	i	Concern	i
	f	be open	f		f
Owning	i	Help other to	i	Individuality	i
	f	own	f		f
Not owning	i	Not help others	i	Conformity	i
	f	to own	f		f
Not open	i	Not help other	i	Antagonism	i
	f	to be open	f		f
Rejecting	i	Not help others	i	Mistrust	i
experimenting	f	to experiment	f		f

i = ideas, f = feelings.

Source: C. Argyris, 1971. Management and Organizational Development. *New York: McGraw-Hill, p. 11.*

a well-developed measurement scheme that can be used to sort out what goes on within groups of newcomers and insiders during socialization (Argyris, 1971).

Two examples should clarify how to categorize interpersonal behavior as shown in Table 7.1. Suppose someone said "I feel tense" to others in a work group. This would be categorized at Level I as *owning f* for "owning one's feelings," i.e., admitting that they exist. At Level II (group norms), such a statement would be categorized as *individuality f* because it signifies that it is permissible in this group for people to talk about their personal feelings. Consider the following statement made to someone else in the group: "Would you please tell me more about your plan." At Level I this represents *help others to be open* [about] *i* [ideas]. At Level II, this statement would be categorized as *concern i* because it signifies the group norm that members are interested in hearing about other people's ideas.

The importance of the coding and category scheme shown in Table 7.1 is that organizational socialization is learning about group or organizational norms from interpersonal interaction. The usefulness of this system should now be clear—it provides a concrete way to *measure* what insiders say to newcomers and to link this face- to-face behavior to what it means in terms of group (or organizational) norms.

In using such a system to make this point, be aware that we need not use these particular categories (owning, openness, and experimenting) because they were specifically developed by Chris Argyris (1971) to assess the climate for learning and change. His interest was in acting as a "change agent" consultant to organizations. This was to be done by increasing the degree of open and honest communication among executives, so he would first "keep score" of their interpersonal behavior and group norms by using this coding scheme to analyze group meetings. Thus his selection of these three categories is appropriate for his purposes.

The three dimensions shown in Table 7.1 do, however, appear to be important for most organizations. In the context of organizational socialization, however, the number of dimensions should probably not be limited to just these three. The main facets of organizational climates should be included, e.g., the climate for service in a bank or the climate for quality in a production organization.

Besides recognizing that all behavior is simultaneously interpersonal and indicative of group norms, it is important to recognize that newcomers to organizations enter quite different interpersonal climates. The types of groups entered can vary dramatically. Sometimes newcomers enter well-established groups, but at other times the groups entered may have short histories and only weakly developed norms. Sometimes newcomers themselves enter as a group. Figure 7.3 indicates the many possibilities.

There are a great many opportunities for organizational socialization to take place, and it takes place in groups that more (or less) need to develop on their own. That is, sometimes the groups entered are almost as "undeveloped" as the newcomers are "unsocialized." It may be true that the "classical" situation of organizational socialization that comes most readily to mind is that where the "lone" newcomer joins an existing and well-established group. Certainly in this situation a maximum of pressure will be brought to bear on the individual. However, socialization takes place in a number of other contexts. The dynamics of socialization

Figure 7.3
The "Overlap" Between Organizational and Socialization and Group Development

Source: J. P. Wanous, A. E. Reichers & S. D. Malik, 1984. Organizational socialization and group development: Toward an integrative perspective. Academy of Management Review, 9, p. 671. *Reprinted by permission of the Academy of Management Association.*

can become difficult to separate from those of group development, as would be the case in military basic training, in an "executive" MBA program, among new fraternity members, or in new groups assembled after a merger, as indicated in Figure 7.3.

Because newcomers join both immediate work groups as well as the organization as a whole, it is possible to consider their "fit" to the norms and values of both groups and the overall organization (Van Maanen, 1976a). For example, a newcomer who conforms to both the group and the organization would be called a "team player." One who conforms to the group but not the organization would be a "warrior." One who conforms to the organization but not the group would be an "isolate." Finally, someone who conforms to neither the group nor the organization would be an "outsider."

Because both organizational socialization and group development occur simultaneously, they have much in common (Wanous, Reichers & Malik, 1984). Groups go through "stages" of development, much as individuals who are being socialized (see the next section for stage models of socialization). Both processes can be represented as shown in Figure 7.4, which shows the most *basic processes* common to socialization and group development.

The significance of Figure 7.4 is that organizational socialization (or group development) can be broken down into three basic components: (a) the *process*—learning from other people who are trying to "persuade" newcomers to adopt organizational norms and values, (b) the *focus*—learning specific and acceptable roles, norms, and values, and (c) the *unique dynamic of conflict* — the socialization process occurs in a cauldron of conflict. (Although each of these three elements is briefly described here, a more complete explanation can be found in Wanous et al., 1984.)

The *process of learning* in organizational socialization is called "social learning" because newcomers "learn the ropes" from other people by listening to them and observing their actions. This type of learning is considered to be the most important way in which humans learn, as contrasted with earlier theories that emphasized reinforcement from the environment (the work of B. F. Skinner), or the "innate instincts" of people. Although there certainly is evidence that "reinforcements" from the environment affect learning and that some instincts do exist, the key here is that organizational socialization concerns *interpersonal* relationships at work (Reichers, 1987). Thus the emphasis on social learning is important to understanding how newcomers become socialized.

A good specific example of how social learning takes place has been provided by Weiss (1977). In this study, pairs of bosses and subordinates were analyzed to see how much the subordinates "modeled" their bosses' leadership style (the subordinates were managers, too). The more the bosses were seen as competent by the subordinates, the more the subordinates were likely to model their own style after that of their boss. (However,

Figure 7.4
Overview of Organizational Socialization

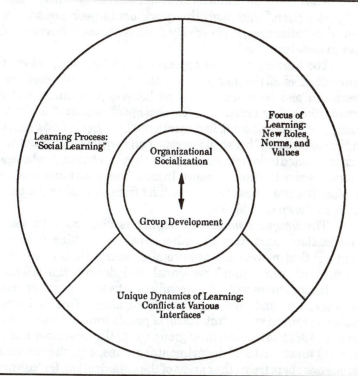

Source: Adapted from J. P. Wanous, A. E. Reichers & S. D. Malik, 1984.
*Organizational socialization and group development: Toward an integrative per-
spective.* Academy of Management Review, 9, *p. 682. Reprinted by permission of
the Academy of Management Association.*

subordinates who had very high self-esteem tended to develop
their own style and not necessarily model the boss.)

The *focus of learning* is the new role to be adopted, the new
group or organizational norms (what to do), and the new organizational values (why you are supposed to behave in certain ways).
A vast research literature exists on the learning of roles, the
impact of roles on behavior, and so on. Probably the best source on
learning a *new* role upon organizational entry is the accumulated
work of George Graen and his colleagues (Graen, 1976). In these

studies, the authors followed newcomers and their specific inter-
actions with their immediate supervisors. They show how bosses
can typecast newcomers into certain roles such as "winner," "loser,"
or "good citizen." Although this work omits peer pressure and
co-worker influences, it effectively documents the influence of the
boss in socialization.

The learning need not appear to be all "one way," where the
newcomer does all the changing in an atmosphere of strict conformity.
There can also be mutual influence between newcomers and the
organizations they enter. The "psychological contract" is the best
example of this. This term, first mentioned by Schein (1965), refers to
an "understanding" between newcomer and organization about what
each is expected to do for the other. Unlike legal contracts, psychological
contracts are not written on paper. In fact, there are a number of ways
in which the two types of contracts differ from each other (Rousseau,
1990), as shown in Table 7.2.

The *unique dynamic of conflict* is distinctive in setting
socialization apart from the other types of learning (e.g., skill
training) that newcomers acquire after entry. Despite efforts at
selection of "compatible" personnel and despite the effects of
self-selection, there will still be conflicts between newcomer expec-
tations/values and those of the organization. This is because
conflict is caused by the "interface" of people from different groups
(Brown, 1982): (a) hierarchical groups, e.g., the newcomer and the
boss, (b) functional and departmental groups, e.g., the newcomer
versus members from other areas of the organization, (c) "cultural"
groups, e.g., race, age, sex, and nationality differences between
newcomers and insiders, or among the newcomers themselves. A
newcomer is *simultaneously* a member of all three types of groups:
hierarchical, departmental, and cultural. In fact, a newcomer is
also simultaneously a representative of *all* the cultural groups
(Brown, 1983). The potential for conflict increases as the number
of differences between newcomers and insiders increases, which
is why organizations do try to select people who are similar to those
already inside (Schneider, 1987).

Stages of Socialization

This section traces the similarities among various forms of socialization as a series of *stages*. The concept of a *stage model* is quite
popular throughout the social and behavioral sciences. In economics

Table 7.2
*Differences Between a Psychological Contract
and a Typical Legal Contract*

Legal Contract		Psychological Contract
	Focus	
Economic, extrinsic		Economic and non-economic, socio-emotional, intrinsic
	Time Frame	
Close-ended, specific		Open-ended, indefinite
	Stability	
Static		Dynamic
	Scope	
Narrow		Pervasive
	Tangibility	
Public, observable		Subjective, understood

Source: *Adapted from D. M. Rousseau, 1990. New hire perceptions of their
own and their employer's obligations: A study of psychological contracts.* Journal
of Organizational Behavior, 11, p. 390.

there are models of how developing countries grow into "fully"
industrialized economies. In psychology there are stage models
that describe the growth of human personality. In vocational
psychology, career stages have been an important concern. The
stages through which organizations pass during "organizational
development" have been the concern of organizational psychologists. Thus it's hardly surprising that those interested in organizational socialization also view this process as proceeding
through several stages.

If it is to be useful in understanding a process as complicated as organizational socialization, a stage model must answer three crucial questions. The first, and most basic, is to define the stages composing the model. This is not as easy as it might seem since there are two basic ways to go about doing this: (a) stages may be based on the passage of time, or (b) stages may be based on the occurrence of certain events. These are not completely separate ways of defining stages, however. For example, in order for several events to have happened, some time must elapse. On the other hand, the mere passage of time does not guarantee that certain crucial events will have occurred. It is for this reason that *events* are chosen as the better way to define organizational socialization. The events composing each stage should be *homogeneous within* that stage. That is, they should have more in common with other events of a particular stage than with events in different stages.

A second question that a stage model should answer is how the stages are related to one another. Any sequence among stages should be spelled out, e.g., the *direction* of movement from stage to stage should be clear. The third, and final, question that must be addressed concerns what accounts for movement from one stage to another.

Before developing a single comprehensive model of the stages in socialization, four recent and well-known stage models are presented. Several themes are common to all four stage models. First, each is defined in terms of the individual's view during socialization, rather than that of the organization. This is consistent with the view that the direction of influence runs from the organization to the individual in the case of socialization, but it goes the other way in the personalizing process. Second, each of the models includes a preentry stage. This is briefly mentioned here, but it has been extensively covered earlier in this book. Third, the respective definitions of stages are rather broad and are defined somewhat differently across the four examples. Fourth, these stage models are primarily based on events that occur, rather than just on the passage of time.

Feldman's Three-stage Entry Model

Feldman (1976a, 1976b) proposed a three-stage model of organizational entry and socialization based on his analysis of the previously published research literature and on his study of newly hired hospital employees.

Stage 1: Anticipatory Socialization—"Getting In"
Two events occur in this stage. One is the degree to which the expectations of *both* individuals and organizations are realistic. The second concerns the degree to which the newcomer is well matched in *both* senses of the Matching Model. The more realistic the expectations and the higher the congruence between newcomer and organization, the easier the transition from outsider to insider will be.

Stage 2: Accommodation—"Breaking In"
Four events compose this postentry stage. The first is being initiated to the job. An individual's abilities to do a good job have a strong influence on the initial level of the newcomer's self-esteem. Second, the newcomer is typically initiated into a group of fellow employees and begins to establish new interpersonal relationships. The primary indicator of success here is how well the newcomer is accepted. Third, the full definition of the newcomer's role in the organization begins to unfold. For example, the degree to which newcomers can make effective use of their time, and the degree to which they can deviate from strict organizational policy are two examples of learning how things "really" work on the inside. The last event in this stage concerns the degree to which newcomers' self-evaluation of work performance is congruent with that of the organization. The first formal evaluation of job performance can easily be viewed as the termination of "breaking in."

Stage 3: Role Management—"Settling In"
The final stage is typified by the resolution of two conflicts that inevitably crop up. The first is how work in the new organization fits in with the newcomer's life interests outside of work. The second is how the newcomer resolves all the varieties of conflict at the work place itself.

Buchanan's Three-stage Early Career Model

Buchanan (1974) studied new managers from five governmental agencies and three large manufacturing concerns. His objective in this research was to study the level of a person's *commitment* to a new organization as influenced by early socialization experiences. This stage model differs from Feldman's in the sense that it is concerned only with postentry events and because it covers a much longer span of a person's early work career.

Stage 1: First year—Basic Training and Initiation
The first year on the job is characterized by a focus on the newcomer's security and existence needs. The first event is the establishment of *role clarity* by the newcomer. It is similar to Feldman's Stage 1. The second is the establishment of *cohesion* within the newcomer's peer group—an event similar to Feldman's view that newcomers must be accepted by their own work group. Third is the *relationship of the newcomer's immediate peer group to the rest of the organization,* that is, the extent to which it is in harmony or conflict with other parts of the organization. Fourth, Buchanan discusses the degree to which *expectations are realized* and the possibility of reality shock when they are not. Fifth, the degree to which the new job provides a *challenge* to the employee was found to be crucial for new AT&T managers (Berlew & Hall, 1966) and is included by Buchanan as well. Finally, he goes so far as to include *loyalty conflicts,* both within the organization and between the organization and outside interests. In contrast, Feldman had put the resolution of these conflicts in a later stage.

Stage 2: Performance—Years Two, Three, and Four at Work
Buchanan's second career stage concerns the achievement or growth needs of newcomers. There are four events that define this particular stage. First, the degree to which the newcomer feels *personally important* is crucial for long-run commitment to the new organization. Closely related to this is a second factor—the extent to which the new organization *reinforces the newcomer's self-image.* Third, the newcomer must *resolve the internal conflict* between needs for achievement and the fear of failure. Finally, at this stage, newcomers are *sensitive to organizational norms* regarding commitment and loyalty. The issue of the newcomer's future internal mobility may rest on the degree to which the newcomer can adopt the desired degree of loyalty.

Stage 3: Organizational Dependability—The Fifth Year and Beyond
Buchanan chose to lump all succeeding years into this stage since he believes that later events are much harder to predict than earlier ones. In essence, Stages 1 and 2 contain events that

are common for most newcomers. By Stage 3, however, quite a lot of diversity occurs that makes it much harder to identify any particular set of experiences as typical for this group of insiders.

Porter-Lawler-Hackman Three-stage Entry Model

Porter, Lawler, and Hackman (1975) base their stage model on review of research conducted by others in contrast to the first two stage models that grew out of a research study conducted by each author.

Stage 1: Prearrival

The major event of this stage concerns the newcomer's personal values (or desires) and expectations. The degree to which these are subsequently matched to reality (in the next stage) is considered a crucial event. The second event of this stage is the degree to which the newcomer was actively recruited by the organization, compared with those who worked very hard to convince the organization that they should be hired.

Stage 2: Encounter

At the point of entry into the new organization, the emergence of discrepancies begins between (a) expectations and reality and (b) values (human needs /specific job wants) and reality. The authors point out that the organization responds to the newcomer in three ways: reinforcement, nonreinforcement, and punishment. These three reactions can be intentional or completely unplanned. Reinforcement is provided to those facets of the newcomer that are confirmed and valued by the new organization. Nonreinforcement is shown by ignoring certain characteristics of the newcomer. Finally, punishment is meted out to the newcomer who engages in behaviors that the organization actively discourages, such as joining a union. (See Nissen, 1978, for an account.)

Stage 3: Change and Acquisition

Borrowing from Caplow (1964), the authors list four areas of change for newcomers. First, the newcomer's *self-image* is altered. This depends on the newcomer's age and previous work experience. The younger and less experienced someone is, the greater the change in self-image during socialization.

Second, *new relationships* are formed. Third, *new values* are adopted. Fourth, *new behaviors* are acquired.

Schein's Three-stage Socialization Model

In a book on careers, Schein (1978) develops a three-stage model of entry–socialization–mutual acceptance to describe the sequence of events that confronts the typical newcomer to an organization. The second two stages are relevant for this discussion of postentry experiences. Schein's view of these events is particularly appealing for two reasons. First, he has adopted the distinction between individual and organizational perspectives used throughout this book. Second, he goes into greater detail than some others in describing the flow of events from both these viewpoints.

Stage 1: Entry
Schein identifies four "problems" that confront both the individual and the organization during this stage. The first is *"obtaining accurate information in a climate of mutual selling"* (1978, p. 85). Chapter 2 contained a detailed discussion of the four conflicts that occur during "traditional" recruitment and selection practices (see Fig 2.1). Second, there is a mutual problem of creating false expectations about the early part of the newcomer's career in the organization. Both parties tend to focus on long-term matches, but they may overlook the fact that the responsibilities encountered in early months or years may be quite different from later job responsibilities. Third, recruitment practices often build incorrect images of the organization, as discussed and documented at length in Chapters 2 and 3. Fourth, the organizational choices made by job candidates cannot be optimal when they are based on biased or deficient information, as discussed in Chapter 4.

Stage 2: Socialization
During the postentry period, both the individual and the organization face difficult issues. From the individual's viewpoint, five "tasks" (to use Schein's term) must be tackled. First, the newcomer must accept the reality of the human organization. The managers Schein studied often underestimated the difficulties of learning to work with others. Second, newcomers must learn how to deal with resistance to change, i.e., good ideas are *not* always accepted.

Third, newcomers must learn "how to work" in their particular job. This may mean coping with either too much or too little organizational structure, and too much or too little job definition. Fourth, the difficult tasks of learning to work with one's own boss and comprehending the "real" working of the organizational reward system also confront the newcomer. Two key issues with respect to the newcomer's boss concern the degree of trust/mistrust, and independence/dependence. The final task is for the newcomer to locate his or her "place" in the organization and to develop an identity around it.

From the organization's viewpoint, three basic issues underlie the assessment of the newcomer. First, will this person fit into the organization, i.e., will there be a congruence between the needs and personality of the newcomer and the present climates of the organization? Second, will the newcomer be able to be an innovative contributor to the organization? Finally, will the newcomer be able to learn and grow throughout a career in this particular organization?

Stage 3: Mutual Acceptance

This is the major transition from newcomer to insider. Schein has done a fine job of describing the "signals" that individuals and organizations send to each other to communicate mutual acceptance. Organizations send six types of signals to newcomers indicating acceptance (a) a positive performance appraisal, (b) a salary increase, (c) a new job assignment, (d) organizational secrets are shared, e.g., how things "really" work, what "really" happened in the past, and how others evaluate the new person, (e) initiation rites confirm the passage to a new status, e.g., a party or the granting of a special privilege, and (f) actual promotion. This last one is often the only one that some employees trust, yet this is surely not the only way organizations signal acceptance.

Newcomers also send signals that indicate they accept the new organization. The most obvious of these is not quitting. However, the mere fact that a newcomer elects to remain does not necessarily mean he or she has accepted the organization or feels any commitment to it. A second category of signals includes all the indications that the newcomer is highly motivated, for example, working long hours, doing extra tasks, and being enthusiastic about work. Since some newcomers may be highly involved with their *work* (and not with the organization), this high work motivation may sometimes be misread as commitment to the organization. The organization must try to distinguish between loyalties felt toward the work itself and those felt toward the organization. The last category includes the acceptance of doing undesirable work, tolerating delays, and putting up with organizational "red tape." The most common case is for the newcomer to accept a temporary starting position with little challenge and responsibility in order to attain a much different job after "paying one's dues."

An Integrative Approach to Stages of Socialization

Table 7.3 combines all four of these models into a single, integrated view of postentry organizational socialization. The first three stages refer to the socialization process proper, and the final stage exemplifies the transition from newcomer to insider. It would be wise at this point to study the events of each stage since this comprehensive model will be used to interpret the events of several case studies from rather diverse organizations at the conclusion of this chapter.

The stage models just described can be directly compared to each other in terms of how much they overlap. Remember, two of the stage models (Feldman, 1976a, b; Porter et al., 1975) have *preentry* stages, and one model (Buchanan, 1974) has a late career stage. Table 7.4 was developed as a way to make these comparisons.

The accumulated research on stage models of socialization has been previously reviewed twice (Fisher, 1986; Wanous & Colella, 1989). The type of research that is relevant for the validity of these stages varies between the reviews. The first review (Fisher, 1986) included research that pertained to a single stage, but not the links among them. The second review (Wanous & Colella, 1989) included only research that attempted to examine *all* the stages together because these were the only types of studies that could assess the sequencing of stages.

The research done to date suggests there may be stages of socialization, but that they do not necessarily unfold in a "lockstep" fashion as implied by the models' originators. Furthermore, organizational differences may be greater than the authors of the

Table 7.3
Stages in the Socialization Process

Stage 1: Confronting and accepting organizational reality

    a) Confirmation/disconfirmation of expectations
    b) Conflicts between personal job wants and the organizational climates
    c) Discovering which personal aspects are reinforced, which are not reinforced, and which are punished by the organization.

Stage 2: Achieving role clarity

    a) Being initiated to the tasks in the new job
    b) Defining one's interpersonal roles
       i) with respect to peers
      ii) with respect to one's boss
    c) Learning to cope with resistance to change
    d) Congruence between a newcomer's own evaluation of performance and the organization's evaluation of performance
    e) Learning how to work within the given degree of structure and ambiguity.

Stage 3: Locating oneself in the organizational context

    a) Learning which modes of behavior are congruent with those of the organization
    b) Resolution of conflicts at work, and between outside interests and work
    c) Commitment to work and to the organization stimulated by first-year job challenge
    d) The establishment of an altered self-image, new interpersonal relationships, and the adoption of new values.

Stage 4: Detecting signposts of successful socialization

    a) Achievement of organizational dependability and commitment
    b) High satisfaction in general
    c) Feelings of mutual acceptance
    d) Job involvement and internal work motivation
    e) The sending of "signals" between newcomers and the organization to indicate mutual acceptance.

stages anticipated, such that there are important differences between, say, military recruits in basic training and MBA students at Harvard. (See the last section of this chapter).

From the point of view of the organization coping with an influx of newcomers, the important learning from looking at these stage models is to keep track of the important events that newcomers will face. Even if research has yet to establish the *precise sequence* of events, it is probably correct to consider the issues raised by the stage models to be relevant for most newcomers at some point early on in their careers with an organization.

The third and final question a stage model must answer is what determines how fast a person moves through the stages. This question is, however, *not* answered by any of the models shown in Table 7.4. The answer to this important question depends basically on how much newcomers *and* insiders take the initiative to interact with each other (Reichers, 1987). As was seen earlier in the overall model of socialization (Fig. 7.4), the learning of new roles, norms, and values is done *interpersonally*. The more that both insiders and newcomers "proact," rather than react, to each other, the faster socialization will occur. The faster a newcomer "moves through the stages" of socialization, the faster the newcomer will fit into the new organization (Reichers, 1987).

The next question is to determine what factors will likely increase the *rate* of socialization. Figure 7.5 summarizes these factors. The figure shows three groups of factors that cause a high degree of interaction frequency between insiders and newcomers: (a) newcomer characteristics, (b) insider characteristics, and (c) situational factors. Reichers (1987) described the three characteristics that insiders and newcomers need to have for increased interaction frequency. First, "field dependence" means that the individuals depend on information *external* to themselves. People rely on various cues and messages from other people and the physical environment in order to understand—or "make sense of" (Louis, 1980)—the new situation. Second, people who *cannot* tolerate a fairly high degree of ambiguity in a situation are more likely to jump to premature conclusions about the new situation as a way to reduce their own anxiety. The premature conclusions— even though likely to be incorrect—comfort these people because they now believe that they "know what's going on." Third, people who have a great need for affiliation with other people (or high

Table 7.4
Stages of Organizational Socialization

Feldman's (1976a, 1976b) Three-Stage Entry Model	Buchanan's (1974) Three-Stage Early Career Model	Porter, Lawler & Hackman's (1975) Three-Stage Entry Model	Schein's (1978) Three-Stage Socialization Model	Wanous's (1980) Integrative Approach to Stages of Socialization
Stage1: Anticipatory socialization—"getting in" Setting of realistic expectations Determining match with the newcomer		Stage 1: Pre-arrival Setting of newcomer expectations Reward and punishment of behaviors		
Stage 2: Accommodation—"breaking in" Initiation into the job Establish interpersonal relationships Roles clarified Congruence between self and organizational performance appraisal	Stage 1: First year—basic training and initiation Establish role clarity for newcomer Establish cohesion with peers Clarify relationship of peers with rest of organization Confirmation/disconfirmation of expectations Loyalty, conflicts with organizational and outside interests	Stage 2: Encounter Confirmation/disconfirmation of expectations Reward and punishment of behaviors	Stage 1: Entry Search for accurate information Creation of false expectations by both parties Inaccurate information is basis for job choice	Stage1: Confronting and accepting organizational reality Confirmation/disconfirmation of expectations Conflicts between personal values and organizational climates Discovering rewarded/ punished behaviors
Stage 3: Role management "settling in" The degree of fit between one's life interests outside of work and the demands of the organization. Resolution of conflicts at the work place itself	Stage 2: Performance—years two, three, and four at work Commitment to organization according to norms Reinforcement of self-image by organization Resolution of conflicts Feelings of personal importance	Stage 3: Change and acquisition Alteration of newcomer's self-image Form new relationships Adopt new values Acquire new behaviors	Stage 2: Socialization Accept organizational reality Cope with resistance to change Congruence between organizational climate and person's needs Organization's evaluation of newcomer's performance Cope with either too much ambiguity or too much structure	Stage 2: Achieving role clarity Initiation to the job's tasks Definition of interpersonal roles Coping with resistance to change Congruence between self and organizational performance appraisals Coping with structure and ambiguity

Table 7.4 Continued
Stages of Organizational Socialization

Feldman's (1976a, 1976b) Three-Stage Entry Model	Buchanan's (1974) Three-Stage Early Career Model	Porter, Lawler & Hackman's (1975) Three-Stage Entry Model	Schein's (1978) Three-Stage Socialization Model	Wanous's (1980) Integrative Approach to Stages of Socialization
				Stage 3: Locating oneself in the organizational context Learning behaviors congruent with the organization's desires Outside and work interest conflicts resolved Job challenge leads to work commitments New interpersonal relations, new values, and altered self-image
			Stage 3: Mutual acceptance Signals of organizational acceptance Signals of newcomer's acceptance Commitment to the organization Commitment to work	Stage 4: Detecting signposts of successful socialization Company dependability and commitment High general satisfaction Feelings of mutual acceptance Job involvement and intrinsic motivation increases
	Stage 3: Organizational dependability— the fifth year and beyond All succeeding years are in this stage Diversity due to individual experiences			

Source: J. P. Wanous, A. E. Reichers & S. D. Malik, 1984. Organizational socialization and group development: Toward an integrative perspective. Academy of Management Review, 9, *p. 672. Reprinted by permission of the Academy of Management Association.*

relatedness needs—see Chapter 1) are the type who will seek out others. When both newcomers and insiders have these profiles, a very high degree of interaction is likely to occur, which facilitates rapid socialization.

Figure 7.5
Determining the Rate of Newcomer Socialization

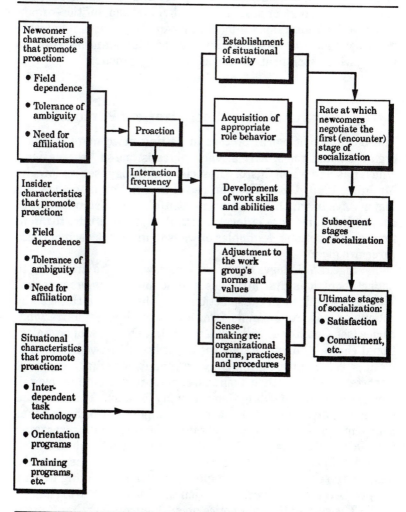

Source: A. E. Reichers, 1987. An interactionist perspective on newcomer socialization rates. Academy of Management Review, 12, *p. 284. Reprinted by permission of the Academy of Management Association.*

Besides these characteristics of insiders and newcomers, several factors in the "situation" can also increase interaction frequency. First, the more that work task design and technology forces people to interact, the more likely it is that they will be forced to talk to one another. Thus projects requiring team efforts hasten socialization. Second, orientation programs (see Chapter 6) also increase interaction. Third, training programs that are primarily aimed at improving the individual capabilities–organizational job requirements match-up can also create an environment conducive to interaction between insiders and newcomers during which socialization can occur as a by-product.

The Psychology of Socialization: Persuasion

The basic psychological process in getting newcomers to adopt organizational roles, norms, and values is one of "persuasion," which has had a long history in social psychology (see reviews by McGuire, 1969, 1985). The purpose of this section is to show the major ways in which a newcomer's attitudes and behavior can be changed. A framework is developed that relates attitudes to intentions and to actions. Examples of ways to influence each of these three are given.

Figure 7.6 shows the overall framework. The first thing to notice about it is that attitudes and actions are *interconnected*. That is, attitudes can cause actions, but they can be changed by actions as well. An example from the research on organizational choice (see Chapter 4) will make this point. One view of organizational choice (the expectancy theory position) showed how individuals' beliefs about a company and the factors that were most important to them (their feelings) *combined* to create an overall motivational force leading them to apply for a job. This is a good example of attitudes causing actions. Chapter 4 also showed that the "unprogrammed" view of organizational choice incorporated the effects of choosing an organization on an individual's later attitudes. Specifically, after a person had made a choice, commitment to the choice was even higher than prior to making it. This is a good example of a person's action causing attitudes to change.

The second thing to notice about Figure 7.6 is that "intentions" lie between attitudes and actions. Many years of research on the most immediate causes of a person's actions has concluded

Figure 7.6
Persuasion Strategies

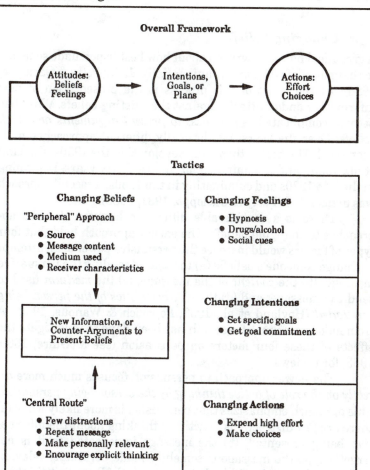

Overall Framework

Tactics

Changing Beliefs

"Peripheral" Approach

- Source
- Message content
- Medium used
- Receiver characteristics

New Information, or
Counter-Arguments to
Present Beliefs

"Central Route"

- Few distractions
- Repeat message
- Make personally relevant
- Encourage explicit thinking

Changing Feelings

- Hypnosis
- Drugs/alcohol
- Social cues

Changing Intentions

- Set specific goals
- Get goal commitment

Changing Actions

- Expend high effort
- Make choices

that specific goals, plans, or intentions are the best way to know what someone is about to do (Locke & Latham, 1990).

The third thing to notice about Figure 7.6 is that persuasion can be targeted at any—or all three—of the attitude-intention-action components of the framework. Methods for persuasion will be briefly described here.

Changing Beliefs

A great deal has been written about how best to persuade someone to change beliefs (Hovland, Janis & Kelly, 1953; Petty & Cacioppo, 1986). At the heart of this process is the presentation of new information and/or attacks against the existing beliefs. What has become complicated is *how best to present arguments or attack beliefs*. Over the years, two basically different approaches have been tried. The first of these was developed in the 1950s (Hovland et al., 1953), and it dominated for almost thirty years. Beginning in the late 1970s and culminating in the 1980s, a second approach was articulated (Petty & Cacioppo, 1981, 1986).

There is a considerable difference between the two approaches to changing beliefs. The earlier approach held that four types of factors would increase the persuasive power of an attempt to change someone's beliefs: (a) the *source* sending the persuasive message, (b) the *content* of the message, (c) the *medium* used to send the message, and (d) the *characteristics of the person being persuaded* (Hovland et al., 1953; Popovich & Wanous, 1982). A tremendous amount of research has been done to investigate the effects of these four factors on persuasion (see McGuire, 1969, 1985, for reviews).

The newer approach to persuasion focuses much more *directly on the role of active thinking by the person being persuaded*. This approach emphasizes that persuasion is more likely when (a) there are few distractions to actively thinking about the information being presented, (b) the message is repeated so it is not forgotten, (c) the message is somehow made personally relevant to the receiver so it will be listened to, and (d) explicit thinking about the information is encouraged (Petty & Cacioppo, 1986). The originators of the newer approach call it the "central route to persuasion," whereas the earlier approach is the "peripheral route." Both routes can get results, and the peripheral route can be successful when the targets of persuasion are either not *capable* of explicit thinking or they are not *motivated* to do so. However, the authors of the central route method argue convincingly that their method produces stronger and more predictable results.

Changing Feelings

A less frequently tried tactic is to try to change a person's feelings *directly*. Of the three examples shown in Figure 7.6, only one example—social cues—can be applied to organizational socialization. The use of hypnosis to change a person's feelings is more commonly seen in attempts to modify bad habits like smoking and drinking/eating too much. I know of no attempts to use it in socialization! The use of drugs or alcohol to change a person's feelings generally results in a short-term mood change. The "glow" of a cocktail party for newcomers may indeed provide them with "warm fuzzy feelings" about the organization during the party and for a period of time afterwards, but I would not recommend this strategy to make the more permanent types of changes implied by socialization.

As a result, the use of social cues to directly change feelings about the organization may be the only viable tactic in this group. Newcomers learn from observing the behavior of others (Bandura, 1977). So, if what they observe is outwardly happy, enthusiastic, energetic insiders, their own feelings will probably be similarly affected. The most obvious example of this is what most readers have probably felt when going to a sporting event like a college football or basketball game where everyone is rooting for the home team. The experience is quite different from watching the same game at home alone on television. The difference is one of feelings, not beliefs, and the feelings are "modeled" by observing the other fans' enthusiasm.

Changing Intentions

The last twenty or so years have seen a tremendous increase in the attention paid to goal setting as a motivational technique (see Locke, 1968; Locke & Latham, 1990). The setting of *specific* goals rather than general (sometimes called "do your best") goals has been shown repeatedly to increase performance. The more committed people are to goals, the more likely they are to achieve them. Thus the key is getting goal commitment. Several things have been tried: (a) using participation to increase commitment, (b) using monetary incentives, (c) having individuals make a public (versus private) commitment to goals, and (d) using role models (see Locke & Latham, 1990).

An unanticipated finding also seems to be that *assigned* goals have almost the same effect on performance as do participatively set goals. Although at first this may seem unusual, the success of assigned goals has been explained as follows (Locke & Latham, 1990). First, assigned goals typically come from the boss, who has the legitimate authority to make such requests. Second, the simple act of assigning a goal to a subordinate also communicates that the boss has confidence in the person to succeed, which increases self-confidence. Third, challenging goals may trigger a person's need for achievement.

Changing Actions Directly

Two basic tactics can be used to change a newcomer's behavior directly, with the consequence that attitudes will change as a result of the change in behavior. When this happens, the attitudes and the behavior tend to reinforce each other. The first tactic is to do anything that will increase the *amount of effort expended*. One of the best examples of this tactic is used by the Harvard Business School and will be described at the end of this chapter. The principle of effort expenditure leading to greater attraction to or commitment to an organization is well grounded in psychology (Festinger, 1957; Lewis, 1965). People need a reason to *justify* the effort expenditure to themselves (Aronson, 1972). The easiest way to do this is to believe that the effort was "worth it." The U.S. Marine Corps has the longest period of basic training (12 weeks versus 8 weeks for the Army and Navy and 6 weeks for the Air Force). It is not surprising that the Marines have been considered to have the highest level of commitment among the various armed forces.

The second basic tactic is to have people make choices. As with effort expenditure, the act of making a choice also means that people must somehow *justify* that choice to themselves. The best example of this principle that most readers are familiar with is buying a car. Automobile salespersonnel are particularly adept at getting customers to make choices right there in the showroom. Some of the typical choices you might have been asked to make are: accepting printed material about the car, filling out an information sheet about yourself, spending some time listening to a sales pitch, choosing to go on a test drive, and choosing to stay in the dealership and "haggle price" even though it looks like they won't budge. Some salespersonnel even try to get customers to make a monetary deposit before they even discuss an offer "with the boss." The list can go on. The point is that each of these is a *choice*—you are always free to simply walk out and go to another dealer.

Combining Tactics: "Organizational Seduction"

Some readers might have considered the tactics just described to be fairly "transparent" attempts to persuade/influence newcomers to adopt organizational norms and values. A "combination" approach has been described that is far more subtle (Lewicki, 1981). The reason for this subtlety is that one danger in getting newcomers to expend a lot of energy is that they will feel the organization "owes" them something in return (Adams, 1965). At the cornerstone of the "seduction" process is getting newcomers to make choices, but the seduction process is not limited to this tactic.

Lewicki (1981) suggests that organizations can induce newcomers to expend effort and make certain choices with two forms of "payoffs": (a) the conferring of status, and (b) the giving of "plentiful hygiene factors." The mere gaining of these payoffs also has the effect of creating a feeling of *obligation* on the part of newcomers, which can lead to even more effort expenditure, and so on.

Organizations achieve high status themselves in a variety of ways. They can be market leaders in a particular segment of the economy. They can employ high-status members, whose status "rubs off" onto the rest of the organization. They can make entry difficult. They can give rewards that are unique to themselves and not available elsewhere. Finally, they can live off past status.

The conferring of status can be done in a wide variety of ways. Some organizations confer status on newcomers immediately upon their entry in the form of a "one of the chosen few" message. Even if the organization sends such a message to the newcomer, the message does not necessarily mean that this person is a fully accepted insider. There may still be a well-defined internal status hierarchy, and the newcomer ("one of a chosen few") is still at the bottom. For example, some Ivy League colleges are rather adept at simultaneously sending these (apparently conflicting) messages to college entrants. On the one hand, there is the message of elitism ("you are one of the chosen few"), but on the other hand, there is the message that you still may be unworthy. This is a form of guilt arousal. That is, the organization communicates to the newcomer that it has taken some risk in admitting him or her and wants the newcomer to know it. The organization then uses the newcomer's resulting gratitude as the basis for future commitment.

A second type of payoff for effort expenditure is what Lewicki (1981) calls the supply of PLUSH—a *Pl*entiful *U*nlimited *S*upply of *H*ygienes. (Hygiene factors (Herzberg, 1968) refer to things such as salary, working conditions, status, security, supervision, peer relationships, and company policies. They are all those factors other than the actual task or work itself.) Examples of "PLUSHness" abound: (1) generous photocopying, telephone, and expense budgets, (2) good secretarial service, (3) free recreational facilities or tickets to events, (4) convenient parking facilities, (5) "flexibility" in using office staff and equipment to conduct personal business (Lewicki, 1981). All of these, plus the normal fringe benefits, are what has been called *system rewards* (Katz & Kahn, 1978) because they are designed to reward *membership in the system* rather than job performance per se. These PLUSH (system) rewards do not directly build internal commitment to the organization because the newcomer can always justify the decision to remain employed in terms of the PLUSHness of the environment. They do, however, create feelings of *obligation* that can be used to initiate a more subtle form of internal commitment.

By feeling a sense of obligation, newcomers are in a position in which they may be *seduced* by the organization (Lewicki, 1981). The seduction process has several elements.

- The individual is induced to make "tempting choices," i.e., there appear to be at least two alternatives, but one of them is clearly more positive than the others. For example, a professor may be given a "choice" either to work on internal affairs of the university (teaching and committees), or to work on external affairs (research or travel).

- Enticement, not force, is used to influence newcomers. That is, promises and opportunities are used rather than threats or punishments.

- The intention of the seducer is not only to entice the person to do something but often to draw the individual away from "principles" as well. It is often an attempt to change the newcomer's values as well as the newcomer's behavior, i.e., it is aimed at building commitment, not just getting compliance.

- The "appearance of a choice" is crucial to the process. Even though the individual may be subject to much inducement (e.g., promises or flattery), the person is always "theoretically free" to say *no*. The significance of this is that the important *internal* changes in a person's beliefs and values occur *after* decisions are made. This is called *postdecisional justification*, i.e., individuals need to *feel* rational and will alter their beliefs to conform to their behavior.

The seduction process (Lewicki, 1981) is one of getting newcomers to make "decisions" such as were just outlined. The building of internal commitment is the *consequence* of these decisions because newcomers justify their choices in terms of their commitment to the organization.

Socialization Tactics

The psychology of persuasion discussed in the previous section is very basic and can be applied to a wide variety of situations—from advertising to politics to parenting. In the unique context of organizational socialization, a set of six "tactical dimensions" has been developed (Van Maanen & Schein, 1979) and refined (Jones, 1986). These six factors, shown in Table 7.5, are ways to categorize various types of socialization experiences that newcomers may face.

The tactical dimensions differ in the types of effects they are likely to have on newcomers. Those on the "institutionalized" end of the spectrum tend to produce newcomers who strictly conform to all organizational norms and values. Those on the "individualized" end tend to produce newcomers who are like the "creative individualists" previously discussed (see Fig. 7.1). In some cases of extreme individualized socialization, "rebels" may be produced as well. It is not easy to predict who will be the creative individualist and who will be the rebel from a socialization program that exemplifies the individualized end of the tactical spectrum.

The first two tactical dimensions concerns the particular context in which socialization takes place. Collective versus individual socialization refers to whether newcomers are socialized in a group or by themselves. (See the earlier discussion on socialization and group development, in particular Fig. 7.3). The formal

Table 7.5
A Classification of Socialization Tactics

Tactics concerned mainly with:	Institutionalized	Individualized
Context	(1) Collective	Individual
	(2) Formal	Informal
Content	(3) Sequential	Random
	(4) Fixed	Variable
Social Aspects	(5) Serial	Disjunctive
	(6) Investiture	Divestiture

Source: G. R. Jones, 1986. Socialization tactics, self efficacy, and newcomers' adjustments to organizations. Academy of Management Journal, 29, *p. 263. Reprinted by permission of the Academy of Management Association.*

versus informal dimension refers to whether the socialization program is an explicit program designed to change newcomers or whether it occurs via interpersonal relationships that are not part of any specific, planned program.

The second two tactical dimensions concern the content of socialization. Sequential versus random socialization refers to whether or not there is any particular pattern to the events of socialization. When events take place in the same order for all newcomers, the process is sequential. If the newcomers' experiences vary greatly, the socialization is random. Fixed versus variable socialization refers to the time element in socialization. When events take place in the same timeframe for all newcomers (like basic training for all military recruits), there is a fixed timeframe. When events unfold in varying amounts of time, as when mental patients are judged to be normal enough to return home, the socialization is variable.

Finally, the third group of tactical dimensions concerns the social aspects of socialization. Serial versus disjunctive socialization refers to the degree of similarity between those who do the socializing and the position the newcomer is to assume later on. When those who do the socializing are basically the same—older professors socializing a new faculty member right out of graduate school—the process is serial, and the mentors serve as role models for the newcomer. When a college graduate from an all women's college goes to graduate school in engineering (virtually all male), the process is extremely disjunctive. A person's college mentors and situation are quite different from that person's subsequent experiences. Investiture versus divestiture socialization refers to how much the socialization process reinforces the newcomer's basic identity (investiture) versus trying to destroy the incoming identity and replace it with a "new identity" considered appropriate for the organization (divestiture).

Since these six tactical dimensions were proposed, only a few research studies (Allen & Meyer, 1990; Jones, 1986; West, Nicholson & Rees, 1987) have attempted to assess their likely effects on newcomers. The first study to assess the effects of these tactics (Jones, 1986) was a study of 102 MBA graduates who were surveyed twice: after graduation and after 5 months on their first jobs. The results of this study support the effects of the six tactical dimensions on newcomers' responses to their jobs. The second study (Allen & Meyer, 1990) was of 105 undergraduate and MBA students taking their first jobs. Surveys were taken after 6 and 12 months on the job. Once again the effects of six tactics shown in Table 7.5 were supported.

A third study of "resocialization" has some relevance here (West, Nicholson & Rees, 1987). This research followed job changers, not newcomers, who moved into newly created jobs, as compared to those who began new jobs that had had an incumbent. The authors of this study assumed that those entering a newly created job experienced a "random, informal, disjunctive, and variable" socialization experience. As would be predicted by Table 7.5, these personnel were judged to be more "innovative" than those who entered new jobs with previous incumbents.

The relative absence of research on the tactical dimensions is easy to understand because such research requires data from newcomers in a very wide variety of organizations. This is important because the tactical dimensions tend to be the same *within* a particular organization. Thus, to assess the impact of the six dimensions requires the researcher to get data from organizations that differ on the dimensions. The problem for the researcher is further complicated in that the six tactical dimensions will occur in different combinations. When this occurs, it is difficult to say *which* of the six factors cause the tendency toward institutionalizing as opposed to individualizing. To ideally test each tactical dimension, it would be necessary to obtain information about newcomers in two organizations that were similar on five of the six dimensions, but differed markedly on the sixth. In this way, the effects of the five dimensions in common would be "controlled." Any resulting differences would be most likely a result of the sixth dimension on which the two organizations differed. This would have to be repeated for each of the six dimensions. To find such organizations and to conduct the necessary research would be very difficult, to say the least.

It is probably not wise to try statistical "short cuts" in assessing the influence of the various tactical dimensions, as has been tried (see Allen & Meyer, 1990). These authors used multiple regression to see the effects of individual tactical dimensions. The problem with doing this is that since the study was of only 105 individuals, the actual number of people representing any particular tactical dimension was quite small. For such statistical approaches to be useful, the researcher would need a much larger sample of newcomers and one that was fairly evenly balanced to represent both ends of all six tactical dimensions. Even if this were to be accomplished, the survey method of having newcomers report their experiences may not be the best way to measure the various tactical dimensions. Without actually going into the organizations themselves, the researcher depends too heavily on the accuracy of the newcomers' recollections of their experiences.

On balance, the six tactical dimensions seem to operate as expected. Even though the research is just beginning to accumulate, that which has been done thus far is supportive. None of the research is so precise, however, that it can guide organizational action in such a way as to produce creative individualists without risking too many rebels.

Examples of Organizational Socialization

Socialization of Students

Accounts of MBA student socialization are available for the Harvard (Cohen, 1973) and M.I.T. (Schein, 1967) graduate schools of business administration. Cohen's (1973) *Gospel According to the Harvard Business School* was a best-seller. In between anecdotal accounts of various classmates, Cohen gives an excellent first-hand description of organizational life for the MBA student at the HBS. The first year at the HBS is quite highly regimented, in contrast to the first year at other schools. It is a "lockstep" program in which all first-year students take the same courses in the same sequence.

Prior to their arrival in the fall, incoming students are sent a package of course reading material. Upon arrival, they discover that the first examination will be Saturday morning at the end of the *first* week.

There are other examples of HBS's attempt to design "up-ending experiences" for this highly select group (776 were admitted from more than 3000 who applied). For example, the opening ceremony for Cohen's class was held in an old gymnasium under rather primitive and crowded conditions. Each newcomer is sent a "suggested" list of materials to purchase for written classwork. The newcomer is assigned to a "section" (Cohen's had 94 students), which takes all classes together for the entire first year. Whatever feelings of elitism that may have existed on arrival in Boston tend to evaporate with this kind of treatment. Completing these "entry shock" experiences is an incredibly tight schedule, which includes four and a half classroom hours per day, all five days a week (about double the typical amount). The students are assigned an average of three cases *a day* (100 or so pages) to be read, digested, understood, and analyzed for oral discussion the next day. Written analyses of cases (WACs) are typed, put in a special large envelope, and deposited in a box for pick-up. At the precise hour of the deadline, the box is sealed and all late papers must be stacked on top of it. Late papers get a full grade lower penalty.

For the newcomer these experiences encourage the formation of "study groups" to pool resources, with the blessing the HBS. As Cohen points out, the "illusion of belonging" is preferable to the "certainty of being on your own." Newcomers are constantly torn between feelings of competitiveness with their fellow students and the need to cooperate to survive the entry shock. As the year progresses, students increasingly know where they stand, and competition among them increases while cooperation decreases.

Newcomers learn to survive, as exemplified by picking up the "rules of the game" for "scoring points" in case discussions. Cohen describes four such strategies. First, *preventive attack* in which the student "lays out the case" for the class is desirable because one usually gets five to ten minutes of uninterrupted "air time." Second, *questioning of premises* is an attack on the original presenter. Third, the *single-point technique* is used by those who don't understand the case, or who are unprepared. It involves waiting for the correct moment when the student *does* have something to say. Fourth, *pseudo-participation* is similar to the single-point technique. One begins by making reference to the case at hand, but then quickly shifts to another point—one that is self-serving. Finally, newcomers quickly pick up the B-school jargon, e.g., "ball-park number," "to eyeball," "to massage data," "the real world," and "hobo problems" (Human Behavior in Organizations, HBO, or "hobo," is a first-year course.)

The degree to which the detached, analytic case study approach was adopted by these newcomers was sharply evident by midyear. When Cohen was a student, a young professor committed suicide at midyear. There was a strong feeling of guilt among students and faculty for contributing to the pressure he was under, but Cohen believes little true emotion was actually expressed. His analysis of this tragic incident is that many newcomers had already adopted the value system of the insiders, i.e., that the suicide was a "case" for detached study and analysis.

The transition from the first to the second year marks the change in status from newcomer to insider. The atmosphere during the second year is quite different. Classes are held on a higher floor, with a better view of Cambridge, the Charles River and the Boston skyline. The curriculum is mostly elective, rather than the required "common core" that all took in their first year. Participation in classroom case discussions is still important, but it is more voluntary than mandatory as it was during the first year. Insider status does not last too long, however, since the job interview process begins at midyear.

The HBS example illustrates practically all of the events listed in the comprehensive stage model of organizational socialization. (See Table 7.3.). Early events dramatically show the disconfirmation of expectations, e.g., newcomers felt "special" because they were admitted to an elite school, but the "messages" they received shattered this feeling. Movement well into Stage 3 (particularly event (d)—the adoption of new values) is exemplified by the reaction of many newcomers to the young professor's suicide as "a case for analysis." The second year at HBS is a good example of the school "sending signals" (Stage 4) to the students that they are now insiders. Being able to take elective courses ("mutual influence") is also a contributing factor to another event of Stage 4 socialization —"high satisfaction."

Schein's study (1967) of attitude changes at M.I.T. does not include a richly detailed description of how students were socialized, but it does provide systematic data about the outcomes of the socialization process. He had members from four different groups complete questionnaires before and after the completion of a year at M.I.T. One group was the faculty and the other three were students, i.e., "regular" masters' degree candidates, Sloan Fellows, and executives in the ten-week program. Sloan Fellows tended to be older than the regular students, had more experience, and were members of an intensive 12-month program, whereas the regular students went through two academic years of nine months each.

Schein grouped the attitude questions as follows: (1) government-business relations, (2) labor-management relations, (3) areas of corporate responsibility, (4) superior-subordinate relationships, (5) theory of how to organize and manage, (6) general cynicism-idealism about business, (7) cynicism-idealism about how to get ahead in business, (8) faith or confidence in workers, (9) attitudes toward individual versus group incentives and decisions, and (10) attitudes toward large versus small businesses.

The initial attitudes of the regular students were about midway between those of the executives and the faculty (executives and faculty differed widely on more than half of the ten areas). At the year's end, student attitudes, as a group, were closer to those of the faculty, however. The main reason for this shift was the *type* of faculty members these students were exposed to during their first year. At M.I.T., as in many business schools, the first-year curriculum is staffed by those professors from traditional academic disciplines such as economics, quantitative analysis, and psychology. In contrast, the second year has more courses from applied areas, e.g., business policy, production management, or marketing. Upon reanalysis of the data, it became clear that faculty from traditional disciplines differed most from the executives. Thus the shift in student attitudes can be attributed to faculty influence from those teaching in the first-year courses when the incoming students were open to influence.

Socializing Police Recruits

Van Maanen (1976b) relates a fascinating and detailed account of police socialization. His description is divided into four stages: (1) self-selection into police work, (2) introduction to the police organization, (3) encounter with actual police work, and (4) metamorphosis into a full-fledged "cop."

Excerpts from Van Maanen's account of this process are as follows:[1]

1. Self-selection: In the large cities, police work attracts local, family-oriented, blue-collar or middle-class white males with military experience. . . . A cultural stereotype exists about police work—high adventure, romance, contribution to society—and this stereotype is shared by virtually all who join a police force. They also enjoy the out of doors, nonroutine, and masculine (that is, "machismo") aspect of the work.

   The stretched-out screening process is a critical aspect of police socialization. From the time he fills out the application blank until he gets the telephone call of acceptance, a recruit passes through a series of events designed for one purpose: to impress him with being admitted into an "elite" organization. There is a written and physical examination, an oral board, a psychiatric interview, and a background investigation (in which an applicant's friends and relatives are questioned about the most delicate matters).

2. Introduction: Once the recruit has "made it," the department quickly and rudely informs him that he is now a "probie." During his trial period, he can be severed from membership at any time without warning, explanation, or appeal. . . . He stands in long lines waiting to receive his departmental issues (rulebook, badge, Smith and Wesson 38-caliber revolver, ticket book, chemical mace, rosewood nightstick). He spends several hundred dollars on uniforms in a designated department store. Even the swearing-in ceremony is carried out en masse, with the words of a civil servant barely audible above the din of a busy public building. . . .

   The recruit's first sustained contact with the police culture occurs at the Training Academy. . . . To be one minute late to class, to utter a careless word in formation,

---

1. J. Van Maanen, 1976b, Rookie cops and rookie managers. *Wharton Magazine* 1: 50–54. Reprinted by permission of *The Wharton Magazine*.

or to walk when he should run may earn him a "gig." And a "gig" costs an extra day of work. . . . . The training staff promotes solidarity through group rewards and group punishments, interclass competition, and by cajoling the newcomers—at every opportunity—to "show some unity." . . . Under the impact of "stress" training the recruit begins to change his high opinions of the department. He learns that the formal rules and regulations are applied inconsistently. . . .

3. Encounter: Following Academy training, a recruit is introduced to the realities and complexities of policing by a Field Training Officer (FTO), the first partner assigned to a rookie policeman. He is a veteran officer who has worked patrol for several years. . . . During the long hours on patrol with his FTO, the recruit is instructed about the "real nature" of police work. First he learns, by word and deed, about the (non) worth of his Academy preparation. . . . Indeed, the rookie discovers on his first tour of duty that he does not know how to handle an unruly drunk, how to spot a traffic violator, or even to negotiate his district's physical and social terrain. . . . At first, the squawk of the police radio transmits only meaningless static. The streets of his sector appear to be a maze through which only an expert could maneuver. So the rookie never makes a move without checking with his FTO.

4. Metamorphosis: As long as the recruit remains with his FTO, his socialization, both psychologically (his own identity) and sociologically (with other officers) will be incomplete. To end the stigma of "trainee" or "rookie," he must take on a patrol partnership with equal accountability. . . . There is an important irony at work. Recruits are attracted to the organization through the *unrealistic expectation* that the work is exciting and dramatic. But an experienced officer knows such times are few and far between. . . .

The patrolman must then sit back and wait and let his experiences accumulate. . . . Socialization always entails the conversion of fantasy to reality. For patrolmen, the reality involves a two-edged disenchantment. One edge is disenchantment with the general public, the familiar "cynical" cop: the other edge is disenchantment with the police system itself, the "abandoned" cop. Both develop rather quickly. . . . In most ways, the squad is a team whose members cooperate in order to project certain impressions. To the so-called law-abiding public, the squad wished to convey the message: "We can take care of everything." To potential adversaries—the "street" people—the message is "Watch your step because we can do whatever we want to you." To the department, the patrol team's message must be "All is going well, there are no problems."

The stage Van Maanen calls "introduction" roughly corresponds to Stage 1 (confronting or accepting organizational reality). His "encounter" stage is about the equivalent of Stage 2 (achieving role clarity). His "metamorphosis" stage is rather broad and appears to include most of the events that compose both Stages 3 (locating oneself in the organization context) and 4 (detecting signposts of successful socialization).

Socialization of AT&T Managers

The Management Progress Study at AT&T (Bray et al., 1974; Howard & Bray, 1988) contains a wealth of pertinent information about factors related to the job performance of newly hired managers. When the 274 men entered the various operating companies of AT&T, there was no uniform set of procedures concerning how they should be socialized. Sometimes the primary responsibility of overseeing the progress of the newcomer was assumed by the personnel department, at other times by the newcomer's own functional area boss, and at still other times by a training supervisor. The content of these early experiences ranged from interviews with insiders to formal sessions with experienced AT&T personnel and, finally, to on-the-job discussions with the newcomer's supervisor. There were some formal management-development courses, but the major means of socializing these new managers was via slow rotation through a variety of jobs in different functional areas of the company.

Their performance was evaluated every six months, but specific feedback to the manager was sporadic. The typical newcomer could expect to be paid about 15 percent more than his or her starting salary about 18 to 24 months after entry. (Inflation was minimal at that time.)

The major focus of this study was to understand what factors significantly affected the job performance of managers. The effect of *first-year* experiences on later job performance was specifically examined. The amount of *job challenge* in the *first* year was significantly related to later job performance and salary.

Job challenge was measured by two psychologists who evaluated the tape recordings of annual interviews conducted by supervisory personnel.[2] The higher the expectations the company had for the newcomer, the more challenging the job was assumed to be. These data also confirmed the fact that "hard" goals (but not impossible ones) do lead to higher job performance, a fact repeatedly found in research (Locke & Latham, 1990).

Thus the net effect of high job challenge in the newcomer's first year at work is to get him or her started in a "success cycle." Challenge in early organizational experiences seems to lead to the adoption of high work standards by newcomers, which in turn leads to high job performance itself. Early success at work, then, seems to lead to more challenging assignments, and the cycle repeats itself.

In fact, early job challenge at AT&T accounted for many of the (so-called) mistakes made in predicting job performance with the assessment center. One type of "error" was the *false positive,* i.e., those who were predicted to reach third-level management in eight years, but who did not. Of the 22 in this group, 14 were on jobs *without high* challenge. The high competence observed in the assessment center was never really given a chance to develop.

The second type of prediction "error" is the *false negative,* i.e., those who were predicted not to reach third-level management, but who actually did. Of the 20 in this group, 11 had high job challenge the first year. Despite their lower assessed abilities, these employees developed managerial competence through the opportunities afforded by high job challenge.

Considered in this context, the predictions made by the AT&T assessment center staff were even more accurate than might first appear since the assessors had no way of knowing what

---

2. Job challenge was a composite of four aspects of one's job environment: (1) the degree to which one's boss set a model for achievement, (2) the degree of job stimulation and challenge, (3) the degree of supervisory responsibilities, and (4) the degree to which one's job included unstructured assignments.

type of job environment each newcomer would enter. This is an excellent example of the interaction between selection and socialization. The issue of why organizations do *not* usually place newcomers on challenging jobs has been investigated. Schein (1964) wrote that the typical company stereotype of college graduate recruits is that (1) they are overambitious and have unrealistic expectations; (2) they are too theoretical, naive, and idealistic; (3) they are immature and inexperienced; (4) they are not risk takers; and (5) they don't understand the distinction between having a good idea and being able to persuade others of its merit. Moore (1974) found that people in superior positions have much longer estimates of the "learning time" for a job than do their subordinates in that particular job. Views such as these often prevent newcomers from being placed in positions of high challenge, until after a "break-in" period. The AT&T study shows, however, that *job challenge should begin immediately,* contrary to usual corporate practice.

Army Socialization: Basic Training

The eight-week period following induction into the army, basic training, is well known to those who have gone through it. Bourne (1967) has divided this socialization into four stages: environmental shock, engagement, period of attainment, and period of termination.

Stage 1, environmental shock, begins at the reception center, where almost everyone is a stranger. One of the biggest shocks is to find yourself *in* the organization for *24 hours a day.* This is particularly stressful to those who have not previously lived away from home. The maximum stress, as measured physiologically by blood and urine analyses, is at its peak on Day One. Bourne noted (1967, p. 189) that the levels reached on the first day are comparable to those found "in schizophrenic patients in incipient psychosis and exceed the levels reached in other supposedly stressful situations." Clearly, this is a lot of stress!

Two factors seem to increase the degree of stress on these newcomers. First, most of the expectations of the new recruits are *dis*confirmed upon arrival. Second, the administrative processing is very time consuming, boring, and ambiguous.

The typical recruit reacts with "dazed apathy." Recruits become very dependent and tend to cling to those in authority. Finally, relatively minor events tend to be overblown in their significance, e.g., the assignment to KP duty can be seen as a catastrophe to some.[3]

After the initial period of a few days at the reception center, the recruits enter Stage 2, engagement, by being assigned to a basic training company. The next eight weeks are spent in this group.

The socialization strategy here is to strip away the newcomer's "old" identity and substitute a new one in its place. This is accomplished by the ritual haircut and wearing of uniforms. There is very little privacy. During this initial period, anxiety levels drop for two reasons. First, this is what the recruits expected, i.e., they typically do not expect the reception center process to last so long. Second, the recruits are now much more active.

During the first four weeks of basic training, the level of anger and resentment rises slowly in the recruits. This is because they see themselves as receiving very little in return from the army for all their sacrifices. (This is a typical danger of the strategy to build commitment via high energy expenditure.) They still feel like outsiders to the army and they are constantly reminded that their own skills are of no value to the army. This anger is directed at many targets; it is hard to vent it on a particular "villain." For those of the highest status in civilian life, the resentment during this period is most acute.

Stage 3, period of attainment, begins the third and fourth weeks as recruits learn how to handle weapons. The scoring of accuracy with rifles is really the first time the army has given the recruit credit for an acquired skill. During the second half of basic training, a weekend pass becomes a possibility. The incidence of upper respiratory illness diminishes dramatically during the second four weeks as compared to the first four. This in itself is reassuring to those who had been ill since it means they will be able to complete the training on time and not be transferred to another group to make up for lost time.

Stage 4, period of termination, begins about one week before the end of basic training. There is a definite shift to feelings of euphoria, self-confidence, and discussion of plans during their upcoming leave from the army.

---

3. KP stands for "kitchen police," i.e., various types of jobs such as cleaning dishes, disposing of garbage, and so on.

The recruits' early fears of failure in basic training are gone. They now realize that the whole experience was designed to ensure a high rate of success. In fact, there are often complaints that the experience was not "tough enough." This has been confirmed by surveys, e.g., Wiskoff's study (1977), of expectation disconfirmation in the various armed services. This disappointment stems from the fact that many young men view basic training as a rite of passage into full manhood. They believe the army when it promises to remake them into superb physical specimens and are disappointed when this is not the result.

Bourne (1967, p. 195) has summarized this type of socialization well.

> The process of basic training is unique in American society, as it represents the only instance when individuals can be forcibly confined against their will, and compelled to perform certain tasks, for other than medical or punitive reasons. It also represents the most radical attempt to change identity and behavior that the average person will encounter.

This account of basic training roughly corresponds to Stages 1 and 2 of the model developed here, with the beginning of events located in Stage 3. Clearly, however, the recruits will need to be in the army much longer to encounter the remaining two events of Stage 3 and those associated with Stage 4.

Conclusions

1. Organizational socialization is how organizations change newcomers. How organizations change as a result of having newcomers join them is called personalization, a process that is rarely studied.

2. Organizational socialization differs from newcomer orientation in two ways: (a) socialization is more concerned with making newcomers conform to the organization, and (b) socialization is a process that unfolds over a period of time.

3. The basic objective of organizational socialization is to maintain control by ensuring that newcomers share the same norms and values as those of the organization.

Socialization and selection are ways for attaining organizational control. They can be substitutes for each other.

4. Newcomers enter new work groups as well as the larger organization Thus newcomer behavior must be examined in both these ways. Group development may occur simultaneously with organizational socialization.

5. Organizational socialization is composed of three basic processes: (a) social learning as the way newcomers learn, (b) new roles, norms, and values as the material that is learned, and (c) conflict as the unique dynamic of this particular learning process.

6. Socialization has been divided into various stages by different authors. A summary and integration of these models includes the following stages: (a) confronting and accepting organizational reality, (b) achieving role clarity, (c) locating oneself in the organizational context, and (d) detecting signposts of successful socialization.

7. The rate at which newcomers proceed through the various stages of socialization is determined by the amount of interaction between newcomers and insiders. Several factors affect the amount of contact they will have with each other.

8. The basic psychology of socialization is how to persuade newcomers to adopt new organizational norms and values. Persuasion can be directed at a newcomer "attitudes" (beliefs, feelings, and intentions) and at their actions. Attitudes influence actions, and actions influence attitudes.

9. Socialization tactics can be categorized on six dimensions, depending on whether the socialization is: (a) done collectively in a group or individually, (b) done formally or informally, (c) done in a specific sequence or randomly, (d) done on a fixed or variable timetable, (e) done by those in positions similar to the one that the newcomer will assume or by others who are quite different, and (f) done in a way that reinforces the identity of the newcomer or in a way that divests the newcomer of some part of his or her identity.

Appendix

The Correlation Coefficient

In personnel testing, the most commonly used statistic to express the relationship between a *predictor* of future performance (e.g., test scores) and actual job performance is the *correlation coefficient*. This is explained in all basic statistics textbooks and in most books on personnel selection. This short appendix is designed for the reader who has had no exposure to statistics.

Figure A.1 shows an example of how the correlation coefficient can be used to express the relationship between test scores and later performance. The example is based on students in a hypothetical MBA program.

The data in Figure A.1 show results from a group of students who took the Graduate Management Admission Test (GMAT) in order to gain admission to graduate school as well as these students' grade point averages during the first year. Figure A.1 shows what these data look like when plotted on a graph. The correlation coefficient is simply a statistic that *summarizes* the degree to which these two variables are related to each other. For our purposes here, we need not know the exact formula for the correlation, but we should know several things about the statistic itself.

One of the first useful properties of the correlation is that it can be used to relate two variables that are *measured on different scales*. In this example, GMAT scores are in the 500 to 700 range. (This particular test has a maximum possible score of 800 and a minimum of 200.) Grade point averages are measured on the familiar scale where A = 4.0, B = 3.0, and so on. This aspect of the

Figure A.1
Example of a .50 Correlation

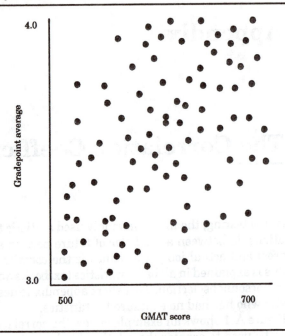

correlation coefficient makes it extremely useful since methods used to *predict* future job performance (e.g., tests) are typically measured on different scales than later performance.

The second thing to know about the correlation is that it has its own maximum and minimum scores. A correlation of 1.0 is the maximum possible *positive* relationship, i.e., as one variable gets larger, the other one does too. A correlation of 0.0 indicates there is *no relationship* at all between the two variables. A *negative* correlation means that as one variable gets larger, the other one gets smaller.

The third thing to know about correlations is that, in the "real world" of selection testing, the values of correlations rarely get much higher than .50 and typically are in the .10 to .50 range, as has been seen throughout this book in discussing the validity of tests, interviews, job previews, and so on. Does this mean that these are "low" values since they are not particularly close to the theoretical maximum of 1.0? The answer is an emphatic *no*.

There are lots of reasons why correlations are typically less than .50 in selection testing. First, in the example shown here, the GMAT supposedly measures a student's *academic abilities* (verbal and quantitative), but a student's grade point average reflects several other factors besides abilities, e.g., motivation or the courses taken (easy versus hard). Second, the test itself does not measure the full range of human abilities that may be relevant for success in an MBA program, e.g., interpersonal skills in class discussion and presentations, or writing skills. Thus it's not hard to see why correlations between test scores and performance are at the levels found in the real world of selection testing.

Validity Generalization Using Meta-Analysis

Years of research in personnel selection have produced a great many studies of various tests being correlated with later job performance. When faced with all these studies, reviewers usually resorted to calculating the *average correlation*, which became known as the average *validity* of the test. A test was "valid" if high scores on the test meant that the person was more likely to have high job performance later on. The higher the correlation, the higher the validity since the correlation coefficient was *the* statistic used to express validity.

After calculating the average correlations between selection tests and job performance (see Ghiselli, 1966, 1973, for the two best examples), it became obvious that the correlations ranged from relatively low values (close to 0.0) up to higher values (close to .50). This variability in results concerned many testing experts because they could never be certain that the test they were using would have a high or low correlation with later performance. Experts began to develop "theories" that would explain when a high versus a low correlation would be likely to be found (e.g., Dunnette, 1963). Underlying all these theories was the assumption that each situation was unique. That is, there was something unique about each organization and job combination that made it impossible to "generalize" the validity of a test from the average test validity (i.e., correlation).

In 1977, two testing/statistics experts (Schmidt & Hunter, 1977) took a hard second look at the usefulness of average correlations and test validities. They discovered that most of the studies done on testing used quite small sample sizes (the average was about 70 people per study). This discovery led them to reason that the variability in results among the different studies was due to the *inherent instability of results from research done on small samples.* Of course, we know that you cannot draw safe conclusions from doing research on only a few people, which is why, for example, political pollsters interview about 1500 persons to estimate a candidate's popularity. Even when the 1500 are carefully selected to be representative of the voting electorate, the typical margin of error is 4 percentage points either way.

The main contribution of these two experts was to devise a way to estimate how much of the variability among studies was due simply to the studies' relatively small size. They were able to show that the studies with the most "extreme" results (very low or very high correlations) were those with the smallest sample sizes. Those studies with larger sample sizes typically reported test validities closer to the overall average for a group of studies. They concluded that the *average validity of test scores is a very good estimate of what will be likely to be found in future use with a test.* They called this "validity generalization" because it meant that researchers could trust the average validity to be a fair and reasonable representation of how test scores will relate to later job performance.

The statistical procedure used to arrive at this validity generalization conclusion is called *meta-analysis* (Hunter & Schmidt, 1990). The term "meta-analysis" refers to the fact that we are actually analyzing a *set* of studies, hence the use of the term "meta." Meta-analysis can be used to assess the results from any group of studies on a particular topic, e.g., realistic job previews (Premack & Wanous, 1985), stress orientation for medical patients (Mumford et al., 1983), structured interviews (e.g., Wiesner & Cronshaw, 1988), and so on. Only when the meta-analysis is done on personnel selection tests is it called validity generalization.

In many cases, the use of meta-analysis has meant that the *average* correlation found in research on staffing is a very good indicator of the validity of the staffing procedure, whether it is a test (Hunter & Hunter, 1984), an assessment center (Gaugler et al., 1987), or a realistic job preview (Premack & Wanous, 1985). This is why I have repeatedly reported the average correlations from various bodies of research on organizational entry issues. In a word, *meta-analysis has shown that we can trust the average results from research and not be too concerned with what looks like variability among different studies because the variability is just a result of using small samples to do the original research.*

References

Adams, J. S. (1965). Injustice in social exchange. In L. Berkowitz (Ed.), *Advances in experimental social psychology* (Vol. 2), pp. 267–299. New York: Academic Press.

Alderfer, C. P. (1971). Effect of individual, group, and intergroup relations on attitudes toward a management development program. *Journal of Applied Psychology, 55,* 302–311.

Alderfer, C. P. (1972). *Existence, relatedness and growth: Human needs in organizational settings.* New York: Free Press.

Alderfer, C. P. & Brown, L. D. (1972). Designing on "empathic questionnaire" for organizational research. *Journal of Applied Psychology, 56,* 456–460.

Alderfer, C. P. & McCord, C. G. (1972). Personal and situational factors in the recruitment interview. *Journal of Applied Psychology, 54,* 377–385.

Allen, N. J. & Meyer, J. P. (1990). Organizational socialization tactics: A longitudinal analysis of links to newcomers' commitment and role orientation. *Academy of Management Journal, 33,* 847–858.

Alutto, J. A., Hrebiniak, L. G., & Alonso, R. C. (1971). A study of differential socialization for members of one professional occupation. *Journal of Health and Social Behavior, 12,* 140–147.

Anastasi, A. (1982). *Psychological testing.* New York: McGraw-Hill.

Anderson, K. J. (1990). Arousal and the inverted-U hypothesis: A critique of Neiss's "reconceptualizing arousal." *Psychological Bulletin, 107,* 96–100.

Anderson, K. O. & Masur, F. T., III (1983). Psychological preparation for invasive medical and dental procedures. *Journal of Behavioral Medicine, 6,* 1–40.

Argyris, C. (1954). *Organization of a bank.* New Haven: Yale Labor and Management Center.

Argyris, C. (1964). *Integrating the individual and the organization.* New York: Wiley.

Argyris, C. (1971). *Management and organizational development.* New York: McGraw-Hill.

Aronson, E. (1972). *The social animal.* San Francisco: Freeman.

Arvey, R. D. & Campion, J. E. (1982). The employment interview: A summary and review of recent research. *Personnel Psychology, 35,* 281–322.

Arvey, R. D. & Faley, R. H. (1988). *Fairness in selecting employees.* Reading, MA: Addison-Wesley.

Asher, J. J. & Sciarrino, J. A. (1974). Realistic work sample tests: A review. *Personnel Psychology, 27,* 519–533.

Auerbach, S. M. & Kilmann, P. R. (1977). Crisis intervention: A review of outcome research. *Psychological Bulletin, 84,* 1189–1217.

Avner, B. K., Gusastello, S. J., & Aderman, M. (1982). The effect of a realistic job preview on expectancy and voluntary versus involuntary turnover. *Journal of Psychology, 111* (1), 101–107

Bakke, E.W. (1953). *The fusion process.* New Haven, CT: Labor and Management Center, Yale University.

Bandura, A. (1977). *Social learning theory.* Englewood Cliffs, N J: Prentice-Hall.

Baron, R. A. (1989). Impression management by applicants during employment interviews: The "too much of a good thing" effect. In R.W. Eder & G.R. Ferris (Eds.), *The employment interview* (pp. 204–216). Newbury Park, CA: Sage.

Barrick, M. R. & Mount, M. K. (1991). The big five personality dimensions and job performance: A meta-analysis. *Personnel Psychology, 44,* 1–26.

Bazerman, M. H. (1990). *Judgment in managerial decision making* (2nd. ed.). New York: Wiley.

Bem, D. J. (1970). *Beliefs, attitudes, and human affairs.* Belmont, CA: Brooks/Cole.

Berlew, D. E. & Hall, D. T. (1966). The socialization of managers: Effects of expectations on performance. *Administrative Science Quarterly, 11,* 207–223.

Birnbaum, M. H. & Sotooden, Y. (1991). Measurement of stress: Scaling the magnitudes of life changes. *Psychological Science,* 2, 236–243.

Bluedorn, A.C. (1982). A unified model of turnover from organizations. *Human Relations, 35,* 135–153.

Bourne, P.G. (1967). Some observations on the psychosocial phenomena seen in basic training. *Psychiatry, 30,* 187–197.

Bowen, D.E., Chase, R. & Cummings, T. (1990). *Service management effectiveness: Balancing strategy, organization and human resources, operations, and management.* Newbury Park, CA: Sage.

Bray, D. W., Campbell, R. J., & Grant, D. L. (1974). *Formative years in business.* New York: Wiley.

Brayfield, A. H. & Crockett, W. H. (1955). Employee attitudes and performance. *Psychological Bulletin, 52,* 392–428.

Breaugh, J. A. & Mann, R. B. (1984). Recruiting source effects: A test of two alternative explanations. *Journal of Occupational Psychology, 57,* 261–267.

Brett, J. M. (1982). Job transfer and well-being. *Journal of Applied Psychology, 67,* 450–463.

Bretz, R. D., Jr., Ash, R. A., & Dreher, G. F. (1989). Do people make the place? An examination of the attraction-selection-attrition hypothesis. *Personnel Psychology, 42,* 561–582.

Brown, L. D. (1983). *Managing conflict at organizational interfaces.* Reading, MA: Addison-Wesley.

Buchanan, B. (1974). Building organizational commitment: The socialization of managers in work organizations. *Administrative Science Quarterly, 19,* 533–546.

Caldwell, D. F. & O'Reilly, C. A. (1990). Measuring person-job fit with a profile comparison process. *Journal of Applied Psychology, 75,* 648–657.

Caldwell, D. F. & Spivey, W. A. (1983). The relationship between recruiting sources and employee success: An analysis by race. *Personnel Psychology, 36,* 67–72.

Campbell, J. P. (1990). An overview of the Army selection and classification project. *Personnel Psychology, 43,* 231–240.

Campion, M. A., Pursell, E. D., & Brown, B. K. (1988). Structured interviewing: Raising the psychometric properties of the employment interview. *Personnel Psychology, 41,* 25–42.

Caplow, T. (1964). *Principles of organization.* New York: Harcourt, Brace and World.

Carlsmith, J. M. & Freedman, J. L. (1968). Bad decisions and dissonance: Nobody's perfect. In R. P. Abelson, E. Aronson, W. J. McGuire, T. M. Newcomb, M. J. Rosenberg & P. H. Tannenbaum (Eds.), *Theories of Cognitive consistency: A sourcebook* (pp. 485–490). Chicago: Rand McNally.

Chaiken, S. & Eagly, A. H. (1976). Communication modality as a determinant of message persuasiveness and message comprehensibility. *Journal of Personality and Social Psychology, 34,* 605–614.

Chatman, J. A. (1989). Improving interactional research: A model of person-organization fit. *Academy of Management Review, 14,* 333–349.

Cherrington, D. J., Reitz, H. J., & Scott, W. E. (1971). Effects of contingent and noncontingent reward on the relationship between satisfaction and task performance. *Journal of Applied Psychology, 55,* 331–336.

Cochrane, R. & Robertson, A. (1973). The life events inventory: A measure of the relative severity of psycho-social stressors. *Journal of Psychosomatic Research, 17,* 135–139.

Cohen, P. (1973). *The gospel according to the Harvard Business School.* Garden City, NY: Doubleday and Company.

Colarelli, S. M. (1984). Methods of communication and mediating processes in realistic job previews. *Journal of Applied Psychology, 69,* 633–642.

Colella, A . (1989). *A new role for newcomer pre-entry expectations during organizational entry: Expectation effects on job perceptions.* Unpublished doctoral dissertation, The Ohio State University, Columbus, Ohio.

Colella, A. & Wanous, J. P. (1989). *Differences in recruiting source effectiveness: A real test of the realism hypothesis.* Paper presented at the annual meeting of the Academy of Management Association, Washington, DC.

Conard, M. A. & Ashworth, D. S. (1986). *Recruiting source effectiveness: A meta-analysis and re-examination of two rival hypotheses.* Paper presented at the annual meeting of the Society for Industrial/Organizational Psychology, Chicago.

Cook, M. (1988). *Personnel selection and productivity.* Chichester, England: Wiley.

Cornelius, E. T., III (1983). The use of projective techniques in personnel selection. In K. M. Rowland & G. R. Ferris (Eds.), *Research in personnel and human resources management* (pp. 127–168). Greenwich, CT: JAI Press.

Crites, J.O. (1969). *Vocational psychology.* New York: McGraw-Hill.

Dalton, D. R. & Todor, W. D. (1979). Turnover turned over: An expanded and positive perspective. *Academy of Management Review, 4,* 225–235.

Dawis, R. V. & Lofquist, L. H. (1984). *A psychological theory of work adjustment.* Minneapolis, MN: University of Minnesota Press.

Dean, R. A. & Wanous, J. P. (1984). The effects of realistic job previews on hiring bank tellers. *Journal of Applied Psychology, 69,* 61–68.

Decker, P. J. & Cornelius, E. T., III (1979). A note on recruiting sources and job survival rates. *Journal of Applied Psychology, 69,* 463–464.

Downs, S. R., Farr, R. M., & Colbeck, L. (1978). Self-appraisal: A convergence of selection and guidance. *Journal of Occupational Psychology, 51,* 271–278.

Druckman, D. & Swets, J. A. (1988). *Enhancing human performance.* Washington, DC: National Academy Press.

Dugoni, B. L. & Ilgen, D. R. (1981). Realistic job previews and the adjustment of new employees. *Academy of Management Journal, 24,* 579–591.

Dunnette, M. D. (1963). A modified model for test validation and selection research. *Journal of Applied Psychology, 47,* 317–323.

Dunnette, M. D., Arvey, R. D., & Banas, P. A. (1973). Why do they leave? *Personnel, 50* (3), 25–39.

Eagly, A. H. & Himmelfarb, S. (1978). Attitudes and opinions. *Annual Review of Psychology, 29,* 517–554.

Eagly, R. V. (1965). Market power as an intervening mechanism in Phillips Curve analysis. *Economics, 32,* 48–64.

Eder, R. W. & Ferris, G. R. (Eds.) (1989). *The employment interview.* Newbury Park, CA: Sage.

Ellis, A. (1962). *Reason and emotion in psychotherapy.* New York: Lyle Stuart.

Ellis, A. (1970). *The essence of rational psychotherapy: A comprehensive approach to treatment.* New York: Institution for Rational Living.

Etzioni, A. (1964). *Modern organizations.* Englewood Cliffs, NJ: Prentice-Hall.

Farkas, A. J. & Tetrick, L. E. (1989). A three-wave longitudinal analysis of the causal ordering of satisfaction and commitment on turnover decisions. *Journal of Applied Psychology, 74,* 855-868.

Farr, J. L., O'Leary, B. S., & Bartlett, C. J. (1973). Effect of a work sample test upon self-selection and turnover of job applicants. *Journal of Applied Psychology, 58,* 283-285.

Feldman, D.C. (1976a). A contingency theory of socialization. *Administrative Science Quarterly, 21,* 433-452.

Feldman, D.C. (1976b). A practical program for employee socialization. *Organizational Dynamics, Autumn,* 64-80.

Feldman, D. C. (1988). *Managing careers in organizations.* Glenview, IL: Scott, Foresman.

Feldman, D. C. & Brett, J. M. (1983). Coping with new jobs: A comparative study of new hires and job changers. *Academy of Management Journal, 26,* 258-272.

Festinger, L. (1957). *A theory of cognitive dissonance.* Evanston, IL: Row, Peterson.

Fieley, D. (1991, August 11). The OSU odyssey: Orientation offers crash course on 15,700 acres, 60,000 students, 11,000 courses. *Columbus Dispatch,* p. F1-2.

Fisher, C. D. (1985). Social support and adjustment to work: A longitudinal study. *Journal of Management, 11,* 43-57.

Fisher, C. D. (1986). Organizational socialization: An integrative review. In K. M. Rowland & G. R. Ferris (Eds.), *Research in personnel and human resources management* (Vol. 4, pp. 101-146). Greenwich, CT: JAI.

Fisher, C. D., Ilgen, D. R. & Hoyer, W. D. (1979). Source credibility, information favorability, and job offer acceptance. *Academy of Management Journal, 22,* 94-103.

Fletcher, C. (1989). Impression management in the selection interview. In R. A. Giacalone & P. Rosenfeld (Eds.), *Impression management in the organization* (pp. 269-282). Hillsdale, NJ: Lawrence Erlbaum.

Foltman, F. (1968). *White and blue collars in a mill shutdown.* Ithaca, NY: New York State School of Industrial and Labor Relations.

Fried, Y. & Ferris, G. R. (1987). The validity of the job characteristics model: A review and meta-analysis. *Personnel Psychology, 40*, 287–322.

Gannon, M. J. (1971). Sources of referral and employee turnover. *Journal of Applied Psychology, 55*, 226–228.

Gatewood, R. D. & Feild, H. S. (1987). *Human resource selection.* Chicago: Dryden.

Gaugler, B. B., Rosenthal, D. B., Thornton, G. C., III, Bentson, C. (1987). Meta-analysis of assessment center validity. *Journal of Applied Psychology, 72*, 493–511.

Gaugler, B. B. & Thornton, G. C., III (1985). *Matching job previews to individual applicant's needs.* Unpublished manuscript, Colorado State University, Fort Collins.

Ghiselli, E. E. (1966). *The validity of occupational aptitude tests.* New York: Wiley.

Ghiselli, E. E. (1973). The validity of aptitude tests in personnel selection. *Personnel Psychology, 26*, 461–478.

Gilroy, C. L. & McIntyre, R. J. (1974). Job losers, leavers, and entrants: A cyclical analysis. *Monthly Labor Review, 97*, 35–39.

Githens, W. H. & Zalinski, J. (1983). *An evaluation of realistic job preview and stress-coping films' effect on Marine Corps recruit training attrition.* (Tech. Rep. No. 83-78). Navy Personnel Research and Development Center, San Diego.

Glueck, W. F. (1974). Decision making: Organizational choice. *Personnel Psychology, 27*, 77–93.

Goldstein, A. P. & Sorcher, M. (1974). *Changing supervisor behavior.* New York: Pergamon.

Gomersall, E. R. & Myers, M. S. (1966). Breakthrough in on-the-job training. *Harvard Business Review, July-August*, 62–72.

Gouldner, A. W., 1957. Cosmopolitans and locals: Toward an analysis of latent social roles--I. *Administrative Science Quarterly, 2*, 281–306.

Gouldner, A. W. (1958). Cosmopolitans and locals: Toward an analysis of latent social roles--II. *Administrative Science Quarterly, 2*, 444–480.

Graen, G. (1976). Role making processes within complex organizations. In M. D. Dunnette (Ed.), *The handbook of industrial and organizational psychology* (pp. 1201–1246). Chicago: Rand McNally.

Greenhaus, J. H., Seidel, C., & Marinis, M. (1982). The impact of expectations and values on job attitudes. *Organizational Behavior and Human Performance, 31,* 394–417.

Guion, R. M. (1965). *Personnel testing.* New York: McGraw-Hill.

Guion, R. M. (1974). Open a new window: Validities and values in psychological measurement. *American Psychologist, 29,* 287–296.

Guion, R. M. (1987). Changing views for personnel selection research. *Personnel Psychology, 40,* 199–213.

Guion, R. M. & Gottier, R. F. (1965). Validity of personality measures in personnel selection. *Personnel Psychology, 18,* 135–164.

Haccoun, R. R. (1978). *The effects of realistic job previews and their position within the selection sequence on telephone operator behavior and attitudes.* Unpublished manuscript, University of Montreal, Quebec.

Hackett, R. D. & Guion, R. M. (1985). A re-evaluation of the absenteeism-job satisfaction relationship. *Organizational Behavior and Human Decision Processes, 35,* 340–381.

Hackman, J. R. & Lawler, E. E., III (1971). Employee reactions to job characteristics. *Journal of Applied Psychology, 55,* 259–286.

Hackman, J. R. & Oldham, G. R. (1980). *Work redesign.* Reading, MA: Addison-Wesley.

Harris, M. M. (1989). Reconsidering the employment interview: A review of recent literature and suggestions for future research. *Personnel Psychology, 42,* 691–726.

Harris, M. M. & Fink, L. S. (1987). A field study of applicant reactions to employment opportunities: Does the recruiter make a difference? *Personnel Psychology, 40,* 765–784.

Heneman, H. G., Jr., Fox, H. & Yoder, D. (1948). Patterns of manpower mobility: Minneapolis, 1948. In D. Yoder & D.G. Paterson, (Eds.), *Local Labor Market Research.* Minneapolis: University of Minnesota Press.

Herriot, P. (1984). *Down from the ivory tower.* Chichester, England: Wiley.

Herzberg, F. H. (1968). One more time: How do you motivate employees? *Harvard Business Review, 46,* 53–62.

Hill, R. E. (1970). A new look at employee referrals. *Personnel Journal,* *49*, 144–148.

Hill, R. E. (1974). An empirical comparison of two models for predicting preferences for standard employment offers. *Decision Sciences, 5,* 243–254.

Hoiberg, A. & Berry, N. H. (1978). Expectations and perceptions of Navy life. *Organizational Behavior and Human Performance, 21,* 130–145.

Hollenbeck, G. P. (1990). The past, present and future of assessment centers. *The Industrial-Organizational Psychologist, 28,* 13–17.

Hollenbeck, J. R. & Whitener, E. M. (1988). Reclaiming personality traits for personnel selection: Self-esteem as an illustrative case. *Journal of Management, 14,* 81–91.

Holmes, T. H. & Rahe, R. H. (1967). The social readjustment rating scale. *Journal of Psychosomatic Research, 11,* 213–218.

Hom, P. W. & Griffeth, R. W. (1985). Psychological processes that mediate the effect of the realistic job preview on nursing turnover. In R. B. Robinson & J. A. Pearce (Eds.), *Academy of Management Proceedings 1985,* pp. 215–219.

Horner, S. O. (1980). *A field experimental study of the affective, intentional, and behavioral effects of organizational entry expectations.* Unpublished doctoral dissertation, University of South Carolina, Columbia.

Hough, L. M., Eaton, N. K., Dunnette, M. D., Kamp, J. D. & McCloy, R. A. (1990). Criterion-related validities of personality constructs and the effect of response distortion on those validities. *Journal of Applied Psychology, 75,* 581–595.

Hovland, C. I., Janis, I. L., & Kelly, H. H. (1953). *Communication and persuasion.* New Haven: Yale University Press.

Howard, A. & Bray, D. W. (1988). *Managerial lives in transition.* New York: Guilford Press.

Hulin, C. L., Henry, R. A. & Noon, S. L. (1990). Adding a dimension: Time as a factor in the generalizability of predictive relationships. *Psychological Bulletin, 107,* 328–340.

Hulin, C. L., Roznowski, M. & Hachiya, D. (1985). Alternative opportunities and withdrawal decisions: Empirical and theoretical discrepancies and an integration. *Psychological Bulletin, 97,* 233–250.

Hunter, J. E. & Hunter, R. F. (1984). Validity and utility of alternative predictors of job performance. *Psychological Bulletin,* *96,* 72–98.

Hunter, J. E. & Schmidt, F. L. (1990). *Methods of meta-analysis.* Newbury Park, CA: Sage.

Iaffaldano, M. T. & Muchinsky, P. M. (1985). Job satisfaction and job performance: A meta-analysis. *Psychological Bulletin, 67,* 251–273.

Ilgen, D. R. & Seely, W. (1974). Realistic expectations as an aid in reducing voluntary resignations. *Journal of Applied Psychology, 59,* 452–455.

Ivancevich, J. M., Matteson, M. T., Freedman, S. M., & Phillips, J. S. (1991). Worksite stress management interventions. *American Psychologist, 45,* 252–261.

Jackofsky, E. F. (1984). Turnover and job performance: An integrated process model. *Academy of Management Review, 9,* 74–83.

Jackson, S. E. & Schuler, R. S. (1985). A meta-analysis and conceptual critique of research on role ambiguity and role conflict in work settings. *Organizational Behavior and Human Decision Processes, 36,* 16–78.

Jacobson, E. (1970). *Modern treatment of tense patients.* Springfield, IL: Charles C. Thomas.

Janis, I. L. (1958). *Psychological stress.* New York: Wiley.

Janis, I. L. (1983). Stress inoculation in health care: Theory and research. In D. Meichenbaum & M. E. Jaremko (Eds.), *Stress reduction and prevention.* New York: Plenum Press.

Janis, I. L. & Mann, L. (1977). *Decision making: A psychological analysis of conflict, choice, and commitment.* New York, Free Press.

Janis, I. L. & Wheeler, D. (1978). Thinking clearly about career choices. *Psychology Today, May,* 67ff.

Janz, T. (1982). Initial comparisons of patterned behavior description interviews versus unstructured interviews. *Journal of Applied Psychology, 67,* 577–580.

Janz, T. (1989). The patterned behavior description interview: The best prophet of the future is the past. In R.W. Eder & G. R. Ferris (Eds.), *The employment interview* (pp. 158–168). Newbury Park, CA: Sage.

Janz, T., Hellervick, L., & Gilmore, D.C. (1986). *Behavior description interviewing.* Boston: Allyn & Bacon.

Jones, G. R. (1986). Socialization tactics, self efficacy, and newcomers' adjustments to organizations. *Academy of Management Journal, 29,* 262–279.

Katz, D. & Kahn, R. L. (1978). *The social psychology of organizations, 2nd ed.* New York: John Wiley & Sons.

Katzell, M. E. (1968). Expectations and dropouts in schools of nursing. *Journal of Applied Psychology, 52,* 154–157.

Kerr, C. (1942). Migration to the Seattle labor market area, 1940–1942. *University of Washington Publications in the Social Sciences, 11,* 151, note 1 August 1942.

Kirnan, J. P., Farley, J. A. & Geisinger, K. F. (1989). The relationship between recruiting source, applicant quality, and hire performance: An analysis by sex, ethnicity, and age. *Personnel Psychology, 42,* 293–308.

Kinslinger, H. J. (1966). Application of projective techniques in personnel psychology since 1940. *Psychological Bulletin, 66,* 134–149.

Klitgaard, R. (1985). *Choosing elites.* New York: Basic Books.

Korman, A. K. (1968). The prediction of managerial performance: A review. *Personnel Psychology, 21,* 295–322.

Latack, J. L. (1984). Career transitions within organizations: An exploratory study of work, nonwork, and coping strategies. *Organizational Behavior and Human Performance, 34,* 296–322.

Latham, G. P. (1989). The reliability, validity, and practicality of the situational interview. In R.W. Eder & G. R. Ferris (Eds.), *The employment interview* (pp. 169-182). Newbury Park, CA: Sage.

Latham, G. P., Saari, L. M., Pursell, E. D., & Campion, M. A. (1980). The situational interview. *Journal of Applied Psychology, 65,* 422–427.

Latham, G. P. & Saari, L. M. (1984). Do people do what they say? Further studies on the situational interview. *Journal of Applied Psychology, 69,* 569–573.

Lawler, E. E., III (1973). *Motivation in work organizations.* Monterey, CA: Brooks/Cole.

Lawler, E. E., III (1986). *High involvement management.* San Francisco: Jossey-Bass.

Lawler, E. E., III, Kuleck, W. J., Rhode, J. G. & Sorenson, J. E. (1975). Job choice and post decision dissonance. *Organizational Behavior and Human Performance, 13,* 133–145.

Lewicki, R. J. (1981). Organizational seduction: Building commitment to organizations. *Organizational Dynamics, Autumn,* 5–21.

Lewis, M. (1965). Psychological effect of effort. *Psychological Bulletin, 64,* 183–190.

Liden, R. C. & Parsons, C. K. (1986). A field study of job applicant interview perceptions, alternative opportunities, and demographic characteristics. *Personnel Psychology, 39,* 109–122.

Locke, E. A. (1968). Toward a theory of task motivation and incentives. *Organizational Behavior and Human Performance, 3,* 157-189.

Locke, E. A. (1976). The nature and causes of job satisfaction. In M. D. Dunnette (Ed.), *Handbook of industrial and organizational psychology* (pp. 1297–1349). Chicago: Rand McNally.

Locke, E. A. & Latham, G. P. (1990). Work motivation and satisfaction: Light at the end of the tunnel. *Psychological Science, 1,* 240–246.

Lockman, R. F. (1980). *The realistic job preview experiments at Great Lakes and San Diego.* (CNA Memorandum No. 80-1885). Center for Naval Analyses, Alexandria, VA.

Lofquist, L. H. & Dawis, R.V. (1969). *Adjustment to work.* New York: Appleton-Century-Crofts.

Louis, M. R. (1980). Surprise and sense making: What newcomers experience in entering unfamiliar organizational settings. *Administrative Science Quarterly, 25,* 226–251.

Louis, M. R., Posner, B. Z., & Powell, G. N. (1983). The availability and helpfulness of socialization practices. *Personnel Psychology, 36,* 857–866.

Lubliner, M. (1978). Employee orientation. *Personnel Journal, 57,* 207–208.

Ludwick-Rosenthal, R. & Neufeld, R. W. J. (1988). Stress management during noxious medical procedures: An evaluative review of outcome studies. *Psychological Bulletin, 104,* 326–342.

MacDonald, M. R. & Kuiper, N. A. (1983). Cognitive-behavioral preparation for surgery: Some theoretical and methodological concerns. *Clinical Psychology Review, 3,* 27–39.

Macedonia, R. M. (1969). *Expectations—press and survival.* Unpublished doctoral dissertation, New York University, New York.

Machen, J. B. & Johnson, R. (1974). Desensitization, model learning, and the dental behavior of children. *Journal of Dental Research, 53,* 83–87.

March, J. G. & Simon, H. A. (1958). *Organizations.* New York: Wiley.

Maslow, A. H. (1943). A theory of human motivation. *Psychological Review, 50,* 370–396.

Mathieu, J. E. & Zajac, D. M. (1990). A review and meta-analysis of the antecedents, correlates, and consequences of organizational commitment. *Psychological Bulletin, 108,* 171–194.

Mayfield, E. C. (1964). The selection interview: A re-evaluation of published research. *Personnel Psychology, 17,* 239–260.

McCall, M.W., Jr. (1983). Leaders and leadership: Of substance and shadow. In J.R. Hackman, E. E. Lawler, III, & L. W. Porter (Eds.), *Perspectives on behavior in organizations* (pp. 476–485). New York: McGraw-Hill.

McCall, N. M., Jr. & Lombardo, M. M. (1979). *Looking Glass, Inc.: The first three years* (Tech. Rep. No. 13). Greensboro, NC: The Center for Creative Leadership.

McClelland, D. C. (1961). *The achieving society.* Princeton, NJ: Van Nostrand.

McClelland, D. C. (1975). *Power: The inner experience.* New York: Irvington.

McClelland, D. C. & Boyatzis, R. E. (1982). Leadership motive pattern and long term success in management. *Journal of Applied Psychology, 67,* 737–743.

McEvoy, G. M. & Casico, W. F. (1985). Strategies for reducing employee turnover: A meta-analysis. *Journal of Applied Psychology, 70,* 342–353.

McEvoy, G. M. & Cascio, W. F. (1987). Do good or poor performers leave? A meta-analysis of the relationship between performance and turnover. *Academy of Management Journal, 30,* 744–762.

McGarrell, E. J., Jr. (1984). An orientation system that builds productivity. *Personnel Administrator, October,* 75–85.

McGuire, W. J. (1964). Inducing resistance to persuasion: Some contemporary approaches. In L. Berkowitz (Ed.), *Advances in Experimental Social Psychology, Vol. 1* (pp. 191–229). New York: Academic Press.

McGuire, W. J. (1969). The nature of attitudes and attitude change. In G. Lindsey & E. Aronson (Eds.), *The handbook of social psychology* (Vol. III, 2nd ed., pp. 136–314). Reading, MA: Addison-Wesley.

McGuire, W. J. (1985). Attitudes and attitude change. In G. Lindsey & E. Aronson (Eds.), *The handbook of social psychology* (Vol. II, 3rd ed. pp. 233–246). New York: Random House.

McHenry, J. J., Hough, L. M., Toquam, J. L., Hanson, M. A., & Ashworth, S. (1990). Project A validity results: The relationship between predictor and criterion domains. *Personnel Psychology, 43,* 335–354.

Meglino, B. M., DeNisi, A. S., Youngblood, S. A., Williams, K. J. (1988). Effects of realistic job previews: A comparison using an "enhancement" and a "reduction" preview. *Journal of Applied Psychology, 73,* 259–266.

Meglino, B. M., DeNisi, A. S., Youngblood, S. A., & Williams, K. J., Johnson, W. E., Randolph, W. A., & Laughlin, J. E. (1983). *Formulation and analysis of counter attrition strategies in the U.S. Army* (Tech. Rep.). Columbia: University of South Carolina, College of Business, Division of Research.

Michaels, C. E. & Spector, P. E. (1982). Causes of employee turnover: A test of the Mobley, Griffith, Hand, & Meglino model. *Journal of Applied Psychology, 67,* 53–59.

Miller, G. A. & Wager, L. W. (1971). Adult socialization, organizational structure, and role orientations. *Administrative Science Quarterly, 16,* 151–163.

Miller, S. (1981). Predictability and human stress: Toward a clarification of evidence and theory. In L. Berkowitz (Ed.), *Advances in experimental social psychology: Vol. 14* (pp. 203–256). New York: Academic Press.

Miner, J. B. (1978). Twenty years of research on role-motivation theory of managerial effectiveness. *Personnel Psychology, 31,* 739–760.

Mobley, W. H. (1982). *Employee turnover: Causes, consequences, and control.* Reading, MA: Addison-Wesley.

Moore, M. L. (1974). Superior, self, and subordinant differences in perceptions of managerial learning times. *Personnel Psychology, 27,* 297–305.

Morrison, R. F. (1990). Personal communication.

Morse, J. J. (1975). Person-job congruence and individual adjustment. *Human Relations, 28,* 841–861.

Motowidlo, S. J., Dunnette, M. D., & Carter, G. W. (1990). An alternative selection procedure: The low-fidelity simulation. *Journal of Applied Psychology, 75,* 640–647.

Mulford, C. L., Klonglan, G. E., Beal, G. N. & Bohlen, J. M. (1968). Selectivity, socialization, and role performance. *Sociology and Social Research, 53* (1), 68–77.

Mumford, E., Schlesinger, H. J., & Glass, G. V. (1982). The effects of psychological intervention on recovery from surgery and heart attacks: An analysis of the literature. *American Journal of Public Health, 72,* 141–151.

Myers, C. A. & MacLaurin, W. R. (1943). *The movement of factory workers: A study of a New England industrial community.* New York: Wiley.

Myers, C. A. & Schultz, G. P. (1951). *The dynamics of a labor market.* Englewood Cliffs, NJ: Prentice-Hall.

Nathan, B. R., Ledford, G. E., Bowen, D. E., & Cummings, T. G. (1990). *Personality as a predictor of performance and satisfaction in high involvement organizations: A construct validation study.* Unpublished manuscript, University of Southern California, College of Business, Los Angeles.

Nissen, B. (1978, July 28). At Texas Instruments, if you're pro-union, firm may be anti-you. *Wall Street Journal,* p. 1.

The Office of Strategic Services Assessment Staff (1948). *Assessment of men.* New York: Rhinehart.

Novaco, R. W., Cook, T. M., & Sarason, I. G. (1983). Military recruit training: An arena for stress-coping skills. In D. Meichenbaum & M. E. Jaremko (Eds.), *Stress reduction and prevention.* New York: Plenum Press.

O'Reilly, C. A. (1977). Person-job fit: Implications for individual attitudes and performance. *Organizational Behavior and Human Performance, 18,* 36–46.

Orpen, C. (1985). Patterned behavior description interviews versus unstructured interviews: A comparative validity study. *Journal of Applied Psychology, 70,* 774–776.

Parnes, H. S. (1954). *Research on labor mobility: An appraisal of research findings in the United States.* New York: Social Science Research Council.

Parnes, H. S. (1970). Labor force and labor markets. In W. L. Ginsburg, E. R. Livernash, H. S. Parnes, & G. Strauss (Eds.). *A review of industrial relations research* (Vol, 1 pp. 1–78). Madison: University of Wisconsin, Industrial Relations Research Association.

Petty, R. E. & Cacioppo, J. T. (1981). *Attitudes and persuasion: Classic and contemporary approaches.* Dubuque, I A: W.C. Brown.

Petty, R. E. & Cacioppo, J. T. (1986). *Communication and persuasion: Central and peripheral routes to attitude change.* New York: Springer-Verlag.

Petty, M. M., McGee, G. W. & Cavender, J. W. (1984). A meta-analysis of the relationship between individual job satisfaction and individual job performance. *Academy of Management Review, 9,* 712–721.

Pierce, J. L. & Dunham, R. B. (1987). Organizational Commitment: Pre-employment propensity and initial work experiences. *Journal of Management, 13,* 163–178.

Popovich, P. & Wanous, J. P. (1982). The realistic job preview as a persuasive communication. *Academy of Management Review, 7,* 570–578.

Porter, L. W., Crampon, W. J., & Smith, F. J. (1976). Organizational commitment and managerial turnover: A longitudinal study. *Organizational Behavior and Human Performance, 15,* 87–98.

Porter, L. W., Lawler, E. E., III, & Hackman, J. R. (1975). *Behavior in Organizations.* New York: McGraw-Hill.

Porter, L. W. & Steers, R. M. (1973). Organizational, work, and personal factors in employee turnover and absenteeism. *Psychological Bulletin, 80,* 151–176.

Posavac, E. J. (1980). Evaluations of patient education programs. *Evaluation & the Health Professions, 3,* 47–62.

Powell, G. N. (1984). Effects of job attributes and recruiting practices on applicant decisions: A comparison. *Personnel Psychology, 37,* 721–732.

Powell, G. N. (1991). Applicant reactions to the initial employment interview: Exploring theoretical and methodological issues. *Personnel Psychology, 44,* 67–83.

Power, D. J. & Aldag, R. J. (1985). Soelberg's job search and choice model: A clarification, review, and critique. *Academy of Management Review, 10,* 48–58.

Premack, S. L. & Wanous, J. P. (1985). A meta-analysis of realistic job preview experiments. *Journal of Applied Psychology, 70,* 706–19.

Randall, D. M. (1990). The consequences of organizational commitment: Methodological investigation. *Journal of Organizational Behavior, 11,* 361–378.

Rees, A. (1966, May). Information networks in labor markets. *American Economic Review*, Papers and Proceedings, pp. 559, 562.

Reichers, A. E. (1985). A review and reconceptualization of organizational commitment. *Academy of Management Review, 10,* 465–476.

Reichers, A. E. (1987). An interactionist perspective on newcomer socialization rates. *Academy of Management Review, 12,* 278–287.

Reichers, A. E. & Schneider, B. (1990). Climate and culture: An evolution of concepts. In B. Schneider (Ed.), *Organizational climate and culture,* (pp. 5–39). San Francisco: Jossey-Bass.

Reid, G. L. (1972). Job search and the effectiveness of job-finding methods. *Industrial and Labor Relations Review, 25,* 479–495.

Reilly, R. R., Brown, B., Blood, M. R., & Malatesta, C. Z. (1981). The effects of realistic previews: A study and discussion of the literature. *Personnel Psychology, 34,* 823–834.

Reilly, R. R. & Chao, G. T. (1982). Validity and fairness of some alternative employee selection procedures. *Personnel Psychology, 35,* 1–62.

Reilly, R. R., Tenopyr, M. L., & Sperling, S. M. (1979). Effects of job previews on job acceptance and survival of telephone operator candidates. *Journal of Applied Psychology, 64,* 218–220.

Reynolds, L. G. (1951). *The structure of labor markets.* New York: Harper Bros.

Rhodes, S. R. & Steers, R. M. (1990). *Managing employee absenteeism.* Reading, MA: Addison-Wesley.

Robertson, I. T., Gratton, L., & Rout, U. (1990). The validity of situational interviews for administrative jobs. *Journal of Organizational Behavior, 11,* 69–76.

Robertson, I. T. & Kandola, R. S. (1982). Work sample tests: Validity, adverse impact, and applicant reaction. *Journal of Occupational Psychology, 55,* 171–183.

Rousseau, D. M. (1990). New hire perceptions of their own and their employer's obligations: A study of psychological contracts. *Journal of Organizational Behavior, 11,* 389–400.

Rynes, S. L. & Boudreau, J.W. (1986). College recruiting in large organizations: Practice, evaluation, and research implications. *Personnel Psychology, 39,* 729–757.

Rynes, S. L. & Miller, H. E. (1983). Recruiter and job influences on candidates for employment. *Journal of Applied Psychology, 68,* 147–154.

St. John, W. D. (1980). The complete employee orientation program. *Personnel Journal, 59,* 373–378.

Salancik, G. R. & Pfeffer, J. (1978). A social information processing approach to job attitudes and task design. *Administrative Science Quarterly, 23,* 224–253.

Schein, E. H. (1964). How to break in the college graduate. *Harvard Business Review, 42,* 68–76.

Schein, E. H. (1965). *Organizational psychology.* Englewood Cliffs, NJ: Prentice-Hall.

Schein, E. H. (1967). Attitude change during management education: A study of organizational influences on student attitudes. *Administrative Science Quarterly, 11,* 601–628.

Schein, E. H. (1968). Organizational socialization and the profession of management. *Industrial Management Review, 9,* 1–16.

Schein, E. H. (1971). The individual, the organization, and the career: A conceptual scheme. *Journal of Applied Behavioral Science, 7,* 401–426.

Schein, E. H. (1978). *Career dynamics: Matching individual and organizational needs.* Reading, MA Addison-Wesley.

Schmidt, F. L. & Hunter, J. E. (1977). Development of a general solution to the problem of validity generalization. *Journal of Applied Psychology, 62,* 529–540.

Schmitt, N., Gooding, R. Z., Noe, R. D., & Kirsch, M. (1984). Metanalyses of validity studies published between 1964 and 1982 and the investigation of study characteristics. *Personnel Psychology, 37,* 407–422.

Schmitt, N. (1976). Social and situational determinants of interview decisions: Implications for the employment interview. *Personnel Psychology, 29,* 79–101.

Schmitt, N. & Coyle, B.W. (1976). Applicant decisions in the employment interview. *Journal of Applied Psychology, 61,* 184–192.

Schneider, B. (1975a). Organizational climates: An essay. *Personnel Psychology, 28,* 447–481.

Schneider, B. (1975b). Organizational climate: Individual preferences and organizational realities revisited. *Journal of Applied Psychology, 60,* 459–465.

Schneider, B. (1983). Interactional psychology and organizational behavior. In L. L. Cummings & B. M. Staw (Eds.), *Research in Organizational Behavior* (Vol. 5), pp. 1-31. Greenwich, CT: JAI Press.

Schneider, B. (1987). The people make the place. *Personnel Psychology, 40,* 437–453.

Schneider, B. & Schmitt, N. (1986). *Staffing organizations* (2nd. ed.). Glenview, IL: Scott, Foresman.

Schwab, D. P. (1982). Organizational recruiting and the decision to participate. In K. M. Rowland & G. R. Ferris (Eds.), *Personnel Management* (pp. 103–128). Boston: Allyn & Bacon.

Schwab, D. P. & Cummings, L. L. (1970). Theories of performance: A review. *Industrial Relations, 7,* 408–430.

Schwab, D. P., Rynes, S. L., & Aldag, R. J. (1987). Theories and research on job search and choice. In K. M. Rowland & G.R. Ferris, (Eds.), *Research in Personnel and Human Resources Management* (Vol . 5, pp. 129–166). Greenwich, CT: JAI Press.

Scott, K. D. & Taylor, D. S. (1985). An examination of conflicting findings on the relationship between job satisfaction and absenteeism: A meta-analysis. *Academy of Management Journal, 28,* 599–612.

de Schweinitz, D. (1932). *How workers find jobs.* Philadelphia: University of Pennsylvania Press.

Sheppard, H. L. & Belitsky, A. H. (1966). *The job hunt.* Baltimore: Johns Hopkins Press.

Sheridan, J. E., Richards, M. D., & Slocum, J. W. (1975). Comparative analysis of expectancy and heuristic models of decison behavior. *Journal of Applied Psychology, 60,* 361–368.

Shuval, J. T. & Adler, I. (1977). Processes of continuity and change during socialization for medicine in Israel. *Journal of Health and Social Behavior, 18,* 112–124.

Smith, F. J. (1977). Work attitudes as predictors of attendance on a specific day. *Journal of Applied Psychology, 62,* 16–19.

Smith, F., Roberts, K. H. & Hulin, C. L. (1976). Ten-year job satisfaction trend in a state organization. *Academy of Management Journal, 19,* 462–469.

Smith, P.C., Kendall, L. M., & Hulin, C. L. (1969). *The measurement of satisfaction in work and retirement.* Chicago: Rand-McNally.

Soelberg, P. O. (1967). Unprogrammed decision making. *Industrial Management Review, 8,* 19–29.

Springbett, B. M. (1958). Factors affecting the final decision in the employment interview. *Canadian Journal of Psychology, 12,* 13–22.

Steel, R. P., Hendrix, W. H., & Balogh, S. P. (1990). Confounding effects of the turnover base rate on relations between time lag and turnover study outcomes: An extension of meta-analysis findings and conclusions. *Journal of Organizational Behavior, 11,* 237–242.

Steel, R. P. & Ovalle, N. K., II (1984). A review and meta-analysis of research on the relationship between behavioral intentions and employee turnover. *Journal of Applied Psychology, 69,* 673–686.

Stevens, D. W. (November 16–17,1977). *A reexamination of what is known about job seeking behavior in the United States.* Paper presented at the conference on Labor Market Intermediaries, sponsored by the National Commission for Manpower Policy.

Strasser, S. & Sena, J. (1990). *From campus to corporation and the next ten years.* Hawthorne, NJ: The Career Press.

Stumpf, S. A. (1990). Using the next generation of assessment centre technology for skill diagnosis. *International Journal of Career Management, 2,* 3–14.

Swaroff, P. G., Barclay, L. A., & Bass, A. R. (1985). Recruiting sources: Another look. *Journal of Applied Psychology, 70,* 720–728.

Tan, S. Y. (1982). Cognitive and cognitive-behavioral methods for pain control: A selective review. *Pain, 12,* 201–228.

Taylor, M. S. & Bergmann, T. J. (1987). Organizational recruitment activities and applicants' reactions at different stages of the recruitment process. *Personnel Psychology, 40,* 261–285.

Taylor, M. S. & Schmidt, D. W. (1983). A process oriented investigation of recruitment source effectiveness. *Personnel Psychology, 36,* 343–354.

Thomas, G. (1953). The mobility of labour in Great Britain. *Occupational Psychology, 27,* 215–221.

Thornton, G. C., III (1992). *Assessment centers in human resource management.* Reading, MA: Addison-Wesley.

Thornton, G. C., III & Cleveland, J. N. (1990). Developing managerial talent through simulation. *American Psychologist, 45,* 190–199.

Ullman, J. C. (1966). Employee referrals: Prime tool for recruiting workers. *Personnel, 43,* 30–35.

Ulrich, L. & Trumbo, D. (1965). The selection interview since 1949. *Psychological Bulletin, 63,* 100–116.

Vandenberg, R. J. & Scarpello, V. (1990). The matching model: An examination of the processes underlying realistic job previews. *Journal of Applied Psychology, 75,* 60–67.

VanMaanen, J. (1976a). Breaking in: Socialization to work. In R. Dubin (Ed.), *Handbook of Work, Organization and Society* (pp. 67–130). Chicago: Rand McNally.

VanMaanen, J. (1976b). Rookie cops and rookie managers. *Wharton Magazine, 1,* 49–55 (b).

VanMaanen, J. & Schein, E. H. (1979). Toward a theory of organizational socialization. In B. M. Staw (Ed.), *Research in Organizational Behavior* (Vol. 1, pp. 209–266). Greenwich, CT: JAI Press.

Vroom, V. H. (1964). *Work and motivation.* New York: Wiley.

Vroom, V. H. (1966). Organizational choice: A study of pre and post decision processes. *Organizational Behavior and Human Performance, 1,* 212–225.

Vroom, V. H. (1969). Industrial social psychology. In G. Lindzey and E. Aronson (Eds.), *Handbook of Social Psychology, 2nd ed.* (Vol. 5, pp. 196–268). Reading, MA: Addison-Wesley.

Vroom, V. H. & Deci, E. L. (1971). The stability of post decisional dissonance: A follow-up study of the job attitudes of business school graduates. *Organizational Behavior and Human Performance, 6,* 36–49.

Vroom, V. H. & Jago, A. G. (1988). *The new leadership.* Englewood Cliffs, NJ: Prentice-Hall.

Vroom, V. H. & Yetton, P. W. (1973). *Leadership and decision-making.* Pittsburgh: University of Pittsburgh Press.

Wagner, E. E. (1949). The employment interview: A critical summary. *Personnel Psychology, 2,* 17–46.

Wahba, M. & Bridwell, L. (1976). Maslow reconsidered: A review of research on the need hierarchy theory. *Organizational Behavior and Human Performance, 15,* 212–240.

Wanous, J. P. (1972a). *An experimental test of job attraction theory in an organizational setting.* Unpublished doctoral dissertation, Yale University, New Haven, CT.

Wanous, J. P. (1972b). Occupational preferences: Perceptions of valence and instrumentality, and objective data. *Journal of Applied Psychology, 56,* 152–155.

Wanous, J. P. (1973). Effects of a realistic job preview on job acceptance, job attitudes, and job survival. *Journal of Applied Psychology, 58,* 327–332.

Wanous, J. P. (1974). A causal-correlational analysis of the job satisfaction and performance relationship. *Journal of Applied Psychology, 59,* 139–144.

Wanous, J. P. (1975a). A job preview makes recruiting more effective. *Harvard Business Review, 53(5),* pp.16, 166, 168.

Wanous, J. P. (1975b). Tell it like it is at realistic job previews. *Personnel, 52(4),* 50–60.

Wanous, J. P. (1976a). Organizational entry: From naive expectations to realistic beliefs. *Journal of Applied Psychology, 61,* 22–29.

Wanous, J. P. (1976b). Who wants job enrichment? *S.A.M. Advanced Management Journal, 41(3),* 15–22.

Wanous, J. P. (1977). Organizational entry: Newcomers moving from outside to inside. *Psychological Bulletin, 84,* 601–618.

Wanous, J. P. (1978). Realistic job previews: Can a procedure to reduce turnover also influence the relationship between abilities and performance? *Personnel Psychology, 31,* 249–258.

Wanous, J. P. (1980). *Organizatonal entry: Recruitment, selection, and socialization newcomers.* Reading, MA: Addison-Wesley.

Wanous, J. P. (1983). The entry of newcomers into organizations. In J. R. Hackman, E. E. Lawler, III, & L. W. Porter (Eds.), *Perspectives on behavior in organizations* (pp. 159-167). New York: McGraw-Hill.

Wanous, J. P. (1989). Installing a realistic job preview: Ten tough choices. *Personnel Psychology, 42,* 117–134.

Wanous, J. P. (1992). Newcomer orientation programs that facilitate organizational entry. In H. Schuler, J. L. Farr, & M. Smith (Eds.) *Personnel selection and assessment: Organizational and individual perspectives.* Hillsdale, NJ: Lawrence Earlbaum Press.

Wanous, J. P. & Colella, A. (1989). Organizational entry research: Current status and future directions. In K. Rowland & G. Ferris (Eds.),

Research in Personnel and Human Resources Management (Vol. 7, pp. 59–120). Greenwich, CT: JAI Press.

Wanous, J. P., Keon, T. L., & Latack, J. C. (1983). Expectancy theory and occupational/organizational choices: A review and test. *Organizational Behavior and Human Performance, 32*, 66–86.

Wanous, J. P., Poland, T. D., Premack, S. L., & Davis, K. S. (1991). *The effects of met expectations on newcomer attitudes and behaviors: A review and meta-analysis* (Working paper 91–41). Columbus: Ohio State University, College of Business.

Wanous, J. P., Reichers, A. E., & Malik, S. D. (1984). Organizational socialization and group development: Toward an integrative perspective. *Academy of Management Review, 9*, 670–683.

Wanous, J. P., Stumpf, S. A., & Bedrosian, H. (1979). Job survival of new employees. *Personnel Psychology, 32*, 651–62.

Wanous, J. P., Sullivan, S. E., & Malinak, J. (1989). The role of judgment calls in meta-analysis. *Journal of Applied Psychology, 74*, 259–264.

Wanous, J. P. & Zwany, A. (1977). A cross-sectional test of need hierarchy theory. *Organizational Behavior and Human Performance, 18*, 78–97.

Ward, L. B. & Athos, A. G. (1972). *Student expectations of corporate life: Implications for management recruiting.* Boston: Division of Research, Harvard Business School.

Weekly, J. P. & Gier, J. A. (1987). Reliability and validity of the situational interview for a sales position. *Journal of Applied Psychology, 72*, 484–487.

Weiss, H. M. (1978). Social learning of work values in organizations. *Journal of Applied Psychology, 63*, 711–718.

Weitz, J. (1956). Job expectancy and survival. *Journal of Applied Psychology, 40*, 245–247.

Werbel, J. D. & Gould, S. (1984). A comparison of the relationship of commitment to turnover in recent hires and tenured employees. *Journal of Applied Psychology, 69*, 687–690.

West, M. A., Nicholson, N., & Rees, A. (1987). Transitions into newly created jobs. *Journal of Occupational Psychology, 60*, 97–113.

Wexley, K. N. & Latham, G. P. (1991). Developing and training human resources in organizations (2nd ed.). Glenview, IL: Scott, Foresman.

Wiesner, W. H. & Cronshaw, S. F. (1989). A meta-analytic investigation of the impact of interview format and degree of structure on the validity of the employment interview. *Journal of Occupational Psychology, 61,* 275–290.

Williams, C. R., Labig, C. E., & Stone, T. H. (1990). *Employee recruiting sources and post-hire outcomes: A test of the differential information and applicant population difference hypotheses.* Unpublished manuscript, Oklahoma State University, College of Business, Stillwater, OK.

Wilson-Barnett, J. (1984). Interventions to alleviate patients' stress: A review. *Journal of Psychomatic Research, 28,* 63–72.

Wiskoff, M. F. (1977). *Review of career expectations research: Australia, Canada, United Kingdom, and the United States.* Technical Note 77-9, March. San Diego: Navy Personnel Research and Development Center.

Woytinsky, W. S. (1942). *Three aspects of labor dynamics.* Washington, DC: Social Science Research Council.

Wright, O. R . (1969). Summary of research on the selection interview since 1964. *Personnel Psychology, 22,* 391–413.

Wright, P. M., Lichtenfels, P. A., & Pursell, E. D. (1989). The structured interview: Additional studies and a meta-analysis. *Journal of Occupational Psychology, 62,* 191–199.

Youngberg, C. F. (1963). *An experimental study of job satisfaction and turnover in relation to job expectations and self-expectations.* Unpublished doctoral dissertation, New York University, NY.

Zaharia, E. S. & Baumeister, A. A. (1981). Job preview effects during the critical initial employment period. *Journal of Applied Psychology, 66,* 19–22.

Index

Adams, J. S., 219
Aderman, M., 6, 80–1
Adler, I., 192
Aldag, R. J., 24, 99
Alderfer, C. P., 10, 57, 113, 114, 191
Allen, N. J., 223, 234
Alonso, R. C., 192
Alutto, J. A., 192
Anastasi, A., 4
Anderson, K. J., 168
Anderson, K. O., 175
Argyris, C., 18, 191, 194–96
Aronson, E., 99, 218
Arvey, R. D., 4, 27–8, 45, 123, 139
Ash, R. A., 13, 192
Asher, J. J., 4, 126, 127
Ashworth, D. S., 15, 36
Athos, A. G., 29
Auerbach, S. M., 175
Avner, B. K., 6, 80, 81

Balogh, S. P., 81
Banas, P. A., 27–8
Bandura, A., 175, 217
Barclay, L. A., 36
Baron, R. A., 120
Barrick M. R., 158
Bartlett, C. J., 79
Bass, A. R. 36
Baumeister, A. A., 79
Bazerman, M. H., 107, 108, 110
Beal, G. N., 192
Bedrosian, H., 6, 11
Belitsky, A. H., 24

Bem, D. J. ,51
Bentson, C., 4, 132, 240
Bergmann, T. J. ,116
Berlew, D. E., 204
Berry, N. H., 29
Blood, M. R ., 64, 75, 79
Bluedorn, A . C., 12
Birnbaum, M. H., 168
Bohlen, J. M., 192
Boudreau, J. W., 113
Bourne, P. G., 168, 232, 234
Bowen, D. E., 158–59
Boyatzis, R. E., 13, 156
Bray, D. W., 25–6, 32, 132, 230
Brayfield, A. H., 18
Breaugh, J. A., 36
Brett J. M., 85
Bretz, R. D. Jr., 13, 192
Bridwell, L., 10
Brown, B., 62, 75, 79
Brown, B. K., 147
Brown, L. D., 57, 200
Buchanan, B., 203–4, 208, 211–12

Cacioppo, J. T., 216
Cascio W. F., 14, 76
Caldwell, D. F., 13, 19, 36–7
Campbell, J. P., 15
Campion, J. E., 139
Campion, M. A., 4, 140, 147
Caplow, T., 205
Carlsmith, J. M., 111
Carter, G. W., 147, 151
Cavender, J. W., 18, 48
Chaiken, S., 62

Chao, G. T., 158
Chase, R., 159
Chatman, J. A., 13
Cherrington, D. J., 18
Cleveland, J. N., 131
Cochrane, R., 168, 172
Cohen, P., 224–6
Colarelli, S. M., 80
Colbeck, L., 129
Collella, A., 28, 36, 39, 40, 76–7,
    83– 4, 113, 115, 208
Conard, M. A., 36
Cook, M., 123
Cook, T. M., 179
Cornelius, E. T. III, 36, 154, 158–
    59, 161
Coyle, B. W., 114–15
Crampon, W. J., 12
Crites, J. O., 90–91
Crockett, W. H., 18
Cronshaw, S. F., 140, 240
Cummings, L. L., 17
Cummings, T., 158–59

Dalton, D. R., 60
Davis, K. S., 31, 84
Dawis, R. V., 7, 57
Dean, R. A., 5, 56, 59, 80
Decker, P. J., 36
Deci, E. L., 33
DeNisi, A. S., 67, 80, 180
Downs, S. R., 129–31
Dreher, G. F., 13, 192
Druckman, D., 175
Dugoni, B. L., 28, 79
Dunham, R. B., 29
Dunnette, M. D., 27–8, 147, 151,
    154, 239

Eagly, A. H., 62
Eagly, R. V., 60
Eaton, N. K., 154
Eder, R. W., 123
Ellis, A., 176
Etzioni, A., 189
Faley, R. H., 4, 45, 123, 139
Farkas, A. J., 12
Farley, J. A., 36
Farr, J. L., 79
Farr, R. M., 129

Feild, H. S., 123
Feldman, D. C., 85, 165, 202–4,
    208, 211–12
Ferris, G. R., 123, 156
Festinger, L., 218
Fiely, D., 166
Fink, L. S., 116
Fisher, C. D., 29, 62, 208
Fletcher, C., 119–20
Foltman, F., 24
Fox, H., 24
Freedman, J. L., 111
Freedman, S. M., 167
Fried, Y. ,156

Gannon, M. J., 36
Gatewood, R. D., 123
Gaughler, B. B., 4, 132, 240
Geisinger, H. F., 36
Ghiselli, E. E., 14, 127, 158
Gier, J. A., 142
Gilmore, D. C., 4, 123, 146
Gilroy, C. L. ,60
Githens, W. H., 78, 80
Glass, G. V., 175
Glueck, W. F. ,103
Goldstein, A. P., 175, 183
Gomersall, E. R., 178
Gooding, R. Z., 14, 126
Gottier, R. F. ,158
Gould, S., 12, 46
Gouldner, A. W., 192
Graen, G., 197
Gratton, L., 141
Greenhaus, J. H., 31
Griffeth, R. W. ,29, 33, 80
Gusastello, S. J., 6, 80, 81
Guion, R. M., 4, 48, 124–25, 158

Haccoun, R. R., 79
Hackett, R. D., 46
Hackman, J. R., 2, 22–3, 57, 156,
    205, 212
Hachiya, D., 60
Hall, D. T., 204
Hanson, M. A., 15
Harris, M. M., 116, 139
Hellervick, L., 4, 123, 146
Hendrix, W. H., 81
Heneman, H. G. Jr., 24

Henry, R. A., 32
Herriot, P., 123
Herzberg, F. H., 220
Hill, R. E., 39, 103
Himmelfarb, S., 62
Hoiberg, A., 29
Hollenbeck, G. P., 132
Hollenbeck, J. R., 158
Holmes, T. H., 168
Hom, P. W., 29, 33, 80
Horner, S. O., 80, 180
Hough, L. M., 15, 154, 158–60, 162
Hovland, C. I., 216
Howard, A., 25–6, 230
Hoyer, W. D., 62
Hrebiniak, L. G., 192
Hulin, C. L., 32–3, 57, 60
Hunter, J. E., 14, 16, 37, 78, 126,
    128, 133, 139, 158, 239–40
Hunter, R. F., 14, 126, 128, 133,
    139, 158, 240

Iaffaldano, M. T., 18, 48
Ilgen, D. R., 28, 62, 70, 79, 80
Ivancevich, J. M., 167

Jackofsky, E. F., 13
Jackson, S. E., 84
Jacobson, E., 176
Jago, A. G., 51
Janis, I. L., 103–4, 106–7, 175,
    183, 216
Janz, T., 4, 118–19, 123, 140, 142,
    146–47
Johnson, R., 176
Johnson, W. E., 69, 180
Jones, G. R., 221–223

Kamp, J. D., 154
Kandola, R. S., 127–28
Katzell, M. E., 30
Keon, T. L., 84, 100
Kelly, H. H., 216
Kendall, L. M., 57
Kerr, C., 24
Kilmann, P. R., 175
Kirnan, J. P., 36
Kirsch, M., 14, 126
Kinslinger, H. J., 158
Klitgaard, R., 123

Klonglan, G. E., 190
Korman, A. K., 158
Kuiper, N. A., 175
Kuleck W. J., 33

Labig, C. E., 36
Latack, J. L., 84, 100, 167–68
Latham, G. P., 4, 61, 118–19, 140–
    42, 147, 215, 217–18, 231
Laughlin, J. E., 67, 180
Lawler, E. E. III, 2, 10, 22–3, 33,
    156, 159, 205, 212
Ledford, G. E., 158
Lewicki, R. J., 219–21
Lewis, M., 66, 218
Lichtenfels, P. A., 140
Liden, R. C., 116
Locke, E. A., 31, 147, 215, 217–18,
    231
Lockman, R. F., 80
Lofquist, L. H., 7, 57
Lombardo, M. M., 134
Louis, M. R., 166, 210
Lubliner, M., 165
Ludwick-Rosenthal, R., 175

MacDonald, M. R., 175
Macedonia, R. M., 70–71, 80
Machen, J. B., 176
MacLaurin, W. R., 24
Malatesta, C. Z., 62, 75, 79
Malik, S. D., 197–99, 212
Malinak, J., 18, 48
Mann, L., 104, 107
Mann, R. B., 36
March, J. G., 1
Maslow, A. H., 10
Masur, F. T. III, 175
Mathieu, J. E., 13
Mayfield, E. C., 116, 139
Marinis, M., 31
Matteson, M. T., 167
McCall, N. M. Jr., 134
McClelland, D. C., 13, 119, 156
McCloy R. A., 154
McCord, C. G., 113–14
McEvoy, G. M., 14, 76
McGarrell, E. J., Jr., 165
McGee. G. W., 18, 48
McGuire, W. J., 48, 62, 64, 214, 216

McHenry, J. J., 15
McIntyre, R. J., 60
Meglino, B. M., 67–69, 80, 180
Meyer, J. P., 223–24
Michaels, C. E., 12
Miller, G. A., 194
Miller, H. E., 114
Miller, S. ,175
Miner, J. B., 155, 157, 159, 161
Mobley, W. H., 43, 46, 84
Morrison, R. F., 6, 81
Morse, J. J., 13
Moore, M. L. ,232
Mount, M. K., 158
Motowidlo, S. J., 147, 151
Muchinski. P. M., 18, 48
Mulford, C. L., 192
Mumford, E., 177–79, 240
Myers, C. A., 24
Myers, M. S., 178
Nathan, B. R., 158
Nuefeld, R. W. J., 175

Nicholson, N., 223
Nissen, B., 205
Noe, R. D., 14, 126
Noon, S. L., 32
Novaco, R. W., 179

Oldham, G. R., 59, 156
O'Reilly, C. A., 13, 18, 19
O'Leary, B. S., 79
Orpen, C., 140

Parnes, H. S., 24
Parsons, C. K., 116
Petty, R. E., 216
Petty, M. M., 18, 48
Pfeffer, J., 17
Phillips, J. S., 167
Pierce, J. L., 29
Poland, T. D., 31, 84
Popovich, P., 216
Porter, L. W., 2, 12, 22, 23, 31, 43,
    205, 208, 212
Posavac, E. J., 175
Posner, B . Z ., 166
Powell, G. N., 115–16, 166
Power, D. J., 97

Premack, S. L., 31, 76–77, 81 84,
    240
Pursell, E. D., 4, 140, 147

Rahe, R. H., 168
Randall, D. M., 12
Randolph, W. A., 67, 180
Rees, A., 24
Rees, A., 223
Reichers, A. E., 11, 84, 194, 197–
    99, 210, 212–13
Reid, G. L., 36
Reilly, R. R., 62, 75–76, 78–79, 158
Reitz, H. J., 18
Reynolds, L. G., 24
Rhode, J. G., 33
Rhodes, S. R., 43, 48
Richards, M. D., 103
Roberts, K. H., 33
Robertson, A ., 168, 172
Robertson, I. T., 127–28, 141–42
Rosenthal, D. B., 4, 132, 240
Rosnowski, M.
Rosseau, D. M., 200–1
Rout, U., 141
Rynes, S. L., 24, 113–14

Saari, L. M., 118–19, 140, 142, 147
St. John W. D., 165
Salancik, G. R., 17
Sarason, I. G., 179
Scarpello, V., 12
Schein, E. H. ,188–89, 200, 206–7,
    211–12, 221, 224, 227, 232
Schlesinger, H. J., 175
Schmidt, D. W., 36
Schmidt, F. L., 16, 37, 78, 239–40
Schmitt, N. 14, 114–16, 123, 126,
    128, 132, 139, 158–59, 161
Schneider, B., 11, 17, 58, 123, 158–
    59, 161, 191, 200
Schuler, R. S., 84
Schultz, G. P., 24
Schwab, D. P., 17, 24, 39
de Schweinitz, D., 24
Sciarrino, J. A., 4, 126, 127
Scott, K. D., 48
Scott, W. E., 18
Seely, W., 70, 80

Seidel, C., 31
Sena, J., 118
Sheppard, H. L., 24
Sheridan, J. E., 103
Shuval, J. T., 192
Simon, H. A., 1
Slocum, J. W., 103
Smith, F. J., 12, 33, 46
Smith, P. C., 57
Soelberg, P. O., 97, 99, 101, 103, 111
Sorcher, M., 175, 183
Sorenson, J. E., 33
Spector, P. E., 12
Sperling, S. M., 79
Spivey, W. A., 36 7
Springbett, B. M. 116-7
Steel, R. P., 81
Steers, R. M., 31, 43, 48
Stevens, D. W., 24
Stone, T. H., 36
Sotoodeh, Y., 168
Strasser, S., 118
Stumpf, S. A., 4, 6, 11, 135, 138
Sullivan, S. E., 18, 48
Swaroff, P. G., 36
Swets, J. A., 174

Tan, S. Y., 175-76
Taylor, D. S., 48
Taylor, M. S., 36, 116
Tenopyr, M. L., 79
Tetrick, L. E., 12
Thomas, G., 60
Thornton, G. C. III, 4, 131-32, 240
Todor, W. D., 60
Toquam, J. L., 15
Trumbo, D., 116, 139

Ullman, J. C., 36
Ulrich, L., 116, 139

Vandenberg, R. J., 12
Van Maanen, J., 187-88, 197, 221, 227-28, 230
Vroom, V. H., 18, 33, 48, 51, 94
Wager, L. W., 194
Wagner, E. E., 116, 139
Wahba, M., 10
Wanous, J. P., 5-8, 10-1, 15, 18, 27, 30-1, 34, 39-41, 48-50, 56-57, 59, 63, 74-77, 79-81, 83-84, 100, 113, 115, 165, 197-99, 208, 211-12, 216, 240
Ward, L. B., 29
Weekly, J. P., 142
Weiss, H. M., 198
Weitz, J., 65, 74, 79
Werbel, J. D., 12, 46
West, M. A., 223
Wexley, K. N., 61
Weisner, W. H., 140, 240
Wheeler, D., 103, 104, 106, 107
Whitener, E. M., 158
Williams, C. R., 36
Williams, K. J., 67, 80, 180
Wilson-Barnett J., 175
Wiskoff, M. F., 30, 234
Woytinsky, W. S., 60
Wright, O. R., 116, 139
Wright, P. M., 140

Yetton, P. W., 51
Youngberg, C. F., 65, 74, 79
Youngblood, 67, 80, 180
Yoder, D., 24
Youngberg, C. F., 27, 74, 79

Zaharia, E. S., 79
Zajac, D. M., 13
Zalinski, J., 78, 80
Zwany, A., 10